About ***WALKING EASY in the World's Best Places:***

For those of us who are into walking as a way to keep in shape, or to really see new country, here is a way to get a taste of what can be experienced on over ***Twenty-five*** long hikes, some classics, others less well-known.

The ***Appalachian Trail*** through Georgia, North Carolina and Tennessee, including the Smokies, is the southern end and customary start for America's best-known and favorite long-walk.

Down in New Zealand ***The Milford Track*** bills itself as the world's finest walk. With 40 hikers a day permitted in the catered huts and another 40 in the independent huts, and MacKinnon Pass open for only four to five months each year, this extraordinary experience takes some planning. Included here are phone numbers for a slot on the trail and descriptions of accommodations along the way.

The author and his wife Angie went through a series of near-death experiences on a high trail bordering 2,000 foot drop-offs in the ***Spanish Pyrenees. The Ordesa Trail*** is surrounded by magnificent peaks with waterfalls spurting out of solid rock escarpments. To enjoy this walk without becoming embroiled in a similar nightmare consider this chapter.

The walk along ***The Thames***, from London to its source, was 171 miles with most of it having been done by commuting from a comfortable flat in London, truly ***'Walking Easy'***.

The walk around ***Grand Cayman*** was punctuated by the terrifying ordeal of a shark attack on the author's son while swimming out to the 6,000 foot deep Cayman Trench.

The 199 miles along ***The Coast to Coast Walk*** of northern England extends from the Irish Sea to the North Sea. It cuts through the heart of the famous Lake District, the Yorkshire Dales of James Herriot, the Pennines and the dramatic North York Moors. It can be hiked in two weeks with B & B's, rented cottages or cozy

The cover shot is from the breathtaking trail cut into the side of the 9 mile ***Rio Cares Gorge*** in the less-recognized other-Alps of Europe, ***The Picos de Europa of Spain***.

The Way of the Gull around the perimeter of ***The Isle of Man*** is 96 miles of old-world charm in pleasant and economical surroundings.

The 94 miles of ***The West Highland Way, in Scotland,*** are filled with lochs and moors and the friendliness of the Scots one meets. It is a walk through centuries of history and at the end a two hour climb up Ben Nevis, Great Britain's highest peak, provides a memorable finish.

The ***Routeburn Track of New Zealand*** can be done in catered huts or independently with excellent facilities and magnificent peaks, rivers, lakes and vistas.

The ***Overland Track of Tasmania*** is a sample of what is one of the world's few remaining outposts yet well-maintained and full of pristine lakes and streams. Friendly Wallabies and shy Tasmanian Devils make it a unique experience.

The ***Tuxachanie Trail and the Black Creek Trail of Mississippi*** are little known walks through national forest land, much of them beside the white sandy beaches of the remote Black Creek.

For a view of a tribe of Howler Monkeys and exotic birdlife the ***Monteverde Cloud Forest and the Nosara Beach along the Pacific Coast of Costa Rica*** are impossible to duplicate.

For catching a bucket of crawfish and enjoying the huge trees of a wilderness area ***The Driftwood Creek Trail in Oregon*** makes a memorable day hike or campout.

Included, too, are a series of long-walks in the ***Sierra Bernia Moutains of southeastern Spain***, one of the author's favorite haunts, many of them with Spanish style dining at remote villages or long picnics with a Mediterranean panorama for company.

The book was written by JAY B. TEASDEL for other walkers considering the long-walks covered.

WALKING EASY
in the
World's Best Places

Also by Jay B. Teasdel:

The Hunt for Mark One
The Last Man's Visitor

WALKING EASY in the World's Best Places

SECOND EDITION, Revised

With additional long walks in COSTA RICA, OREGON, ALABAMA & The Coast to Coast Walk of AUCKLAND, NEW ZEALAND.

★ The APPALACHIAN TRAIL Across Ga., N.C., Tenn. & The Smokies ★

★ ENGLAND ★ THE ISLE OF MAN ★

★ SCOTLAND ★ SPAIN ★ THE PYRENEES ★

★ THE PICOS de EUROPA ★

★ NEW ZEALAND ★ TASMANIA ★

★ GRAND CAYMAN ★ MISSISSIPPI ★

JAY B. TEASDEL

Published in 1995 by:

GULF ATLANTIC PRESS, Ltd.
P.O. Box 8006
Biloxi, MS 39535

Cover by Bryan Dahlberg, Denver, Colorado

ISBN: 0-9633918-3-6

Printed in the United States of America.

First Edition 1992; Second Edition, Revised, 1995.

10,9,8,7,6,5,4,3,2

For Angie

Also, for Beauregard, Benjamin, Duffy and Buck.

CONTENTS

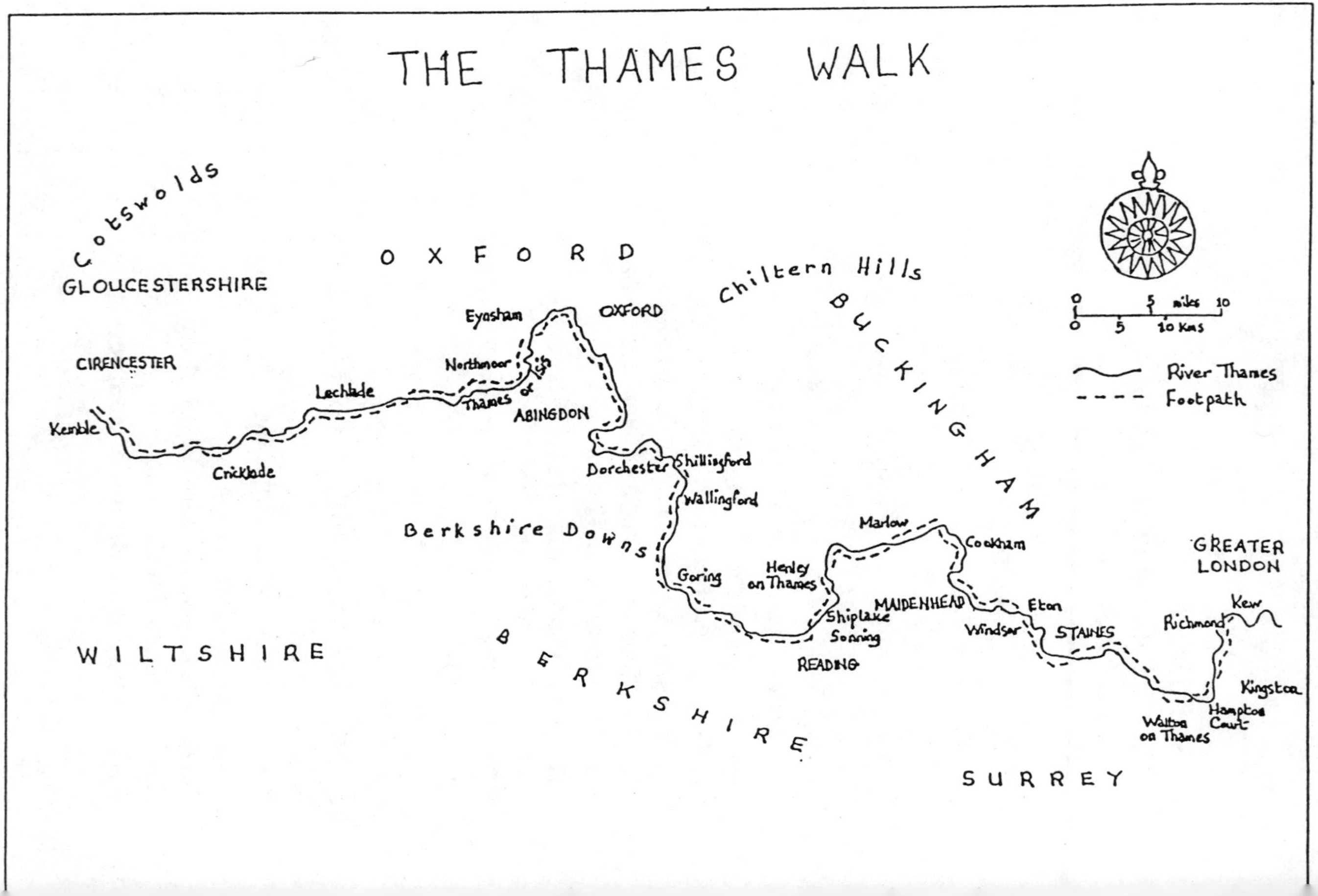
THE THAMES WALK
Cotswolds
GLOUCESTERSHIRE
OXFORD
CIRENCESTER
Kemble
Cricklade
Lechlade
Eynsham
Northmoor
Thames of
OXFORD
ABINGDON
Dorchester
Shillingford
Wallingford
Chiltern Hills
BUCKINGHAM
Berkshire Downs
Goring
Henley on Thames
Shiplake
Sonning
READING
Marlow
Cookham
MAIDENHEAD
Windsor
Eton
STAINES
GREATER LONDON
Richmond
Kew
Kingston
Hampton Court
Walton on Thames
WILTSHIRE
BERKSHIRE
SURREY
0 5 miles 10
0 5 10 Kms
River Thames
Footpath

Introduction

When I first became interested in extended walking as a change from sailing I found it difficult to find info about the walks that I decided to do. Since that time I've enjoyed doing several of the world's classic walks and a good many walks in other places that are equally worthwhile but relatively unknown and seldom hiked. In an effort to help resolve the problem of what to expect and how to go about doing them I put together ***WALKING EASY in the World's Best Places.***

This book shows how to go about obtaining the maps that are essential for doing each of these walks. It provides trailhead directions, types of terrain, what to plan in the way of day-mileages, suggestions for accommodations and an overall view of the trails themselves. It also includes my own day-by-day experiences so that a reader can obtain a general idea of what to expect and how it could be changed to suit an individual's own preferences.

Through the book we have shared this information with other hikers in many different parts of the world. We sold out the first edition but still received requests for the book. Because of this we have done this revised edition which also includes some additional walks in Costa Rica, Oregon, Alabama and an interesting walk in Auckland, N.Z.

Most of these walks take vacation time, a week or two, sometimes three, but they are flexible and they provide a lot more value than the usual sight-seeing, eat-too-much, spend-too-much, sit-on-your-duff-too-much affair. I have always felt that the purpose of a vacation is to produce some mental and physical rejuvenation, to spend a little time taking stock of where I've been and where I'd like to try to go on the path of life. A walk in the woods or through a different type of environment has always been a big help in trying to unscramble it all.

In addition to a sharpened perspective, I find that I come back refreshed, in better shape than when I left, with that little spring in the feet that you only feel after regular jogging or doing several days of a long-distance walk. Apart from these fringe benefits, the principal reason for devoting a vacation to a long walk in a new environment is because it really is fun to do. I never get tired of the anticipation of discovering what is around the next bend.

Most of us are objective oriented so part of the satisfaction in doing a long-distance walk is the accomplishment of having done what we set out to do. It is pleasant to bore friends and associates with snapshots and stories but more important is the realization of having travelled from A to B all on foot and the memory of it, maybe even a map on the wall for a reminder. I have a few maps, framed I confess, of some of them, hanging in my study.

Also stimulating is the anticipation and the logistics of getting organized and scheduled. Nowadays the cost of airfare makes it worthwhile to plan departure dates well in advance. To reserve a flight and book accommodations it is sensible and enjoyable to plot each day on a map in front of a winter's fire, break-in days, full-stride days, goof-off days, sight-seeing days, feet-up days and travel days. I find myself planning the year, and prospective hikes, in January. It's almost as much fun as actually doing them.

In the effort to show what might be expected from each of the walks I put down our own adventures on a day-to-day basis. I am blessed with a wife who has a hobby of searching for vintage clothing. Sometimes Angie will walk with me but as often as not she is content to go off on shopping expeditions of her own after a drop-off at a trailhead.

We are fond of dogs. In the U.S. my middle-aged labrador, Gen'l. G. P. Beauregard, has usually hiked with me. Sometimes Angie's West Highland Terrier, Duffy, has come along and Benjamin, their old black lab roommate, used to go, too, before we lost him to a misadventure not long ago.

At the end of each walk you will find references and information for obtaining the maps that are usually essential for considering them. These long-walks are termed *'easy'* because it isn't necessary to be too far into physical fitness to do them. The day-miles that I covered in a particular walk wouldn't necessarily be quite the same for someone else. They could easily be more and sometimes they might be less. They can serve as a useful guide, though, for planning a day's mileage. Elevation and pack weight are determinants and the beginning 7 to 8 milers can stretch to 15 and 20 milers as a hike progresses and fitness grows. Aerobic benefits from a brisker stride can be weighed against drinking in more of the peace and contentment of nature that unfolds at a slower pace.

The Appalachian Trail is the longest of the easier long walks but I had only space enough to include the southern portion across Georgia and some of North Carolina and Tennessee. Most people make their start at Springer Mtn. on the southern end of the A.T. This will provide a sample of what to look forward to when contemplating a six to eight month commitment for the whole trail or perhaps a section closer to home. I have included the A.T. across The Smokies as well. The bear stories, zoolike shelters and more dramatic terrain make it one of the best segments. On the A. T. it is traditional to use 'trail names'. Mine is Claude Bushwhacker. Beauregard has always just used his real name.

Included in this edition is a delightful walk across Auckland, in New Zealand, called the Coast to Coast Walk. If you plan to do any walks down there in New Zealand, or Tasmania, it is a good way to get acquainted with Kiwis and Kiwi terrain. International flights arrive there and it is a pleasant way to shake off the jet lag.

Costa Rica is also included with a fascinating walk through the cloud forest of Monteverde and other walks along the Pacific coast.

Also added are two walks in Oregon, one along the

seashore and another back into the wilderness area of Driftwood Creek.

In addition a beach walk in Alabama makes a welcome winter break if you are anywhere near the Gulf Coast.

Among all of the walks that follow I hope that there will be some that others will want to consider doing themselves from time to time. I know that they will provide as much pleasure for them as they have given me and for those who have sometimes hiked with me, and for those that I have chanced to meet along the way.

A journey of 2,100 miles, the A.T., begins with but a single step....

JBT

WALK I

I. The Thames Footpath from London to Henley-on-Thames.

(82 Miles)

The walk along the Thames River is a unique experience. It varies from town to town, lock to lock, bridge to bridge, pub to pub, and always there is something of interest to catch the eye. In between the villages it becomes quite remote and rural and often you travel considerable distances without seeing anyone else on the path. Before and after a town you find more people out for a stroll, walking their dogs, jogging, or just sitting by the river.

The Thames fisherman is the most elaborately equipped I've ever seen and always there is the passing parade of boats, some clustered around the locks waiting to go through, some moored by the riverbank and some leisurely cruising by at a stately 4 to 6 knots.

The birdlife is abundant and quite tame. The people are invariably friendly, polite and helpful and never once did I see the bad element that is sometimes found in London. The sense of history is all around you, old history of many centuries. The buildings are often quaint and picturesque and usually the trains and underground facilities are efficient and punctual.

The walk itself is often challenging, particularly in the later stages as it becomes more rural. The towpath right-of-way constantly varies and it becomes necessary to cross from side to side from time to time. Detours are frequently required where land ownership actually borders the river's edge. About 80% of the time, though, the towpath follows along the bank of the Thames, usually over grass or firm ground that is good for walking. There are seldom any hills or elevations to negotiate and these are quite mild anyway so a steady pace is usually possible.

The bibliography that follows is a help in determining which side of the river to follow from time to time and how best to do the detours when necessary. Parts of the riverbank are occasionally occupied by private estates. This makes it necessary to plot a course that will take this into consideration. Often the footpath is clear on the other side of the river.

My own log for the walk is as follows:

The beginning.

Browsing through the books in Harrods, I came across 'A Guide to the Thames Path'. In glancing through it there seemed to be a footpath, more or less, that ran along the banks of the Thames for most of the way. This confirmed a dormant, sort of vague, notion that I had entertained for a long time, namely that a long walk along England's most famous river was possible and that it would be an interesting expedition. Apparently it was some 155 miles from London to the actual source of the river.

The wheels started turning and as luck would have it that same evening I became acquainted with a yachtsman on the houseboat next to that of our old friends, Ann and David. These houseboats were mostly quite elegant. They were part of a flotilla that had permission to permanently moor there on the Thames near Battersea Bridge in Chelsea. I mentioned my interest in the project over a glass of wine and this gentleman was kind enough to loan me his copy of a pocket navigation chart of much of the river beyond London.

The next day Angie and I took a train to Oxford, she to browse for additions to her collection of vintage clothing and me to sample the trail along the Thames. It was reminiscent of my initial expedition on the old A. T. out of Asheville, N. C. That first bite of a new project can be a welcome taste of what is to follow and I looked forward to it with relish.

Oxford to Abingdon. 10 Miles.

It was one of those sometimes sunny days in England when we reached Oxford and everyone who could take the time off was out to make the most of it. The town of Oxford was also full of the international variety of tourists who seem to visit London and the surrounding area more so than any other place in the world. We climbed the Carfax Tower on Queen's street and from its top we enjoyed a bird's-eye-view of downtown Oxford. That done, we wandered through the streets a bit until we came to Folly Bridge, my starting point on the river.

Folly Bridge held a very special interest for me because of a framed painting that hangs on the west wall of my study back in Biloxi. It was done by my father's father, whom I knew only slightly as a toddler. The painting is a scene at Oxford on the river Thames and I feel confident that it was the very site where I set out on my hike. The building in the painting is now a pub called 'Head of the River'. Both the pub and Folly Bridge looked familiar. I don't know quite when he painted it. He probably did it as a young man around 1883 or so because shortly afterward he came to America and settled in Salt Lake City where he stayed for most of his life. It gave me a good feeling to see it and to be starting the walk there because of it.

The path alongside the river was much-used and straightforward. I chose the right side going downstream. It was full of Oxford sights in every direction and soon I came to the Isis Hotel and Pub. The pub was so inviting that I couldn't resist going inside. It was quite busy and the outside tables were located in a garden-like setting near the river. I had a Schweppes orange drink at the bar just to get the feel of it. If Thames hiking was going to have a handy pub like this every so often there would be no need to worry about getting dehydrated along the way.

Next I came to my first Thames river lock. It was

called Iffley lock and everything about it was neat and tidy. A handsome little narrowboat was being locked through. I admired the traditional gold and green lettering, the ornate designs on a tugboat-red background and the colorful flower boxes with fresh flowers that were growing on its roof. An elderly couple were manning the boat and I had the impression that it was a home for them for most of the year.

The path then went beneath a highway bridge and a British Rail bridge. It bordered open fields beside the river and then it came to another lock at Sandford-on-Thames. Across the lock there was an attractive pub that was serving meals. I crossed the lock on its closed gate-end and I went inside. The buffet lunch was tasty and reasonably priced.

The towpath followed the west side of the river along open fields. Three young riders galloped their horses in a field nearby. Then the path narrowed and now became less used. I saw no other walkers. I passed beneath another railway bridge and then a small roadway bridge. Finally I reached a small footbridge across a stream. Here the path became confused and soon it petered out altogether. I managed to make my way through the briars and along the edge of a plowed field until I came to a road that led to a bridge that crossed the river. On the other side of the river was the town of Abingdon.

At Abingdon I found a bus back to Oxford. A fast train took me back to London and that was the start of my Thames walk. I had found it to be an interesting and colorful way to enjoy the English countryside with easy walking on level ground. I resolved to do some more of it in what little time we had left for that trip.

Richmond to Kingston-on-Thames. 5 Miles.

After becoming better acquainted with the London 'Underground' I managed to find my way to Richmond. Here I set out for a sample of Thames walking near urban areas. At first the towpath was a paved promenade for the popular

Richmond suburb for London but surprisingly enough it then bordered pastures and playing fields after that until it reached the Teddington lock. The weir, or dam, there is the longest on the Thames. It is particularly important because it prevents any tidal flow from entering upriver. There was a footbridge across the river that led to two pubs called The Anglers and Tide End Cottage. I managed to keep the feet moving on past the temptation of visiting them.

The towpath then began to enter the suburb of Kingston-on-Thames. It bordered a road and another promenade until it reached a railway bridge. The tracks led me to the station in Kingston where I found that I needed to take a British Rail train to get back to an Underground transfer at Waterloo in London. It had been a short walk with many enjoyable experiences including a leisurely lunch at a riverside cafe in Kingston-on-Thames.

Richmond to Battersea Bridge. 11 Miles.

After the two initial walks I became more and more intrigued with the idea of coming back to walk the whole river. I went to the British Ramblers' Association office at 1/5 Wandsworth Road in London. There I became a member for a nominal fee and I obtained a list of their publications. One of them was a description of the Thames walk itself. My original idea, I promptly found, was far from being original at all. It was, in fact, a perfectly classic walk to do and well described in a little booklet called 'The Thames Walk'. This guide was more direct and easier to follow than the book I had earlier found at Harrods.

The people at the Ramblers' Association were most helpful and they suggested that I visit London's two best bookshops for hikers and yachtsmen, The International Map Centre and Stanford's bookshop in Covent Garden. At these two bookshops I was able to obtain the appropriate maps and also the guide that I eventually used for most of the walk,

Nicholson's 'The Ordnance Survey Guide to the River Thames'. The names and addresses for these guide books and how to order them are listed in the bibliography at the end of the next chapter. These two bookstores are quite inspirational for browsing as they also stock a large assortment of other books describing walks in England and the Continent.

As a result of obtaining this information along with the experience I had had thus far I resolved to do the rest of the Thames walk when next I could. In the short time remaining for this trip I decided to complete the first leg backwards, that is, to walk from Richmond back to the houseboat where we were to have dinner that night. The houseboat was actually moored a couple of miles downstream from the Ramblers' official beginning at Putney Bridge so Battersea Bridge would become my own personal start for it.

It was a nice sunny day again when I set out from Richmond towards London. The start there was an elegant promenade for a bit and then it became more rural as it passed the old Deer Park with its golf course and the magnificent Royal Botanic Gardens. It passed under the two Kew bridges along a grassy path until beyond the Chiswick bridge it skirted the huge Mortlake Brewery and then a large reservoir.

The Hammersmith bridge is probably the prettiest bridge across the Thames. It is a work of art when seen from a distance. It was like something out of a fairy tale. Then I began to see rowing shells that were being stroked with varying degrees of proficiency. One in particular was an all-girl crew who must have been experiencing a first time at the oars. The patient coxswain was doing his best to induce them to stroke together but try as he might each oar hit the water on a different schedule. I have a rowing shell myself back in Biloxi. I use it on the Tchoutacabouffa River where we live. It is a fiberglass affair with aluminum oar rests but it does have some nice wooden sweeps. It is serviceable enough and I manage to get it up to an acceptable speed but I have the feeling that it would cause a raised eyebrow in the company of so many finely crafted wooden shells that scoot through the water like a needle.

Just before Putney Bridge I came upon a series of boat houses and rowing clubs. On the sloping riverbank a large number of spectators were lounging about with the usual glass of lager in hand. They were cheering their favorite shells as they came by in matched heats. These were not the serious college rowing teams who do race there. Rather they were just a number of good friends and clubs out for an afternoon's fun and exercise while their mates watched from picnic blankets with ice chests nearby. This was the official start for the famous Oxford and Cambridge Boat Race and I'm sure that many of the participants rowed with fantasies of being an oarsman in that celebrated event.

At Putney Bridge I crossed over to the other side and I followed the roadway until eventually I reached the houseboat at Battersea bridge. I settled into a welcome bottle of English lager and I realized then that I was hooked on hiking the whole of the Thames when next I could.

Almost a year went by before I came back to London and the Thames walk. I had spent many a winter's night in pleasant anticipation and scheduling and I had gone over each of the guides and the various maps to try to determine how long each day should take. Finally Delta set down at Gatwick and it became possible to take up where I had left off.

Kingston-Upon-Thames to Staines. 14 Miles.

We had made arrangements to rent the same little flat that we had occupied the year before. It is located about two blocks from Harrods and a block from Hyde Park, a handy location. After a reunion with Ann and David and Elizabeth and then a carbohydrate loading at a neighborhood Italian restaurant in Chelsea, I made an 8:00 a.m. start the next morning from the underground in Knightsbridge. The London tube diagram has been meticulously laid out so that even a

Pakistani camel driver can understand it. Knowing this it becomes a bit intimidating when trying to board the right train going in the right direction amidst a sea of people who are all intent on being punctual for work. Like ants. Nobody says a word. Half-asleep, glum, everyone retreats to what innermost thoughts drift up from the sub-conscious.

The tube system really is quite simple when the diagram finally sinks in and, of course, when you've done it a few times you can nap like a regular, getting off with bat-like radar when the door opens at your station. On at Knightsbridge, 2 stops before a transfer at Piccadilly Circus, then the Bakerloo line, colored brown, then 2 more and presto, Waterloo for British Rail. On this first trip I couldn't quite remember the drill from last year but finally it filtered through. The automatic ticket stile gobbled up my ticket, read it and then spit it back at me as the little gate snapped open for entry.

British Rail became a bit more complicated at the Waterloo terminal because of the number of trains to sort through. The people I questioned were friendly, though. I have noticed that this is usually true of Brits. No matter how much of a hurry they seem to be in they always seem to be willing to stop and respond with directions.

There is a huge departure board in the middle of the terminal where you can find the news on your particular train. This told me that the train for Kingston was supposed to leave at 8:33 a.m. but on this particular day it actually left at 9:17 a.m. A train strike from the day before was the culprit. Train schedules at British Rail are almost always sacrosanct. They have to be. The rails are shared at astonishing speeds and frequency. You just put your faith in the Lord and the Engineer's domestic life and hope for the best.

At 10:04 a.m. the fast moving train made its stop at Kingston and by 10:23 a.m. I was finally back to the Thames where I had left it last year. It was a treat to be there. I headed upriver as I would for the rest of the walk.

The chart showed a better path on the other side of the

river. It was labelled a towpath. This is from the old days when barges were towed upriver by men or mule power. I crossed the Kingston Bridge to pick up the towpath on the other side.

This first part of the walk skirted the edge of the extensive fields and gardens of Hampton Court Palace for some two and a half miles. The grounds of the palace comprise 2,000 acres with lots of deer and Versailles-like gardens. I entered the gardens through a gate near the river and I joined the other visitors.

The palace was undergoing extensive renovation because of a serious fire from the year before. A uniformed girl came up and began to ask questions. She wanted to know where I was from and if I was a single. I was afraid that I was being checked for vagrancy because of the jeans, the faded shirt, the worn boots, the beard and the faithful pack. I hoped that the Greek fisherman's cap would somehow connect me with the boat traffic of the Thames. It was only for a questionnaire, though. I guess they were trying to determine the number of visitors and something about them. The buildings date back to 1514 when Henry VIII took it over from his errant cardinal and made it into a royal palace. Today, some 45 royal pensioners live there as well as part of the royal family at times. Hampton Court itself is open to the public for a nominal admission fee but the Thames was waiting.

Once again it became necessary to cross over Hampton Court Bridge to get back to the south side of the river. Here the towpath narrowed and passed beneath shade trees. It skirted the edge of numerous reservoirs and then it came to the Sunbury Locks. Just beyond I found 'The Weir', a pub that looked so inviting that I went in for lunch. The smoked mackerel and salad plate was ample with fresh and varied vegies.

After passing a number of tidy houses the towpath came to the bridge at Walton. Beyond, the chart showed a maze of uncrossable interlocking canals that dictated a stretch of pavement on the right side for the best way to get around them. The B376 to the B375 and then some friendly advice from two ladies out walking their dogs headed me down a lane that went back to the river where I came out just below Shepperton Locks.

On the way to the locks I was amused by a sign that was posted on the door into a Tea Room: 'No bare chests. That goes for the ladies as well.'

Then, too, the elegant names for the pretentious little houses along the way from Walton were relieved by one which was neatly lettered: 'Justa Cottage'.

Continuing along the right side of the river the towpath went from a well-mowed, grassy lane, typical of the area on either side of a town, to a narrow path. Soon I passed two younger men in an orange canoe who were paddling upriver. One of them noticed me, took in the pack and shouted, "How far you going?"

I answered back that I was going to the "Source".

They both stopped paddling and applauded. "Hey that's great," the stern canoeist said, "We are, too."

"Well, then," I said. "I'll see you there". I trudged on. I felt pleased that I was making better progress than the canoe but then they were going against what current the Thames had and besides, they had to pass through all 45 of its locks as well.

Shortly afterward I passed under the M3 Motorway bridge with the roar of its traffic and then I walked along some open fields for a while until the towpath went through an extensive residential area. It was always pleasing to walk by these houses. Invariably they are neatly kept with colorful flower gardens and immaculately manicured lawns. At the time there was bright sunshine and many of the residents were out taking advantage of it. Most of them had brought their folding chairs to the river's edge and dogs and children were in abundance. There were a good many bikers and joggers and walkers out, too, and a friendly greeting was always the response whenever I initiated one. I found that people were often reluctant to say hello to a stranger unless spoken to but once the ice had been broken they were invariably pleased to respond, especially when they had satisfied themselves that it was not someone out for a handout or their goods. A pack and a walking stick seemed to be reassuring. Just some fool out walking around and the U.K. is a country full of walkers.

A little later I fell into conversation with a man about his 6 months old Westie named Monty. He reminded me of our own Duffy when he was that age. Westie owners seem to somehow hang together the world over. I saw at least a dozen of them on the walk that day.

The railway bridge at Staines appeared and the station was not too far off to the right. A train was about to come through for London in only twenty minutes. I made it back to the flat for around seven o'clock. The day produced about fifteen miles of walking over seven hours, fourteen of them on the Thames. It was a pleasant day and it felt good to be back.

Staines to Maidenhead. 15 Miles.

After the tube and train routine I reached the Thames at Staines for 9:27 a.m. I sat on a bench in a little park there and I moleskinned my left toe. It showed signs of a blister, something I hadn't had in a long while. It must have been because of the hard pavement and flat ground walking that I hadn't become accustomed to at the time.

Nearby in the little park were three ne'er-do-wells who were passing a bottle back and forth to start the day. A fourth, suited mate, had joined in the festivities. It was the first time that I'd seen that sort along the river. It made me realize how different the lifestyle was away from the city.

When I reached Staines Bridge the chart showed the towpath as being on the other side again. I crossed over the bridge and then the path narrowed. Soon it passed beneath the busy M25 and beyond I found a group of archaeologists doing an excavation of some size. They appeared to be volunteer university types, serious and industrious, as they dug away in the hard dirt. A matronly woman pushed a wheel barrow full of overburden off to the spoil bank. Tents were pitched next to the excavation and portable office sheds were full of papers and diagrams. The depth was down to only 3 or 4 feet but the trenches were already being carefully swept and filtered and little flags had been stuck here and there. Everyone was busy with a sense of importance and satisfaction in the air. They seemed to be so resolute that I was reluctant to interfere by inquiring what it was they were looking for. I hope that it became a successful dig.

More houses were followed by sweeping fields and in the distance I caught a glimpse of Windsor Castle. Then it became necessary to cross the Albert bridge to avoid the patrolled grounds of the royal residence. A sign proclaimed 'Crown Estate. Entry Not Permitted'.

Windsor Castle is the largest inhabitated castle in the world. It was initially built by Henry II, 1165-79, with other monarchs having left their mark on it over the years. Parts of the castle are open to the public and I could remember when we had been taken to visit it by my London literary agent some three years ago. It is indeed impressive. It is hard not to admire the driving fortitude, shrewdness and salesmanship that have kept one family so successful for so many centuries. I could remember an estimate by Forbes magazine about the world's richest people. Queen Elizabeth was up there near the top with an estimated 8 billion worth of assets. Louis the Sixteenth of France misjudged the fine art of diplomatic give and take with the people and they lopped off his head because of it. The British Royal family were shrewd enough to recognize this possibility and so they continue to survive, prosper and form the cornerstone of the world's most successful and enduring form of government. To look at Windsor Castle with about four city blocks worth of rooms and 4,800 acres of grounds it is hard not to wonder, though, why two people, with the children all grown, need so large a house. And they only live there part time. It is an integral part of the system, though, and the system works well for a large slice of mankind.

At Windsor I stopped to have lunch on the grass by the river. I saw my two canoe friends paddle by near the far bank. They didn't notice me. I enjoyed a siesta there amidst the swans, ducks, people and moored boats.

Eton is across the way but the school was closed for the summer holidays. I crossed the river again on a busy highway bridge just past Windsor. The path was well-maintained and much-used by cyclists and dog-walkers for a short distance after that and then it began to narrow once more as it bordered a huge wheat field that was ready for harvest.

One of the features that helps to make the Thames such a pleasant place to walk or cruise is its speed limit for boat traffic. 8 mph is max. and about 3 mph is customary. This helps to protect the banks from wave erosion, a serious problem, and it precludes any serious accidents or grievances. More than that, though, it ensures a certain element of peace and tranquility that is seldom found in the States where the dictum is flat-out-every-man-for-himself boat operation.

At the Boveney lock the lockkeeper came over to me and told me that two men in a canoe had asked about me. They had wanted to know if I had already passed that way. They had gone through themselves about an hour before. I assured him that it was, indeed, me and that they had overtaken me at lunch.

After passing more wheat fields I caught up with a family of four, all on bikes. The two little girls were on bikes with much smaller wheels but they were keeping up all right. I passed them, they passed me, all of us on the narrow path. An old man was swimming in the river. He told me that he swam there every day. Seldom had I seen any swimmers. Another biker with a pack and a foam pad went charging by. Then, a little later, I passed him as he took a nap on his foam pad beside the trail.

At Bray there was a huge marina full of the customary type of Thames power boat. The boat is typically either 15 or 20 ft. long with a closed cabin and an aft cockpit. This is different from the traditional narrowboat. Moored there next to the gas dock was the orange canoe. It was empty. I surmised that the owners were inside having something cold. I waited for awhile to wave to them but it was getting late so I gathered my weary legs and aching toe together and off I went in the direction of Maidenhead.

The noise of the M4 Motorway could be heard for half a mile away before I passed beneath it. Then the railway bridge came into view and I was about to celebrate my good fortune at having reached my destination for the day when I learned from a couple of friendly boatyard workers that the station was on the other side of town. It was still a mile and a half away.

In town I went to the local Marks & Spencer, the have-everything-chain, and I bought a liter of orange juice. I sat on a bench in the walkway and polished off the whole liter. Practically O.D.'ed on O.J. but nothing ever tasted quite so good. I remembered the days back in the infantry in Texas and the 30 mile forced marches where the only thing that kept me going was the vision of an ice cold pitcher of orange juice that would somehow be waiting at the other end. This was like that. Somehow my shins and calves ached, too, a new experience. I guess it was the walking on the flat and the stretches of pavement that were responsible. Maybe a 16 mile day behind a 15 miler had something to do with it as well.

The train that took me back to London deposited me at Paddington Station instead of Waterloo. The faithful tube delivered me to Knightsbridge, though, albeit with a few more stops. The underground was Saturday-night-crowded with couples out for a good time. A bath in the flat never felt so good.

Maidenhead to Marlow. 9 Miles (7 Miles on the Thames).

After a couple of days off to rest the blister and the not-used-to-flat-walking legs I went back to the tube and train commute to the river. It was a late start for the day because of

Monday morning chores. By the time I made it back to Maidenhead the train's arrival time was 1:51 p.m.

The mile or so from the station back to the Thames didn't seem so long this time. I was wearing the high-topped Reeboks, freshly whitened to look a bit more smart. I thought that they would be more suitable for this type of walking. The river there at Maidenhead was very pleasant with park-like trees beside its edge, many ducks in residence and a paved path.

At Boulter's lock the boats were lined up in a row waiting their turn. An interesting Inn and Restaurant was perched on the island at the far side of the lock. I watched the lock-keeper squeeze nine boats in for the upstream locking when I went by, the busiest lock I'd seen yet.

The path then passed along what was probably the prettiest section I'd seen thus far. It had huge beechwood trees that marched alongside the edge of the river. The opposite bank was a heavily forested hill, the first I'd passed since starting out from London.

Around a bend in the river I discovered two boys who were proudly holding a large perch. They had just caught the fish and it was about two feet long. A third boy had run off to fetch a bucket of water in which to put the fish. The Thames fisherman has more gear and paraphernalia than any fisherman I've ever seen. Not the least of his inventory is a large can of oozing maggots with which he baits his line and chums around his hook from time to time. Not an easy thing to do with a queasy stomach I would imagine. The unsuspecting fish gets a nice feed for his last supper until one of the maggots becomes barbed and difficult to digest.

Farther along I noticed a handsome old varnished runabout of the type that was popular in the twenties and thirties. The name on the transom I noticed, as it went majestically by, was 'Claude', my a/k/a A. T. trailname.

A magnificent house and grounds were noticeable on the other bank. I later learned that the property has had a colorful history. It had been burned down and rebuilt three times and the previous owner had been Wm. Waldorf Astor. In the thirties it produced the 'Cliveden Set' and in the sixties 'The Profumo Affair'. It now belongs to the National Trust and it can be viewed by the public. Tied up at its dock was a very large and tastefully appointed barge that looked to be the ultimate for canal type cruising vessels.

Suddenly the path took a sharp left away from the river. It bordered a private estate that apparently had refused passage through its grounds on the river. It became necessary to trudge down a lane through the village of Cookham. At the bridge there I was startled to see two life-sized mannequins inside the door to a pub on the right. They were animated in a state of perpetual greeting somewhat like royalty waving to the public with fixed smiles and mechanical gestures. On closer inspection I found that one of them was a straw-stuffed scarecrow. He was holding the hand of the attractive maiden next to him who was dressed in her Sunday best.

The path wound along fields beside the river for awhile and then it made another detour toward a nearby hill. On hiking up this welcome hill with a change of pace I was surprised to see a man coming toward me with a huge falcon on his leather-gloved arm. The bird was much larger than I would have imagined. I asked him the age of his bird as an opening gambit. "Six", he said perfunctorily as he continued on his way. He was intent on hunting the bird and he was not in the mood for idle conversation. A huge game bag hung at his side. It seemed partially full of game. A small dog trotted nearby and another ranged up above us on the hill.

Shortly after the falconer had passed on around the side of the hill I saw the falcon take to the air. The bird just hovered in the wind almost motionless. He was waiting for one of the dogs to flush his prey. I thought of the small rabbit I had seen just before I had passed them and I knew I didn't want to see the falcon practice his ancient skill on this peaceful little fellow. I hurried on up the hill.

At the top of the hill a couple of young lovers had just

climbed down from their motorcycle to admire the view and each other. I asked them for the best route to take to get back to the river. They were very helpful and once again I was impressed by the way that everyone tried to make sure that a stranger reached his destination. In this case I was even given the names of each pub along the way. Maybe I looked in need of a pint or two.

After leaving the couple I noticed another path a little farther along that looked like a shortcut. I headed down it and it turned out to be a good way to get back to the river and the bridge that I needed to cross to get to Marlow on the other side. The path took off at the end of the open field at the top of the hill. It wound down past a long wall that bordered beside someone's estate. I took a downhill turn when I came to a fork in the path and then it carried on down some wooden steps until it finally left the woods for a busy road at the bottom. Ahead was a major road with a bridge across the river. I elected to cross under this thoroughfare and continue on to the more picturesque one-lane bridge that led directly into the town of Marlow.

The town of Marlow was quite tudorlike and inviting. At the entrance to the town was a neatly-done sign that proudly proclaimed its award for being the 'Best Kept Town in Buckinghamshire' and rightly so it seemed to me. I found the train station and I sat down gratefully on a bench to wait for the 5:55 p.m. train. Marlow is a two-car end-of-the-line stop but already a crowd had gathered. I was lucky to have had only a five minute wait before setting off for London town.

Marlow to Henley-on-Thames. 9 Miles.

It was 11:00 a.m. before I made it back to Marlow on the end-of-the-line two-car special on the next day. A faulty bridge opening had somehow slowed things down enough so as to miss the regular connection. I was glad that I was not a regular commuter, except that by then I had begun to feel like one.

Moored to The Complete Angler, an attractive Inn, was the Actief, the plush house-barge I had admired yesterday down by Maidenhead. After crossing the one-way take-turns bridge I followed the road around through Bisham, a tidy little village, and I walked on until it was possible to rejoin the towpath. This footpath cut between two estates and went through a low tunnel that stretched beneath a wide road. The path then turned back down to pick up the Thames once again.

At the Hurley locks things became a bit confusing. A charming old lady showed me the way and we fell into conversation. She turned out to be Mrs. Hurley herself and her lovely home was just across from the locks. Her son owned the shipyard and the marina next door. They were very proud of a handsomely restored wooden steam-launch which she showed me nearby. It was a masterpiece of craftsmanship all right, complete with stack and large helm. Its name was The Windsor Belle and it was varnished to a glossy finish.

The path led across the gates of the lock itself to an island and then up an overhead foot bridge back to the same side again. This arrangement apparently assured Mrs. Hurley that she would keep the privacy of her front lawn on the water. Just beyond, the path opened up onto a very large newly-mowed field. Next to the field was a caravan park, the term used for a trailer, camper or RV campground in the States. The caravan park was neat and tidy and not too closely spaced. It had electricity but no other amenities. In fact, none of the caravan parks that I had seen offered the choice of the usual Stateside facilities.

It was a nice sunny day and I flopped down on the grass for a lunch of left-over fettucine with feta cheese, fresh dill, fresh garlic and a bit of Spanish olive oil mixed in. Delicious. During a short catnap afterward five ducks waddled over to check me out for scraps. Maybe the garlic attracted them. The noisy leader quacked me awake. 'Too late, boys, it's all gone.'

The towpath continued along a series of hay fields with

many rickety stiles to negotiate. In the different fields horses and Holstein or Friesian dairy cows peacefully grazed. They brought to mind the days when I used to run a hundred milk cows on the line myself. Most of them were Holsteins for the big volume of milk that they produced but I always had a few Jerseys and Guernseys in order to bring up the butterfat content for an overall premium milk price. Lots of work to a dairy. Those cows need to be juiced twice a day, 365 days a year. Good money, though, if you can handle it. Mine used to support the beef herd, which, in turn, managed to pay the notes each year when it came time to sell calves.

Farming or ranching is a hard way to make a living. It is a good lifestyle if you have a family that likes the outdoors, physical work and the satisfaction of seeing things grow. My own experience was that the profit is all in the land. If you hang onto it long enough the appreciation is a comforting thought. Unfortunately, if you want to keep the place in the family it is a profit that you never see. The places I saw along the Thames must have been in the family for centuries. The appreciation and sentimentality must be astronomical.

The towpath evaporated again and a little green sign pointed in a vague direction across a pasture. It pictured a low stile along with the word 'footpath'. Beneath the sign was the credit which said: 'Erected by East Berks Rambler's Association Group'. This must be a volunteer organization much like the Appalachian Trail Hiking Clubs who maintain the A. T. Those of us who like to walk these out of the way tracks are forever indebted to the people who give of their time and effort to help others enjoy them, too. Someday I am sure that a feeling of obligation will one day put me on a trail work-crew myself. It would be a way to help pay back for some of the benefits that I've had in walking the paths that have been cut by others.

Around three-thirty I crossed the bridge and entered the lovely town of Henley-on-Thames. I remembered that many years previously I had been friendly with a family from there when I had had my boat in Puerto de Pollensa, Mallorca. I had given one of their youngsters a job of helping to clean the topsides so that he would have the experience of earning some pocket money for himself. They owned an old farmhouse in the valley near Pollensa which they used on holidays and where I had visited and had dinner with them. I had wanted to touch base with them again. A salesman at the automobile dealership that they used to own told me that they had sold out and moved permanently back to the farmhouse in Pollensa. I was happy for them and on the way back to London I indulged in some of the memories of those Mallorca days.

WALK
II

II. The Thames Footpath from Henley-on-Thames to the Source of the River Thames

(89 Miles)

Henley-on Thames to Reading. 9 Miles.

British Rail suffered the humiliation of being subjected to a one day train strike again and I took the day off from hiking to take in a play, one of the fringe benefits of staying in London. The next day I made an early start for Henley-on-Thames. More sunshine. I was beginning to wonder if the notorious London weather was only a myth. It became necessary to take a complicated detour route on the tube because the Bakerloo line was out of service. An Arab terrorist had blown himself up along with three floors of his hotel in an attempt to rig up his bomb. Police had shut down the area, including the tube. My congratulations went to the terrorist, with only the reservation that he hadn't taken the rest of his mates along with him.

It was a good feeling to set out from Henley on the old towpath again. I found that I was becoming attached to it. The town itself is a madhouse around the 31st of July as that is when they have the famous Henley Regatta and Rowing Races each year. I had just missed it by a few days. Pity. Had I known I could have done that section on that date and seen some of the shells in action.

The walk started out on a promenade next to golfcourse-like fields, freshly mowed. Then it continued along a grassy bank beyond. An iron bollard had been set in the ground at one spot. The date of 1904 had been inscribed in its head. The bollard was only a couple of feet away from the water at the time. It had been placed there originally to delineate a fourteen foot wide towpath next to the river. This indicated that the riverbank had eroded or washed away some twelve feet during that time. No wonder the river traffic is restricted to a snail's pace.

The towpath was next relegated to a stretch on the road behind some elegant estates facing the river. From one of these fashionable homes with their extensive and well-kept gardens an old woman set forth with the help of her cane. At the railway crossing for Shiplake we fell into conversation while waiting for the train to pass. She was a spry 83 years of age and she was on the way to the 'bookmobile' that was parked nearby. The bookmobile was making its once a week visit and I could see others who were headed toward it. They seemed keen to make selections for their weekly read. It was nice to see people who still liked to read instead of letting the television do all of it for them.

At a large house with a flag proclaiming it to be the Andrew Duncan British Red Cross Society I found an obscure footpath that crossed a field holding a small herd of very large Holsteins. They were placidly stretched across the path. I threaded my way among them. They weren't the least bit concerned or inclined to move out of the way. After three more stiles and a turn down a lane to the right I found the river once again at Shiplake lock.

The walk became a real pleasure now as it followed along through one large pasture after another for the next two and a half miles. At a bend in the river I came upon a dozen young students being taught how to paddle the kayaks that were about to be launched. The instructor was a grey-bearded man with a concerned look on his face as he patiently helped a youngster to appropriately waggle the double-edged paddle from a standing position. As I passed them I observed to him, "You're very brave."

He thought about it for a moment and good-naturedly said, "Sometimes I think so myself."

There was a college nearby and I assumed that this was probably a summer camp activity.

The grassy path fetched up at an interesting bridge with five arches. The bridge had been put together with brick and the middle arch was larger than the others but still narrow and agonizingly low. It was a perfect illustration of the dimensions that limit the width and the height of the Thames narrowboat or cruiser. The road itself was a one-way affair and the traffic waited at a stoplight on either end to take turns going across.

On the other shore of the bridge there was a splendid restaurant with patio tables outside and it was tempting to visit it for lunch. I had my sandwiches, though, which I'd made myself, and I felt obliged to eat them.

The simple pleasures in life are often the best. It was a bit of luxury to stretch out on the grass with my back to a garden wall for a support. Then the shoes came off for a barefoot breather and I brought out the smoked turkey sandwich that I had been looking forward to for the previous hour. In front of me was a narrow slice of river with a changing parade of boats that constantly passed by. It was a delicious moment.

After lunch the path continued along to the Sonning lock. I enjoyed a boat name there, 'Second Gnome'. I overtook a couple on the path beyond and I happened to notice 'The Thames Walk' booklet in a mesh bag that one of them carried. I asked them if they were walking the Thames, too. They said that the they had done only a couple of sections so far.

In retrospect I couldn't actually remember having seen anyone else that I could have readily identified as having the appearance of a London to Source walker. There had been many walkers but none of them carried packs. This should have been the season for it and England is a country of walkers, too. Maybe the walkers I had seen just hadn't felt the need for a pack. There are things that you need from time to time on a long walk, though, and you can only carry them in a decent pack. It would have been nice to have found someone who was doing the same thing.

Reading is a bustling industrial city with office buildings and commerce all around. I made my way up to the busy train station and I purchased a ticket for Paddington. Whoopee! The fast train to London! I had seen them go whizzing by on the outside through-track without deigning to stop at the lesser towns along the way. Now it was my turn.

The Intercity Special made it back to London in only 28 minutes. It was a smooth ride, too, like a bullet. When these trains passed the old many-stop commuters that I had been riding they sent out a solid shock wave that rattled the windows and shook the car where I was seated. It was startling to be sitting on the side next to them, almost as if someone had slammed a heavy door in your face. I was back to the flat early and it had been a nice day indeed.

Reading to Goring. 11 Miles.

The night before we had been given tickets to a concert at the Royal Albert Hall. What a magnificent structure it was. With excellent accoustics and very large it had been built in the round and even the seats behind the orchestra had been all taken. In the British tradition the floor of the hall is used by the impoverished who stand during the performance. Before and in between they sit on the bare floor. The price to them is only two pounds, though. Something for everyone. The swells feel good because they are above it all and the struggling masses feel good because the big discount can be used for a few pints after the concert. Royalty feels good because there's a place for everyone and everyone is in his place. I felt good because I figured all of this out while sitting there listening to some very good music. The program was well played by the Bournemouth Symphony Orchestra. The orchestra was something over 80 strong and it was quite well-known. The conductor was actually a young New Yorker who also performed as piano soloist for Ravel's Piano Concerto in G. He was an extraordinary and well-liked talent.

It was a surprise to reach the underground before it had opened. Then I realized that it was because it was a non-commute Saturday. I took a cab to Paddington for only three pounds sterling and as luck would have it, I boarded the fast train to Reading only four minutes before its scheduled departure. In only an hour's time from leaving the flat I was back to Reading where I had left off and it was only 7:41 a.m.!

After leaving Reading I set out along a grassy promenade. This was on the left bank. I noticed an apparent backpacker who had crashed on the park grass with nothing but a mat and a blanket that he had pulled over himself. This was the only backpacker that I would see on the whole walk.

Shortly afterward I came to a series of fishermen with all of the customary paraphernalia. One of them had just pulled in a huge two footer and he was very pleased with himself. The fish are kept fresh in a long collapsible net that stays half underwater. Everybody dips into the wriggling mass of maggots from time to time to toss a few out around the hook to attract whatever is cruising by. It killed my appetite to watch them do this but I guess Thames fish are big on maggots.

Many of the walkers and fishermen that I'd seen had been taking the sun and it was interesting to observe the extensive number of elaborate tatoos. The quality was quite impressive. It seems to be an English characteristic. I didn't see any with a succession of women's names crossed out, though, like the sailor in Norman Rockwell's well-known painting.

The walk along the river was the usual pleasant grassy footpath all the way to Purley and then it became necessary to detour through a residential area until crossing the bridge at Whitechurch. This was actually a toll bridge, the only one on the Thames. A sign said not to complain to the bridge tender about a recent toll increase but to go and take it up at the city council when they met. Pedestrians go free. Something for everyone again.

The route went up a hill then onto a bridle path sign and down a dirt road until it turned off into some forest. The next two and a half miles were probably the prettiest of all of the Thames walk that I'd done so far. Apparently it is the only stretch of hillside trail in the whole walk. For a while there I thought I was back on the Appalachian Trail.

Finally, the delightful path emptied out onto a country lane and by 12:07 p.m. I had reached the train station at Goring. Then it became necessary to wait an hour for the slow Goring train that connected with the Oxford bullet at Reading. I contented myself with lunch and a nice rest on a comfortable bench near the rails. Lunch was punctuated by the various bullets that came zipping past from time to time. They were too important to stop at the little station of Goring. I ignored them and just munched on my sandwiches.

Goring to Shillingford. 10 Miles.

The commute from London was becoming too long to do and still wind up with enough time for a good day's walk. We rented a car and moved to Oxford. The car was a brand new Ford Fiesta with only 37 miles on it. I had found that Europa Car Rentals had the best deal. Angie dropped me off for an 8:09 a.m. start on the following day. I left the railway station at Goring where I had stopped before and then I crossed the railway bridge that went over the active tracks. I took a right at the second street and went down it until I came to a gravel lane that said 'Bridle Path', i.e. footpath as well, just watch out for horses.

A friendly cat was out for a morning stroll. He came over for a pat and a rub against my leg and then I noticed that he had lost most of his tail. He looked like a manx cat but he didn't care.

The trail dipped down to the river and went past the local pub, 'Ye Olde Leatherne Bottle', and then it carried back up to the lane again until it came to a section where it used a part of the well-known Ridgeway Path. This is one of the many long-distance walks in England.

The path now followed a worn track across fields. It then entered the town of South Stokes. This little residential village with its thatched roofs and gabled windows was one of the most picturesque that I'd seen on the whole walk. The houses were very old and well-maintained and all of them had colorful gardens to set them off.

At the entrance to South Stoke I met a distinguished looking Englishman who was out walking his two little Yorkshire terriers. He kindly gave me directions which I didn't really need at the time and then, about a block later, he caught up with me, having turned around and come back, and he asked me if I'd like to have some company for an hour or so.

This gentleman turned out to have been the President of a large pipeline construction company, now retired, and he had done business with many of my old customers, including Brown & Root, J. Ray McDermott and Williams Bros. His daughter had, in fact, been married to the grandson of George Brown himself, the founder of Brown & Root, now merged into Halliburton. He had also been raised in the area, complete with nanny, five gardeners and the manor house. He was very knowledgeable about the history of the country through which we walked and he maintained a fascinating commentary about the people who had lived there and the events that had taken place, some of them back to the 8th century.

The Ridgeway Path followed the bank of the Thames all the way to North Stoke. The little yorkies had a great time scampering off of the lead. Occasionally they had to be helped over the fence stiles where the brambles were bad. We saw a huge flock of Canadian Snow Geese. Apparently they had been introduced only 25 years ago and with no predators and plenty of feed they had multiplied rapidly, preferring to stick around and lead the good life on the Thames, none of this international travel for them, they knew when they had it made.

My new English friend told a good story about the time

a colleague of his had determined to drive himself home from a party. He had realized that he had had too much to drink when the headlights of the approaching cars appeared to be shining in sets of fours. He had resolved the problem by holding his hand over one eye and sticking close to a large car in front of him. Finally, the large car came to a sudden stop and he crashed into the rear of it. He decided to take the initiative about it as a way to minimize the situation. He climbed out of his car and he accosted the Dutchman whose car he had hit by saying, "What do you mean by stopping so suddenly?" The Dutchman had replied with admirable control, "Well, you see, my friend, I always come to a stop when I park the car in my garage!"

The Ridgeway Path actually cut right through a churchyard with its collection of tombstones. We all went inside the little church, yorkies included. The door was some five hundred years old, thick, grey and weathered. It felt good just to open and close it. Inside, the pews were worn shiny and the memorial headstones were for people gone centuries before. It was a working church and it would be hard not to feel a deep sense of history during any sermon attended there.

North Stoke was another charming little village. Here my acquaintance left me to walk back to South Stoke again to check on his car. He actually lived in London but he had been going to the same mechanic in South Stoke for over 25 years and he had driven out to have his car serviced there. I'm glad he did, otherwise I wouldn't have had the pleasure of meeting him.

At Wallingford I left the Ridgeway Path and I crossed the bridge to the other side. It looked as though the towpath could be used as far as the locks at Benson and then the river could be crossed across the top of the lock gates. At Benson there was a huge sign, though, which said that this was not permitted by the Thames Water Authority. Also, there was mention of this problem in both of my Nicholson and Rambler guides. Ours not to reason why...I gave up and plugged along a field path on the left side of the river.

The path petered out completely. I crawled under some barbed wire fence and I joined some cows in a field. I worked along the edge of the field by the river. I realized I was 'trespassing' but what the hell, I thought, what else am I supposed to do? Then I came to an impassable slough and more serious barbed wire. It seemed to be a huge farm. I doubled back alongside a high brick wall that must have been a moat a few centuries ago. I crossed over a locked gate and I headed for the main road which was about a half mile away.

In the middle of the huge field I suddenly noticed a formidable four-story brick building off to my right. There were many cars parked around it and a doubly-fenced lane that led down to it. In the distance was a high stone wall that ran next to the main road. 'Oh, oh,' I thought. 'Now I've done it, probably MI5 or something and here I am with a pack on my back. They'll think I'm an I.R.A. terrorist out to blow up the place. Dogs'll be coming any minute.'

Anxiously I made it to the stone wall. There was an iron fence with spikes on it that butted into the far end of the stone wall. Somehow I managed to get over the iron fence, spikes and all, and then I was on the road. Phew!

In walking past the entrance to the lane that led to the building I noticed a sign which said 'Rush Court Nursing Home'.

'Well,' I placated myself, 'it could have been a cover for MI5. Anyway, there doesn't seem to be any better way to get from Wallingford to Shillingford without doing a couple of miles of pavement on a busy highway on either side, something even more dicey.'

Shillingford to Abingdon. 10 Miles.

Angie dropped me off for an early start from the bridge at Shillingford. I crossed the bridge where I had stopped the day before. Then I turned down the first road to the left but I missed the footpath and I wound up in someone's front yard. The resident was leaving and he said something about the path being just around the next bend back the way I'd come. Then I found it and I walked along between high walls that screened the houses on either side. The path soon ran into the busy A423 highway but fortunately there was a sidewalk along the far side. Soon the sidewalk came to a stile and a footpath sign that pointed off to the left. I was relieved to once again be headed back for the river.

On the river the passing boat parade had begun to start already. The boats go in small groups of 3 to 6 or so depending on how many made it through the last lock together. It is always nice to see them and to watch the variety of passengers on board. Everybody is friendly, polite and relaxed. No skinheads, druggies or crazy hairdos, all of that seems to stay in the city. Usually families or couples, many with their dogs hanging over the bow like a hood ornament.

At Little Wittenham I crossed on the footbridge to find the usual dilemma again. The guide warned that there is no towpath connection between it and Clifton Hampden. It became necessary to do a nerve-wracking slog of a couple of miles down country lanes with little or no shoulders to avoid any oncoming traffic. Just past the town of Little Wittenham the first footpath sign that appeared turned out to be the wrong one. It led to a church yard cemetery. I retraced my way back to the road. The second, just beyond a picturesque pub called 'The Plough', was correct.

After carefully following the path across a little footbridge the route completely evaporated. I tried to get better oriented with the compass but nothing made sense. Then a couple of bounding retrievers came loping across the field ahead. They were soon followed by a leggy blonde in shorts and halter. She was cutting diagonally across the winnowed hay field with its rows of cut straw. I waited for her to reach where I was standing by the little footbridge.

The tall blonde was from Scotland. She was camping

somewhere in the vicinity with her two dogs. When I asked her for directions she pointed toward a church steeple in the distance and told me that I should head in that direction. I thanked her for the advice and I started out across the winnowed rows of hay. On close inspection I could see that there had been a trail diagonally across the field at one time but now it had been planted over and cut for hay. I couldn't very well blame the farmer. He needed a crop from the land more than an itinerant walker needed a footpath.

The church spire direction eventually brought me to a main road that crossed the railway at Appleby station. Another hike down country lanes took me away from the Nuke plant in the distance and to the town of Courtenay Sutton. Here a river crossing on the Sutton bridge brought me back to a usable section of the towpath on the other side.

The river then wound around to the beginning of Abingdon. At the cricket field near the bridge a game of cricket was in full swing. I watched the game for quite awhile trying to understand the scoring involved. It was a complete mystery to me. Everyone was dressed in white flannels. The pitcher seemed to be doing all of the work. The batter would swat at the ball protecting his wicket, I guess, and every once in a while he would get a decent slug at it. If the other side didn't catch it he would get to run down to the opposite wicket at a sort of leisurely pace. Everyone would then walk over to congratulate him with a good handclap all around, 'Jolly good show, old chap,' that sort of thing. Then there was a break for fresh orange juice, or squash, served on silver trays at the neat little tent that had been set up for the visitors. Everything was very elegant and proper.

At the car park next to the bridge I met Angie where I had ended my first introductory hike from Oxford last year. We found a spot on the grass beneath an inviting shade tree, not far from the mysterious game of cricket. We picnicked while we watched the ongoing play, still doing our best to keep up with the scoring.

Oxford to Newbridge. 14.5 Miles.

At Folly Bridge I returned to where the Thames walk really started for me a year ago. I made an 8:15 a.m. start along the path that follows the river through Oxford. The path from Oxford to King lock, about 4 1/2 miles, was easy walking with many interesting scenes along the way. Past the lock the path became a DIY over grass. After awhile it became better defined as it passed through some woods next to the river.

A group of cows were grazing near the river. As I went by a hefty cow with horns I reached over to pat her on the head and to scratch her behind the horns. She wasn't having any of that. She lowered her horns and pushed into me. I had to fend her off and sidestep out of the way like a novice toreador. What an ignominious way to go, 'Oh, Claude?. He was taken out by an old cow in a field beside the Thames.'

More DIY over fields until I reached a boatyard where we had stopped the day before in search of a narrowboat to live aboard while completing the hike. The girl on duty there had informed me that the river crossing by ferry at Bablock Hythe, mentioned in both guides, was no longer in operation. This was a blow because the right-of-way for the towpath switches sides there and I dreaded the problem of dealing with a heavily-travelled highway that would be necessary to use to get to my destination of Newbridge.

There was no way out of taking the highway for a short detour around the boatyard area and the houses just beyond it. It was a sample of the traffic on the road that I wanted to avoid. The path then took up again beside the river.

When I reached the lock at Pinhill I went through the 'Private' gate and I strode across the lock-gate to the lockkeeper on the other side. This was a sort of critical maneuver because it was the only way to cross over to the good side of the river. I went up to him and asked about the ferry problem at Bablock Hythe as though it was the reason that I had crossed over on the lock gates. I showed him the Nicholson guide which said that the ferry up the way could be utilized to get across the river at that point. This is a very accurate and detailed series of charts and descriptions in an easy to read form with lots of helpful information but we noticed that it was five years old. He suggested that I just take off on his side, which is where I then was, and he pointed me in the right direction.

The lockkeeper was very cooperative and sympathetic even though I can understand why The Thames Water Authority doesn't usually want the public walking across the top of their lock gates. It does seem to vary from lock to lock, though. Anyway, in this case the scam worked and I made it to the other side, the good side, and I hoped that I could avoid the highway torture.

After the lock it got a bit tricky since there were only a series of hay fields with no path. Nicholson's was not much help here but I dug out the Thames Walk guide and I followed their instructions for a change.

After many fields and gates and some two miles I finally made it back to the good towpath at Bablock Hythe. I stopped for lunch along the way. I was doing a can of tuna on croissants then, since we no longer had a kitchen and nothing more exotic was possible.

The 'Ferry Inn and Pub' at Bablock Hythe had closed, too, along with the ferry. A low-cost sort of trailer-park housing development was located there, the first I had seen that is akin to what we have all over the South in the States. Everyone had his own few feet of lawn and garden and everything was neat and tidy, quite different from what one often sees in the backwoods of Mississippi.

The rest of the way to Newbridge was easy walking beside the river. The Thames had narrowed considerably by then and I could see the need for shoal draft craft.

At four o'clock I finally reached the Revived Rose Pub and Inn where we were staying at Newbridge. This little inn is a very pleasant place and our room was nicely furnished and decorated. It overlooked the river with its quaint old bridge that was actually built in 1250 A.D. It is called Newbridge because the bridge there is a bit newer than the one down the way. British history and names are often entertaining. There is always a reason for everything if you take the trouble to dig for it. The restaurant at the Revived Rose was excellent, too, and I felt revived as well after dining there that night.

Newbridge to Buscot. 14.5 Miles.

It rained that night. It was the first time in the two weeks since we had been in England. It was overcast at 8:00 a.m. when I set out from The Revived Rose at Newbridge. (The pub had been the location for a television production of an Alan Ayckbourn play called 'Three Men in a Boat', which we happened to see on the BBC later on).

After crossing the 'new bridge' at Newbridge I walked along the edge of the river to Shifford lock. It was a bit muddy and the old boots became caked with mud. The path was not used much on this section but it was still okay. I saw a sign that said 'Beware of the Bull!' This was right after passing across a pasture with some young bulls in it. Across the way on the other bank two young bulls were practicing lock-heads, butt and push. Nobody was winning. It was just good fun.

The little power boat 'Miss Marple' passed me by just before the locks. Her skipper was grey-bearded with a greek fisherman's cap like mine. He reminded me of an old shipmate friend. I remembered him from the day before when we had waved to one another as kindred souls. It is funny how you can instinctively like someone you don't even know. We waved again.

The path ran along the edge of a field. The overgrowth was wet against my jeans so I trudged through the burned barley stubble gathering mud on my boots that made them look like a size that would have been favored by Frankenstein. Suddenly a pair of pheasants broke cover and flew off in front of me. Immediately five more pairs each took their turn. They would have been easy shots. They had waited too long. I never was much of a hunter, though. I can appreciate a good shot but I hate killing birds or animals.

The path came to a fork with a wading 'ford' across a wandering division of the Thames. Then it followed a country lane that ended in a farmer's barnyard. A sign said 'bridle path' and vaguely pointed along a hedgerow beyond a gate. This was a cross-country ramble in the general direction of the town of Tadpole. I had to cross a deep water-filled ditch with the help of some hanging branches from a strategically placed tree, go up the other side and then plod along a field track toward a distant paved road with traffic.

When I went by two large combines that were idle I stopped to talk with a couple of farmers who were waiting for it to dry enough to finish harvesting a 200 acre field of barley. They were friendly and they seemed interested in my walk. Then I reached the road and I headed for the bridge that would take me back to the other side where I could resume walking beside the river again.

As I came to a pub called The Trout Inn that was located just before the bridge I saw a familiar face in a recognizable Ford Fiesta. As coincidence would have it Angie had happened to be crossing the bridge just then. She was scouting for our next place to stay. We repaired to the pub for a cup of coffee.

In the pub a Westie pup named Holly was prancing around the room endearing herself to the customers. It was a treat for us to be able to enjoy her and it helped us to remember Duffy when he was that age.

Angie left me and I crossed the Tadpole bridge and headed down a narrow little road that was just then being tarred and graveled. The road led to Rushy lock where I crossed on the lock-gate which was permissible there and also the weir (dam). Then the path began a delightful stretch of pasture walking beside the river that continued for three miles.

At Radcot bridge it became necessary to switch sides

again but by now the sun had come out and it had turned into a beautiful day. The river narrowed some more as it twisted and turned. After another three miles of grass-cushioned walking the path crossed the Eaton footbridge to the other side again.

After the footbridge a little yellow arrow pointed straight across some poor farmer's wheat field. A mashed-down path led through the wheat which was about three feet high.

On the other side of the wheat field the path hit a freshly plowed area and naturally it then evaporated. I headed in the general direction of Buscot where I was to meet Angie. After crossing two more freshly plowed fields I finally made it to a paved road with a sort of sidewalk path beside it. I was about a quarter of a mile off target there but when I finally noticed a sign down the way that pointed encouragingly in the direction from which I had come I noticed that it led through another crop of something that looked like huge weeds about four feet high. They, too, were trodden down as though somebody knew where they were going. This was a field I had rejected as being too troublesome to cross. 'Oh well' I thought, 'What are a few more steps on such a fine day?'

At the little village of Buscot I settled down beside the road and I began to write up my log. Fifteen minutes later Angie turned up with the welcome news that she had found a nice inn for us in the neighboring town of Fairford. It was called 'The Bull'. The Bull? Yep, no bull, The Bull.

Buscot to Cricklade. 12.5 Miles.

We took a day off to visit old friends at the village of Willersey, near Broadway, in the Cotswolds. Philip and Pamela own the old farmhouse in Altea, Spain, that we have rented in the past. We had a delightful lunch at their charming old home with its two acres of well-kept gardens and ancient slate roof.

Back at Buscot I made a 9:30 a.m. start the next day. I walked through the village and across the Buscot lock to the other side of the river. It was a nice stroll beside the river on the right side for a short distance and then I made the biggest boo-boo of the whole Thames walk.

A large cornfield left no right-of-way beside the river. In making a detour around it I turned left down the road that carried around its border. I came to a bridge over what I thought was the Thames. I crossed the bridge and I came to a footpath sign. Instinctively I turned right. After about a mile of following this river and going down a couple of country lanes I came to a highway and I headed down it as the ordnance survey map seemed to indicate. Everything had fallen into place I thought until I came to a sign post, fortunately, which indicated that I had actually wound around and managed to walk in the reverse direction for over a mile!

The river that I had been following was actually the river Leach which drained into the Thames at the cornfield. The Thames itself was just a little beyond where it flowed under a second bridge. After getting out my compass and verifying all of this I sheepishly walked back along the road until I reached the cornfield again. I passed the footpath sign at the scene of my big mistake and I carried on to the real Thames beyond.

After rejoining the Thames with a pleasant walk beside it for a bit the path reached a point where it became necessary to abandon the river and to head for a busy highway, the A361, as the only way to keep going. Not only that but the rest of the six or seven miles to Cricklade showed on the ordnance survey map and in the guides as a sort of treasure hunt of trying to find different roads, farm lanes and footpaths, which I had learned by now were usually plowed over, intermingled with cattle trails or used too seldom to follow. When I reached the A361 I discovered that there was no shoulder to walk along and the oncoming traffic was headed straight for me at about 70 miles an hour with only inches of good driving between me and oblivion.

The situation was such that I just went to orienteering. I followed the direction of the highway for about a mile and a half on the inside of the fields next to the road. The fences I crossed by going over or under them, usually over wherever there was a gate. The gates were usually padlocked or tied shut but they were proper metal or wood gates and easy to cross over.

At the town of Upper Inglesham I headed off in the direction of a path shown on the map but it was not marked or used even though I found the spot where it was supposed to start. So, I just laid a compass course of 260 degrees and I followed that.

The rest of the day I spent crossing field after field. It was really very satisfying. Sometimes it became necessary to alter course to deal with hedgerows and ditches but English fences are not difficult to negotiate. The barbed wire is usually loosely strung because dairy cattle are well-fed and not prone to stray. It is easy to slide under it, through it, or even over it. The sheep fields were often separated by a single-strand electric wire fence but this is only 12 v. current and the battery was seldom connected or recharged. It was easy to step over it. I was careful to stay to the edge of planted fields, away from farm houses, and I tried not to disturb the livestock. I was careful to close what few gates I could open and I carried my lunch litter back in my pack. I never saw a farmer or another soul the whole way.

At one point I saw a fox. He was about 100 yards away and when he noticed me he headed for a hedgerow.

When finally I reached the busy A419, just before Cricklade, the traffic was so continuous that I couldn't get across it. There was a path beside the river for a short distance that passed under the highway. I took this for a solution and it soon deposited me in a farmyard. I asked an attractive young blonde in jeans for permission to pass through her corrals. She was gathering hay from the barn to feed her horse nearby. She was very cordial and friendly. She led me around the barn and she even took the trouble to make sure that I took the right street that would get me to the center of the town.

When finally I reached the little bridge across the trickle that was all that now remained of the once mighty Thames I sat down on a convenient park bench. The bench had a plaque nearby which said:

'This bench is in memoriam for a very special milkman who died whilst on duty in 1988.'

It was an eight-hour walking day and because of the cross-country orienteering, the fence climbing and the extra two miles of boo-boo in the beginning I was 45 minutes late for the rendezvous that day. It was okay, though, because Angie was late herself. The traffic from Oxford, where she had gone, had been exceptionally heavy. A bottle of Spanish rioja at the old Bull's Inn that night never tasted so good.

Cricklade to The Source (At last). 12.5 Miles.

After identifying where we would meet, at the closest parking spot near The Source, it was a 9:00 a.m. start at the little bridge back in Cricklade. I sat down on the milk man's bench and I tried to second-guess the day's route. It didn't look too bad, not like the orienteering of yesterday, but it was going to be another treasure hunt type of walk, of that I was sure.

After crossing the bridge I turned left into a large meadow which was a nature reserve for rare plants and grasses. I couldn't tell any difference between it and the many other fields that I'd walked across but a sign posted on the edge of the meadow was quite keen about it. The people of Cricklade have common grazing rights from August 12th to Feb. 12th when it then reverts to the owner who cuts it for hay, a peculiar arrangement that no doubt has a typically British reason. It was then the 13th of August, the day after the Cricklade residents could feel proprietary about it, and perhaps this explained the half-dozen people that I encountered who were out walking their dogs in the meadow. It was also a Sunday so that may have helped, too. Anyway, it was a pleasant meadow to walk across. It had no identifiable footpath and I wondered if I should feel guilty about treading on the special plants and grasses. Nobody else seemed to give it any thought, though, and at least I wasn't down grazing on it which was supposed to be permissible if you were a Cricklade resident.

The Thames was only three to four feet wide now and only three or four inches deep.

A well-trained lab trotted up. He was proudly carrying his canvass retrieving bag in his mouth. 'Odin' was a veteran of many a competition. I had a nice chat with his owner.

Just beyond the meadow I had resigned myself to some more cross-country orienteering when I came upon a new bridleway with a sign that said 'Ashton Keynes 2 1/2 miles'! I felt like dancing a jig, particularly so since this was an area of quarries and old ponds that had been formed from previous digs. It would have been time-consuming to work around them. The bridleway was 3 to 4 feet wide and judging from the horse tracks it was widely used.

On the new bridleway I made good time to Ashton Keynes. It had been mentioned in the Thames Walk guide as being in the planning stage but not then completed. One of the ponds along the way had had an ominous sign posted that said, 'Danger. Quicksand. Stay on Bridleway!' Right. No place for orienteering.

After passing through the charming little village of Ashton Keynes I found a footpath that followed the river, now a creek, with the help of the Thames Walk guide. For the rest of the way I used this guide and my ordnance survey map. The faithful Nicholson guide stops at Cricklade since that is a complete dead-end for even a canoe. In fact, if you can prove that you paddled from Lechlade, the end of the journey for a powered cruiser, to Cricklade you can get a nice commemorative scroll for it.

Just beyond Ashton Keynes I was shocked to discover that the Thames, now a trickle, had completely dried up. It had become just a clean, dried-mud ditch!

Shortly afterward I met a man with a one-year old

golden retriever, by now I was convinced that everyone in England owns a dog, certainly everyone who walks. I stopped to talk for awhile and he informed me that the river had dried up there about two weeks ago. He said that this had been the driest summer that he had known in a long while.

Just for the anomaly of it I walked the dry streambed for awhile. I finally came to a long sloping field with a sort of brushy section in the center. Just beyond was reputed to be an ancient spring where, at many times of the year, some of the original Thames water was supposed to rise.

The true source, though, was said to be farther up the valley and on the other side of the busy A433 highway. I continued walking.

At the agreed upon parking spot off the highway I met Angie and we walked together toward The Source. We climbed a gate, passed through another and then went down a dirt track. There before us, at long last, after some 158 miles or more of walking beside it, was the river's beginning. The spring was a small rock-clustered basin about three feet in diameter. It was completely dry! Nearby was a stately old ash tree and it was surrounded by farm meadow. Just beyond was a large stone. Imbedded in the stone was a bronze plaque which read:

> 'The Conservators of the River Thames
> 1857 - 1974
> This stone was placed here to mark
> the source of the River Thames.'

At 3:17 p.m. on the 13th of August I had reached The Source of the River Thames. And of all times for the faithful Olympus camera to suffer a break-down this was it. No amount of fiddling with it would induce it to take a picture of the historic occasion. No matter. I had walked the Thames. It was a good feeling to sit there for a bit and recall some of the highlights of the long walk and all of the pleasure I had experienced in doing it.

That night I wrote in my log:

'It is hard not to comment that I find it difficult to believe that the reputed spring is the true source of the river. Where it lies appears to be considerably downhill from the A433 that crosses the swale up which it would have to flow. I can only think that perhaps it flows underground somehow to join the area beyond the highway, a long distance and a notion that is not very comfortable.'

The quandary over the source having to flow uphill was so disturbing that I decided to revisit it once more. We were scheduled to leave to visit friends in Wales but I could work it in before we left. Then, too, Angie had found a very good camera, used, that was similar to our old Olympus. It would be nice to have a picture of the river's beginning, wherever it was, and I could examine the terrain again, hopefully with more satisfaction.

In the morning I hiked out to the source once more. I took my pictures, including a picture of the plaque. It seemed just as improbable that it could, in fact, actually be the true source of the Thames.

Still puzzled I went back to the busy A433 highway and I crossed to the other side. I examined a drainage tunnel that passed under the roadbed from the other side. Then I worked down the gently sloping field to where I could readily picture enough of a fall for a stream to form. In fact a meandering ditch soon began to take shape. Surely, this was the true source and the other was an imposter, someone with political clout had wanted it to be on their land and the plaque had been located there to appease them.

As luck would have it I noticed two men working on a fence at one edge of the field. One of them turned out to be the farmer who actually owned this land. He had, in fact, lived for 20 years in the nearby stone house which used to be the old pumping station for an abandoned canal whose historic remains I had already identified. "Yes," he said, "that spring really is the source of the Thames. It is deceiving, I know, but in the wintertime it puts out a stream of water that actually floods this pasture. Not just a trickle, I mean a proper flood!" We visited some more and I thanked him for putting my mind at rest. I knew now that I had truly stood at the very beginning of the great river up which I had walked.

Bibliography for the Thames Walk.

1. Nicholson: The Ordnance Survey Guide to the River Thames. (This is the most detailed and easiest to use).
Order from: International Map Centre, 23-24 Caxton St., London S.W.1. U.K. Tel. 071-222-4945.

2. Ordnance Survey Maps:
Landranger 176 West London Area
Landranger 175 Reading, Windsor & surrounding area.
Landranger 164 Oxford & surrounding area.
Landranger 163 Cheltenham & Cirencester area.
Order these from the National Map Centre, address above.

3. Stanford's River Thames Map. (Good for train connections).
Order from Stanford's Travel Bookshop, 12-14 Long Acre, London WC2E 9LP, U.K. Tel. 071-836-1915

4. The Thames Walk. (Very good for upper end of the Thames; could substitute for Nicholson if necessary).
Order from: The Rambler's Association, 1/5 Wandsworth Road, London SW8 2LJ, U.K.

5. A Guide to the Thames Path, by Miles Jebb. (History and literature of interest are also included; most recently published). Order from: Constable & Co., Ltd., 10 Orange Street, London WC2H7EG, U.K. (I bought mine at Harrods, which makes a good excuse to go there, especially around lunchtime when the huge buffet is waiting).

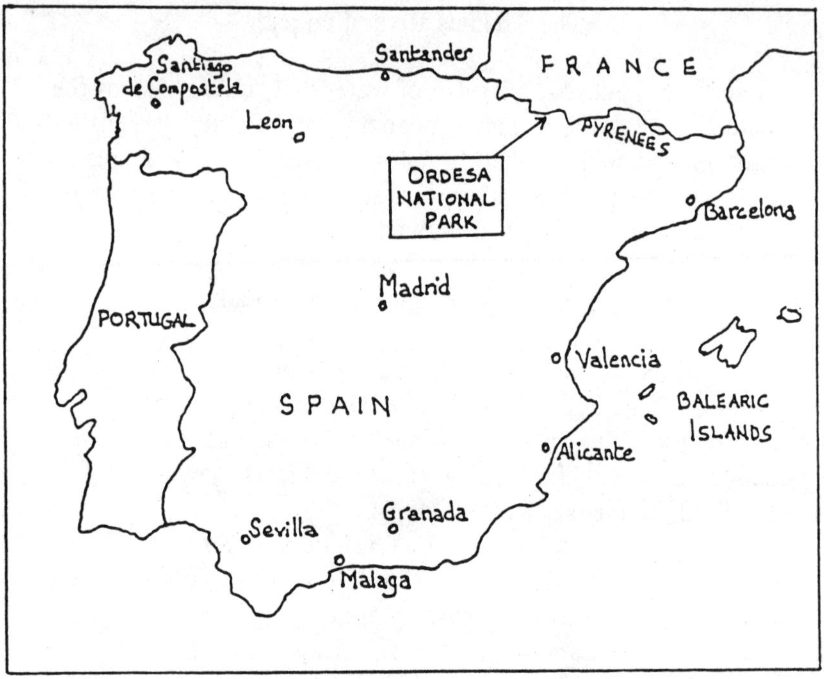

Santiago de Compostela
Santander
FRANCE
Leon
PYRENEES
ORDESA NATIONAL PARK
Barcelona
Madrid
PORTUGAL
Valencia
SPAIN
BALEARIC ISLANDS
Alicante
Granada
Sevilla
Malaga

Ordesa in the Pyrenees

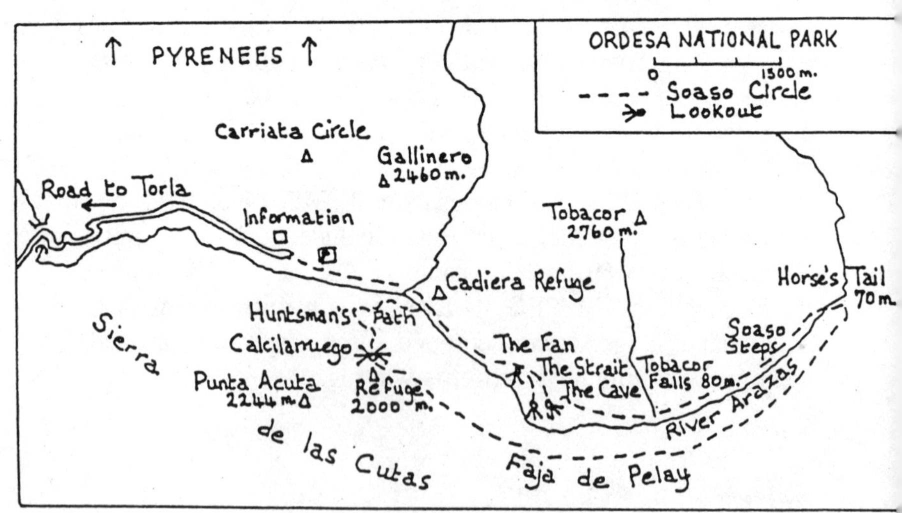

WALK III

III. Ordesa in the Pyrenees.

(16 Miles)

If you hike in the mountains long enough I guess you are apt to someday find yourself in a life and death situation. This finally happened to us in the mountains of the Spanish National Park, Parque Nacional de Ordesa, which is situated in truly magnificent terrain on the south side of the Pyrenees. How we survived the nightmare in which we found ourselves is still a mystery to both of us. To put it together in the proper sequence of events the log follows.

Soasa Circle. 16 Miles.

The little town of Torla, at the gateway to the west side of the Valle de Ordesa, is one of the most charming of the hundreds of villages we have visited in Spain. Its buildings are made of ancient stone with the hand-hewn rock slab roofs, twisting alleys, interesting levels and cobbled streets that are so picturesque. Some five inns, half a dozen bars, a couple of small groceries and a savings bank are intermingled with the livestock occupants of the lower levels. It is a daily event to see the small herds of cattle plodding through the streets en route to their quarters in the village.

We had checked into the Edelweiss Hotel, a very pleasant and well appointed inn with nice food and comfortable rooms which overlook the river from private balconies. On Monday morning it was necessary to wait until 10:30 a.m. for the savings bank to open so that we could replenish a dwindling inventory of pesetas. The bank is only open on Mondays and

Fridays. Then we had to wait for the bread delivery truck to make his rounds and finally we reached the take-off point at the park itself, only ten minutes away, for 11:30 a.m. Ten minutes later we were underway on the wide path that leads up the valley between tremendously imposing bluffs on either side. All around us and beyond were snow-clad peaks in the distance. The river Araza came cascading down the floor of the canyon nearby.

The hike up the shallow valley was pleasant and interesting. The river itself presented two series of tumbling waterfalls, one with a close lookout point where we were suddenly inundated by a company of Guardia Civil soldiers who were apparently on an outing together. They were well-mannered and clean-cut with packs and boots and many cameras were produced to take one another's photographs near the perilous edge overlooking the falls. They were all young and seemed to be in training. This is right in the heart of the Basque country and we had noticed an uncommon number of well-armed patrols on the way in to the area.

On either side the steel-grey and ocher colored limestone escarpments rose some 6,000 to 7,000 feet high. Huge poplars and beeches and pines forested the early part of the walk and down each side tumbled numerous other waterfalls from dizzy heights. Often these waterfalls and side streams would originate straight out of the rock itself with no apparent source to them, a phenomenon that invariably amazed us.

At the upper end of the valley a circle of bluffs, known as the Soasa Circle, majestically ring the end of the huge canyon. Above them is the Mount Perdido Massif at some 10,000 feet. It was mostly covered in snow. Pouring down into this basin is the falls known as the Cola de Caballo, the Horse's Tail. They are quite spectacular as they fan out towards the bottom like the tail of a horse, hence the appropriate name.

We reached the Soasa Circle by 3:15 p.m. and we found a large rock for shelter from the prevailing breeze. A friendly heifer came over for a visit but soon left when she discovered we had nothing in the way of a handout. Here we had our lunch. This was about 6.5 miles up the valley. The trail up had been a gradual climb with nice switchbacks, well-maintained and much-used, a thoroughly delightful walk, the kind you always hope to find.

During lunch we had discussed the possibility of taking what showed on the map to be a high route trail back. It would be longer and it would present us with a steep drop from off of what seemed to be a sort of a bench high up on the other side of the canyon. It didn't appear to be too much more of a climb, though, since we had already worked our way on up to what we thought was a goodly elevation. Rather it seemed to generally follow the contours where we were already. It would be a change from going back the same way that we had come up and we would have some splendid views from up there. Then we noticed a couple with red sweaters who had taken the route. I watched them for a long time as they seemed to go higher than we had anticipated while still heading toward the noticeable bench beyond.

We packed up and left at 4:19 p.m. I had some reservations about doing the high route but it seemed feasible enough. There was actually a sketch map of the route in our Michelin guide with the encouragement that the whole hike, including the upper return, would take around seven hours. Then we noticed a solitary hiker come down from that same direction and we decided to do it. As we crossed the little log bridge over the stream a young Scandinavian couple passed us and they, too, headed up that same trail. Surely the trail was being used then and we put any apprehension out of our minds.

After an hour and a half up the trail we had covered almost four miles and we had climbed some thousand feet above the canyon floor. We hit our first snow bank just above the trail and Angie climbed up to make a snow ball and throw it at me. The view was magnificent. Shortly afterward we spotted four chamois. They were quite close, about fifty feet away, and they were not shy like the others I had seen on our hikes in the Picos de Europa. We watched them for a bit while they watched us. They are a sort of a cross between a goat and a small deer with sharp curving horns, white blazed faces and light brown hides. These were well-fed and grazing on the tough grass that grows on the precipitous side of the bluff there.

Four minutes later we rounded a bend, still climbing, and we hit our first disaster. A large snow bank had covered the trail. The trail at that point was running across a sixty degree slope. This snow bank continued on down to a precipice edge that was only ten yards away. The drop-off there was one thousand feet straight down to the canyon floor below. There were footprints in the snow where others had crossed.

Now we were faced with a difficult dilemma. We had come some ten miles and by now it was six o'clock. To go back would mean a twenty mile day and the probability that darkness would overtake us was almost certain. We were just not prepared for a night out in low temperatures in case we strayed from the trail or something else went wrong. We did not know what lay ahead of us but we could not see any other snow banks on what we could see of the trail beyond. We kept thinking that it would begin to head down soon.

We decided to try to get across the snowbank. Angie went first. She managed to get out on it for about a third of the way and then her boots began to slip when she placed them in the footprints that she tried to follow. I had followed right behind her, trying my best not to think about the drop-off so agonizingly close to us. We decided to work our way back to the trail itself. She walked backwards, past me, and she managed to make it back to the trail without slipping. I had the same problem. The snow was icy and slippery and I had to dig in with my hands and the walking stick as I gradually retraced backwards the footprints that we had tried to dig into the snow on our way out onto it. I made it, too, with a rush of relief when my boot finally hit the trail.

At that point we both asked ourselves, as usual, what is the right thing to do? We went back three more times to the edge of the snowbank to study it carefully. The more we looked at it the more determined we became that to cross it was not the right thing to do. We reasoned, of course, that five others that we knew about must have somehow made it by there that same day. This was what made the crossing so difficult to reject. Perhaps it had become icier in the interim with the freshening wind, though, or maybe they had found another way around it. We thought about the alternative of the ten miles back the way we had come. It seemed preferable, even in the dark and cold, but it was risky,too. Then we decided to somehow try to claw our way up above the snow bank, cross the gravel slide that led to it, and then try to regain the trail on the other side. We walked back to a spot that had some shrubs growing out of the side of the mountain. These could be used for purchase and we hauled ourselves up the sixty degree slope and over toward the rock slide. It was hard going on all fours but we reached what looked to be a reasonable crossing just above the snow bank. This was loose gravel about three feet from a perpendicular drop of around ten feet down onto the snow bank. A slide would have sent me right on down to the sixty degree snow bank and thence out into space like a giant ski jump.

Right there was where I came as close to death as I have in a long time. I inched my way out onto the gravel with my pack on my back. As I was halfway across I felt my right foot give. It was unable to gain any purchase or to support me. The gravel just gave way and rolled on down the side of the mountain. I felt my whole body give but the weight of the pack somehow kept everything in place. I knew I couldn't work my way back. I tried not to panic, to just keep still. Gradually I found a little more purchase with my right foot a little further forward and I dug it into the gravel. I eased over gingerly, trying to keep my weight evenly distributed. Little by little I made progress until I reached the solid earth side of the mountain on the other side of the rock slide. I told Angie to stay where she was.

I crossed over to where I could see a way to slide back

down to the trail by holding onto the shrubs that were somehow growing out of the side of the mountain pretty much the same as on the other side. Then I worked on up alongside of the rock slide until I found a better place to cross that was much higher up. I crossed over there without any trouble and I urged Angie to go back and to work her way on up to where I then was.

Angie didn't panic or hesitate although she was in a terribly precarious position herself. Thank God she has the press-on-regardless type of courage of the typical Brit. She turned around and made it back to where she could make uphill progress by clawing her way up the mountain using the same scrub brush that grew there. We crossed the gravel rock slide again and then we worked our way around to where we could inch our way back down onto the trail below. The threat of a slide from here was just as grim but now we had solid earth to dig into. We made it back down to the trail only to find the same situation staring us in the face around a bend fifty feet farther on. There another snow bank was located that was just as dangerous with the same thousand foot drop-off right next to it.

Again we made it up and over onto another rock slide. This one was even more worrisome because running water could be heard beneath it and I wondered about the base beneath us as I crossed over. We made it, though, and again we worked on down to the trail as before.

Now the trail began to climb more steeply. We rounded another bend and we found another snowbank covering the trail. This one was not as wide, though, and the footprints were better dug into the snowbank. We didn't hesitate this time and Angie went first while I went right behind her with the bamboo walking stick that I tried to use as a poor substitute for an ice axe. We made it to the other side all right and then the trail continued its climb.

We passed over three more of these snowbanks. They were not as extensive as the first two but the mountain had become so precipitous that there was no way to work on up above them anyway. The drop-off was right next to the trail all along this section. By then the canyon floor below was going down while the trail was going up. The drop-off had long since passed the two thousand foot mark, not that it mattered, the dive would have been more spectacular but the mess you made on the bottom would be about the same.

Then we reached the bench and here we found small pines and relief from the ever present drop-off to the right of us. We continued along this bench for about a mile until we came to a shelter and a wide clearing out over a point. The shelter was tiny, about six by six, and the ground inside of it was as wet as that on the outside. I could see no evidence of its ever having been used and the open side faced out over the canyon where it would be exposed to the prevailing wind. The shelter looked like a convenient place to die from hypothermia without sleeping bags. We were elated, though, because we thought we had reached the place on the map that showed a shelter and a lookout point and just beyond the trail was supposed to head downward.

Shortly afterward we were dismayed to discover the trail heading up again and now it had left the bench and the drop-off was once again next to us. Now the drop-off had graduated to several thousand feet. We came to another snowbank that crossed the trail but just before we reached it a huge boulder came crashing down the mountain about twenty-five feet in front of Angie. We waited for more to follow but it seemed to be a maverick. We then headed across the snowbank.

The trail continued to climb and it was beginning to get dark, twilight with an overcast threatening sky. It was around eight o'clock and it was getting difficult to come up with words of encouragement. We couldn't understand why the trail refused to head down and we worried about whether we had somehow missed the junction where one trail headed up and the one we wanted headed down, except that this didn't seem to make sense because we knew that there had been nothing but precipice next to us for the whole distance. We crossed three more of the snowbanks that covered the trail with the now several thousand foot drop-off beside us. By now we refused to worry about the consequences of a false step and we just headed across them.

Finally we reached the real refuge and the lookout. The shelter that we had reached earlier was not marked on the map, probably it had been built since the map had been printed. This refuge was large, built out of stone with windows and a fireplace inside. It would have provided good protection in spite of the open door if one could have scrounged up some wood for a fire. We probably could have survived there. I refused to go out to the crumbling lookout which the Michelin guide said overlooked the canyon straight down for a depth of 6,000 feet. The lookout was only about thirty feet away from the refuge. I asked Angie not to go out there either, one side of the path had crumbled away. It had a cable with yellow danger flags that was stretched across it.

The trail at last headed down. By now it was after 9:00 o'clock and the threat of darkness was a serious worry. We elected to continue down, though, and our next obstacle was yet another large snowbank. This time we were able to negotiate around it by inching our way down the seventy degree slope on our rear ends. We could see where others had done the same thing. Still others had apparently crossed it on their bottoms, the sitz marks were obvious.

The rest of the next hour was a continuing nightmare. The trail was cut into the side of the mountain in a succession of rocky, perilous switchbacks which were worse than any I have ever experienced in all of my miles on the Appalachian Trail. Any wrong move on this narrow trail and you would keep tumbling forever. Angie's knees were beginning to trouble her, understandably so after nine hours of continuous walking and scrambling. It started to rain and we broke out the Gortex jackets from the pack. Then darkness fell. The mini-flash that I always carry for just this sort of an emergency I gave to Angie. I could pick out the trail ahead from the reflection of the light. Somehow we made it down to the canyon floor and we found the one bridge that crosses the river. Our faithful old Renault was waiting not far beyond.

At the car we found a bottle of cognac and we each took a double slug and then some. We drove back toward the inn. It was somehow like being born again and life suddenly became sweeter than it had been for a long time. The dining room stayed open for us and after dinner we stayed up until two in the morning reliving those moments we had been through. If either one of us had fallen it would not have been likely the other would have made it back alive. Had it been me I would have taken the pack down with me and Angie would have been unable to survive the freezing cold without the few survival clothes that we had. Had it been her I would have gone with her trying to make a grab to save her.

With all due respect and being aware of the casual Spanish attitude toward death I think that a simple sign up there at Soasa circle could have been justified under those conditions. It could have been placed where the trail began below the crude sign that says ‘Faja de Pelayo’ and it could have said either ‘Senda cerrada’, trail closed temporarily, or even ’Senda peligrosa’, dangerous trail.

It was late May when we were up there and possibly this is still a little early to use the upper trail. During summer, when the snow has completely melted and the trail is free from this problem it would make a breathtaking adventure. It would be well to make an early start of it and to allow some eight or more hours to complete it. It is a difficult and dangerous hike, though, and not to be undertaken lightly. A return by the well-maintained trail along the canyon floor is stimulating enough to satisfy most hikers anyway and you see all of that magnificent scenery with much the same perspective albeit a little lower down.

Bibliography.

The Michelin Guide for Spain is the tourist bible for roaming around the countryside. The actual trail itself is outlined under Ordesa National Park in the Aragon section.

The Michelin Guide can be obtained from: International Map Centre, 22-24 Caxton St., London, SW1H 0QU, U.K. Tel: 071-222-4945. Or, Stanford's as well, Tel. 071-836-1915.

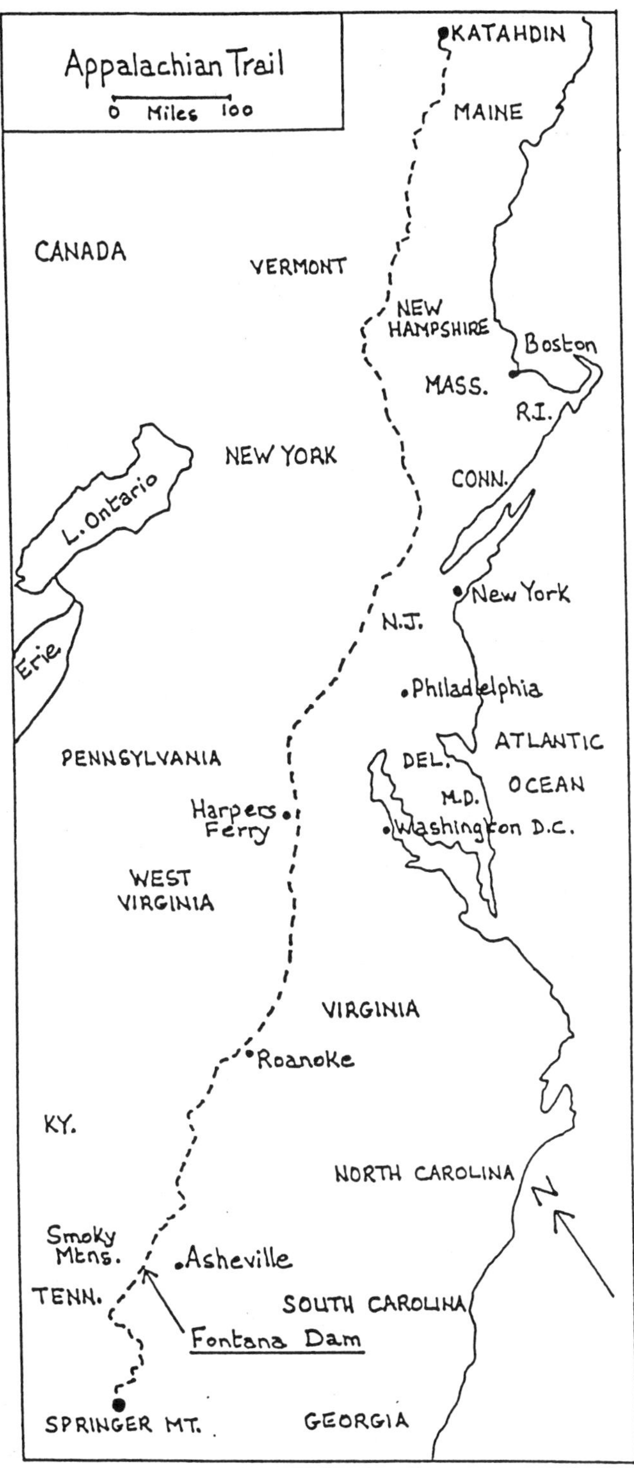
Appalachian Trail
0 Miles 100
KATAHDIN
MAINE
CANADA
VERMONT
NEW HAMPSHIRE
Boston
MASS.
R.I.
NEW YORK
L. Ontario
CONN.
New York
N.J.
Erie
Philadelphia
ATLANTIC
OCEAN
PENNSYLVANIA
DEL.
M.D.
Harpers Ferry
Washington D.C.
WEST VIRGINIA
VIRGINIA
Roanoke
KY.
NORTH CAROLINA
N
Smoky Mtns.
Asheville
TENN.
SOUTH CAROLINA
Fontana Dam
SPRINGER MT.
GEORGIA

WALK IV

IV. The Appalachian Trail from Springer Mtn. to Wallace Gap.

(113.4 Miles)

Springer Mtn. in Georgia is the beginning of the A. T., or ending, if you are one of the few who do the whole trail. About 90% of the 'thru-hikers', those attempting to hike the whole 2,100 miles of trail from Georgia to Maine, start there. The reason for this is that it is possible to start earlier in the south, usually around the first of April, and it is less buggy than it is in Maine in the springtime.

Only about 10% of those who attempt to do the whole trail all in one go actually succeed. Most of them peter out somewhere before the Smokies. Only some 2,000 hardy souls have actually hiked the entire trail in its fifty years of history. And this includes those who have put it together year after year as time permitted.

The vast majority of the 3 million hikers who actually walk on some part of the A. T. each year do it in sections at a time as dollar obligations at home will allow. I'm one of these. I've hiked several hundred delightful miles of it, always headed north.

We have learned to use our 19' Prowler trailer and our K-5 Chevrolet Blazer with four wheel drive for getting up to the trailheads, although paved roads usually cross the A. T. at sufficient intervals. We use the trailer as a base for when I'm not camping out on the trail and Angie drops me off with one of the dogs and picks us up at a prearranged rendevous. It tends to make the whole experience more enjoyable for us because we have most of the amenities of civilization, we get to enjoy

Appalachia itself in the area around the trail, and the logistics are a whole lot easier. I guess this best illustrates the book's title because it really is Walking Easy.

Straight backpacking for extended periods has its own rewards, too. It is the best way to really climb into limbo, become truly at one with nature, make new friends and taste the intoxication of real freedom.

13 Sept. Springer Mtn. to Hightower Gap. 9.1 Miles.

The actual start of the A. T. was a bit tricky to find. After a long struggle with wrong roads we discovered Hwy. 42 out of Suches, Ga. It is an innocuous little gravel road but after about fifteen miles and around an hour of driving it took us past Hightower Gap, where the trail crossed, and then to the take-off juncture for Springer Mtn. We left the Blazer there and we headed up the trail to the left for the official start.

At 7:40 a.m. Angie and Duffy and Beauregard and I headed for Mecca which is only 9/10th of a mile away. This beginning hike on the famous trail is not without a certain amount of emotion somehow. How many others had gone before us? And how many of them had been fired up with that initial commitment to do the whole walk, all the way to Mt. Katahdin in Maine? And how many more would come after us, too? And how about all of the volunteers who keep it up year after year? Will they continue to go on giving unselfishly of their time and effort to keep it maintained year after year for others? And will the government someday figure out a way to charge a fee for walking on it?

The top of Springer Mtn. seemed a fitting place for the start of the Appalachian Trail. It was rocky with light woods and an old campsite much-used. A regular RFD mail box housed the 'Register' to keep it dry. The 'Register' was a plain spiral notebook. It was filled with around a hundred entries.

We signed the register with our adopted trail names. Mine was Claude Bushwhacker, then General P.T. Beauregard, then Meandering Madeleine and finally, Madeleine's MacDuff. The trail names and the register signing was like an initiation or tribal rite where we sort of joined a huge club that had no attendance requirements, no dues and no restrictions. Its only obligation was a respect for the wilderness and a consideration for others.

There was a nice piece in the register by someone who had finally completed the trail north to south over a five year period. It was very eloquent. It spoke of the serenity and the respite from man and machines below the crest line and the heightened sense of appreciation for the basics in life that a life in the wilderness produces. A lot of thought had gone into it and a sense of reluctance was apparent, too, now that the long quest would no longer be a strong part of each year's plans.

We admired the bronze plaque that had wisely been imbedded in a rock overlook that had a magnificent view of receding ridge lines in the distance. It was a scene showing a hiker with a pack ascending a mountain. It had been made and installed in 1959 by the Georgia Appalachian Trail Conference. It said: "Appalachian Trail - Georgia to Maine. A footpath for those who seek fellowship with the wilderness."

When we returned back to the road Angie and Duffy left in the Blazer and Beauregard and I set out down the trail. The trail passed through a large stand of huge hemlocks for quite a long distance and eventually it reached a shelter. The shelter had a much-used fire pit just in front of it and off to one side a picnic table had been provided. This picnic table was a rare piece of furniture because A. T. shelters invariably come completely unfurnished. Free, though. One of the few things in life that is still free anymore.

After the shelter the Trail followed down an old logging road that bordered a rushing stream. There were numerous camp spots beside the stream. They showed evidence of use in days gone by. I met a lone hiker coming the other way. We stopped to chat for a bit. He seemed to be someone I wouldn't mind sharing a shelter with.

We stopped for lunch at a place called Long Falls in a fern and moss covered little glen. There was a pool beneath the falls and it was cool and misty because of the spray from the falls.

When we reached Hawk Mtn. shelter it already had a solo occupant, an older man. He apologized for not going farther. Said he was overweight. Said he was headed for Fontana and that he had done it before some 12 years ago.

Going up a little draw we noticed an army plane that was making a pass overhead and then we saw a command post that was nicely camouflaged. Army Rangers. The only thing that gave it away was the captain's bars on the back of his cap. His radio was speaking Spanish, gringo Spanish that I could understand. When the trail reached a dirt road that it crossed we passed a sentry with a rifle at the ready. I was glad that he hadn't taken me for a spy in the exercise and then hauled me in. It must have been a bubble-burster to have had an A. T. hiker stroll by a secret command post like that.

We came swinging into Hightower Gap well ahead of schedule and I was pleased that we had made this first leg of the trail without any problems.

14 Sept. Hightower Gap to Woody Gap. 12.1 Miles.

Angie and Duffy left us at Hightower Gap early on the following morning. Beauregard and I climbed a steep ascent through heavy woods. No army rangers were around this morning.

We walked along a ridgeline just at sunrise. It was an eerie and dramatic sensation with the sun shining through the trees in the lifting mist and tulle fog. It was just cool enough for the Gortex jacket. I couldn't think of any place else I'd rather be at that moment. We broke cobwebs on the trail with no sign of other tracks before us. Beauregard never ran out of scents to check out and only seldom did he make the mistake of doubling back around a tree. When this happens, and it still does, his retractable lead that is fastened to my belt gets tangled. One of us has to resolve the problem, usually me.

A dog's sense of smell is 200 times more acute than a man's. We see better than he does. He sees in black and white and it is from close to ground level so his sense of smell and his hearing are more receptive for compensation. This is why a dog companion stays so busy in the early stages of a long walk.

We finally reached Sassafras Mtn. summit after a long uphill slog. The committee who planned the layout of the meandering course of the trail deserves a lot of credit. Generally it follows an interesting variety of terrain and there is always something to see around the next bend. It upholds the basic objective of heading north across the crests of the Appalachian range but sometimes, every now and then, it becomes hard not to wonder if maybe they had had a perverse sense of humor at times. This usually happens when the trail stretches ever upward out of sight and there is a tendency to speculate about the merits of maybe going around the side of the mountain instead of always climbing up and over the top each time. Oddly enough, though, I always seem to forget about the struggle getting up there in the exhilaration of actually reaching the top. And once up on top any question about the committee's wisdom or ancestors quickly evaporates in the celebration of a spectacular view to enjoy, the sense of achievement in having made it up there and the anticipation of the downhill section now to come.

Around mid-morning I met a young hiker from Florida. He had spotted the $100 reward mark on Beauregard's collar, the offer of payment for information leading to his arrest and return, and he wanted to know if that was what I'd paid for him. I guess he figured that I'd acquired him at a garage sale somewhere nearby and that I had just forgotten to remove the price tag. Or had he read it as $1.00? I hadn't the heart to tell him that I'd actually raised him from a pup.

At Gooch Gap shelter I had lunch and a quick nap. 8.2

miles in about four hours. We had passed several beautiful camp sites that morning, some with streams running next to them and one under a rock ledge with a view that was completely protected from the weather.

That afternoon I passed two young men with a youngish woman companion. They were all moving rapidly down the trail. They looked sharp with newly purchased packs and clean cut-offs.

Just before reaching our destination we came to a barefoot young woman in white shorts who was perched on a rock by herself. She was writing a letter. She was attractive with a trim figure and an engaging smile. Had I been single it would have been tempting to try to help her to resolve whatever problem had taken her out there in the woods by herself.

At the Woody Gap rendezvous we were both very thirsty after about six hours of walking. A heavily bearded man gave me directions to a clear spring some 200 yards away. The water there was cool and delicious. Beauregard and I drank our fill.

In talking to this bearded man, whose name was John, I found that he made a precarious living of sorts by shuttling trail hikers from Woody Gap to wherever they would like to leave their car. He mentioned an older couple from Baton Rouge whom he had helped with their shuttle earlier that summer. They had made the hike all the way from Springer Mtn. through the Smokies. The husband was 74, his wife 70. They had told him that it had been the adventure of a lifetime.

As I was talking to John a man came out of the woods and joined us. He had been hunting squirrels he said. There was a big discussion about two others who had come out just previously. They had been carrying digging tools and buckets and they had left in a big hurry. Ginseng! They had been hunting ginseng illegally, without a national forest permit. The stuff would bring $125 a lb. And I had thought it only grew in China.

Apparently the ginseng trade is a way to supplement

income in the back woods of Georgia. We later saw others making this same effort, usually surreptitiously it seemed.

15 Sept. Woody Gap to Neels Gap. 11.3 Miles.

John, the bearded man, lived in his car there at Woody Gap for much of the time but the next morning when I started on the Trail he was gone. That day's section worked its way up and over the top of Bloody Mtn., the highest point on the Trail in Georgia. It went from 3,150 ft. to 4,461 ft., and then on down to Neels Gap.

We made good time, up and down, mostly up, some steep, some gradual, until we reached Slaughter Gap. The two streams and the spring that I was looking forward to for water were all dry. In fairness, though, they were termed intermittent in the guide but ever the eternal optimist I never figure that that is going to apply to my own visit. Enough of a pool had accumulated from the spring remnants there for Beauregard to get a drink so we stopped for a lunch of Taboule and Capon chicken with a Georgia peach for dessert. I saved most of the rest of the iced tea for the onslaught up Blood Mtn.

The remaining trail up Blood Mtn. was not as difficult as I had anticipated. There were some rocky parts but we made it up to the top for a little after 1:00 o'clock. There is a stone shelter up there with a fireplace in the front room and the customary plywood raised floor for togetherness sleeping in the back room. The year before a man had died there from hypothermia. He must not have had waterproof matches, spare clothes or a poncho.

On the rocky top of the mountain extensive views could be seen across mountain ranges that rolled away in the distance. A handsome couple from College Park, Ga., appeared. They had hiked up from Neels Gap. I took their picture. They took mine with Beauregard, in front of the shelter. Later I sent them a copy of the picture. It proved that they had climbed to the top of Blood Mtn.

On the way down I came to some blue blazes that indicated a side trail which led to a spring. The spring turned out to be dry but I continued on following the trail in the hope that it was a shortcut to Neels Gap. We reached a small stream where Beauregard gratefully wallowed and drank his fill. When I checked the compass it became obvious that we were headed north, a wrong direction. I had to back track to the regular trail. It was a good lesson. Never second guess the regular trail for a gamble of a short cut.

The trail emptied out onto the main highway and then it crossed over to go through an arched opening at Walasiyi Inn of Neels Gap. This building included a very comprehensive backpacker's store. The store was run by very friendly and knowledgeable people who had a good selection of hiking and nature books as well as the latest in backpacking equipment. I downed two bottles of orange juice and then a couple of grape juice bottles as well. When Angie came with the ice cold beer I put away two more cans of that, too. I must have become dehydrated from not finding any water along the way.

It was super nice to come back to the camper for a hot shower, clean clothes, a home-cooked meal, even TV and a comfortable bed. A civilized way to backpack. 'Walking Easy'.

While I was hiking the trail Angie was able to pursue her hobby of collecting vintage clothing and accessories. She has a very interesting collection and she is quite knowledgeable about it. There were many towns in the area that were worth combing for rare and unusual items. Helen was one of them. It was full of people for its 'Oktoberfest', too. We made it over for a good meal one night and we watched the cloggers perform. We worked the meal off afterwards by joining the group doing polkas. The town is a Bavarian-like village with good restaurants and accommodations and not far from the A. T. itself.

Other interesting towns in the area include Clarkesville, which was then rated No. 2 on the list of most desirable places in the U.S. in which to retire. Cleveland and Dahlonega were two more. All of them have interesting shops and restaurants to enjoy for a change from life on the trail. And this whole area is not far from Atlanta, one of the largest of get-anything, do-anything places in the country.

18 Sept. Neels Gap to Tesnatee Gap. 5.7 Miles.

This was a pleasant hike that Angie and Duffy made with Beauregard and myself. We managed to get a shuttle from an older man at the campground. It was a nice day and we found some good hiking including a steep climb up to a place called Wolf Laurel Top. There was a lovely view from up there and we had a fine picnic on a grassy spot near some trees that produced enough shade for comfort. We indulged ourselves in the luxury of a bottle of vino and a siesta Spanish-style.

Duffy enjoyed his hike and so did Angie. We didn't see anyone on the trail during the whole time that we were out. It was a treat to be able to wind up with the car already there and waiting for us.

19 & 20 Sept. Tesnatee Gap to Low Gap to Unicoi Gap. 15 Miles.

For quite some time I had wanted to try an A.T. campout alone. The next fifteen miles seemed to be a bit much at the time then without breaking it up and there was no road available for a meeting point in between. This seemed to be a good place to have the experience.

That morning it was raining hard and I decided to wait to see if it would let up or whether to consider myself weatherbound. After a couple of hours it stopped long enough for me to feel obliged to give it a go. We managed to get to the trailhead for 11:00 a.m. It was misty, damp and the pack was heavy. In those days I tended to take a lot of unnecessary things that all add up in the weight department. A plastic trash bag over the pack served as a cover for rain protection. The adios to Angie and Duffy was not altogether enthusiastic because it spelled commitment to the next two days in overcast weather. But that is what backpacking is all about. Freedom. With nothing but the goods on your back to worry about. Come rain or come shine.

It was a steep climb up Wildcat Mtn. with Beauregard checking out the many scents as usual. As soon as I started moving, though, I began to enjoy the beauty of the wilderness as always in spite of the miserable weather. After only two hours and twenty minutes we found ourselves headed down the descent into Low Gap. Then it became time to make a decision. There was a shelter there, the only one that would be practical, and it looked bad overhead.

After checking it out, I decided to stop and make camp at Low Gap Shelter. There was a stream nearby and it was a tranquil place in an openly wooded hollow. It would mean a longish hike the next day but the pack would be a little lighter. We made ourselves comfortable along one wall of the shelter. I figured that there wouldn't be anyone else out in this rain, even though it was the weekend, so we would have our solo campout in a good spot.

Damn! Voices, clanging noises and then more rain, too. Down the shelter trail they came. A party of eight! The shelter only sleeps eight. "Mind if we share the shelter with you?" The leader had a heavy dark beard. He was not big, in his late thirties, and he seemed pleasant enough. He carried a huge cook pot on the top of his pack. "Glad to have the company!" I answered. It was a lot more company than I had expected and it wasn't going to be a solo campout after all.

One of the party had a hammock that he was anxious to try out. It had a tarp rig that fitted over the top so as to keep out the rain. This resolved the problem of no more room at the inn. They seemed a nice enough group, all of them from Smyrna, Ga. I surmised that they belonged to a church group of some kind but Frank, the leader, carried a pistol. In those early days I packed one, too, until I finally realized that it really isn't the least bit necessary and the weight is a real nuisance. Most of the repartee was okay men-type talk, mostly cracks about one another, the trail, the rain, the usual double negatives. They were friendly and they all seemed like hardy, responsible types who liked the outdoors and being with one another. Frank, the organizer of the group, gave me a cup of hot Russian tea and he invited me to share in their spaghetti dinner. I declined because I was looking forward to my own menu that would help to lighten the pack. We talked for awhile and I liked him.

We all lined up like sardines in the shelter, feet facing out, goods at the back wall. Everyone hung his pack high on the rear of the shelter to keep it safe from mice and bears. Just at dusk another group came down the shelter trail. More customers. A scout group. They were a noisy lot. The scout masters were good-natured, though. They were disappointed to find the shelter taken but they tented out up above, in the rain. There must have been 15 of them altogether.

On the little one burner pack stove I cooked some fettucine. It turned out to be fairly good, with onions and garlic and mushrooms and even freshly ground parmesan cheese to perk it up a bit. A salad and fried bread with a coffee and cognac helped it along. Frank came over for more of a visit. He told me that he worked for a box mfg. company and that he had a couple of rental houses that he owned. He seemed like he had his act pretty well put together.

Beauregard downed the balance of the fettucine with his supper. I had to wash him in the creek so as not to track his mud and dirt onto the sleeping bag. Then I did the dishes.

By 7:00 o'clock almost everyone was in the sack watching the dying embers of the fire. Three of the group played cards for a while but they soon folded in favor of the warmth and comfort of their bedrolls. Conversation went on until around 9:30 p.m. when everyone finally drifted off.

There was not much sleep for me that night. The boy next to me was a snorer with a touch of asthma and Beauregard tossed and turned down at the foot of my bed. He had the usual nightmares with the feet-in-the-air muffled-barks routine. I was afraid that he would wake everybody up so I'd give him a good nudge whenever he got himself into that mode. I tried counting from 100 backwards, using my own mantra, then the OM mantra, thinking pleasant scenes, whatever, but there was just too much competition around me and nothing worked very well.

It was a welcome relief when six o'clock rolled around and I could get up. I was careful not to disturb anyone. It was fun getting breakfast together and organizing the pack for the trail, especially with everyone else sawing away. Coffee and cereal and fried toast made a good meal. It took an hour and a half to get on the trail. It was still dark when I left. Only Frank was awake. We said goodbye, quietly, knowing we would never see one another again, which is one of the nice things about life on the trail in a way because it is one of the few places where anonymity allows you to say whatever you want to say without its coming home to roost.

For the next five hours we pushed fairly hard through the cloud and mist to make our 12:00 o'clock rendezvous. It was not too bad in spite of some rocky parts and some steep bits. In fact, it turned out to be an inviting section with plenty of water from springs and small streams. I like the feeling of progress that I get from checking off the various features as they are outlined on the map or in the guide as I go along. It is almost like celestial navigation where you make each successive line of position entry on the chart, or where you check off the islands as you pass them by when you are sailing in the Bahamas, or the buoys that you run on the Intracoastal Waterway.

We made it to Unicoi Gap for 12:30 p.m., about 10 miles in five hours with the heavy pack and no breaks. I was grateful that Angie and Duffy had waited past the agreed upon tentative 12:00 o'clock meeting time. The next rendezvous was for three o'clock. Two cold beers from the igloo were welcome thirst quenchers. Nothing ever tasted so good. Then we headed back to the camper for barbecued 'lamberginis', Angie's ground-lamb patties in a sour-dough muffin cooked on the Hibachi.

This was the end of this starting expedition on the A.T. I had to go back to do chores. It left me with some reflections about the experiences I had had in this initial get-acquainted period. It was easy to acknowledge that I had enjoyed many pleasant miles of walking in the wilderness and that I had seen a part of the country that I would never otherwise have seen. I felt better for it mentally and physically and I recognized that it was a true vacation where you didn't tend to bring the work and problems along. I liked the logistics of packing the pack and planning each day's hike. It was nice to do something where the dogs could be included, too. They tend to be amusing and cheerful and they have a way of making each day a little better in spite of the trouble they sometimes get into.

The people that I had briefly met along the trail thus far had invariably seemed to be friendly and stable with an absence of malice within. There is nothing to be bought or sold in the wilderness, no reason for promotion, and relationships are not going to carry over into everyday life so everyone can relax and hang loose. By not using a real name on the A. T. nothing can come back to roost if the skeletons in the closet back home are revealed and some times it can be therapeutic to talk about them. A sympathetic and interested listener invariably has his own problems and a good ear, in turn, can help him as well. Commiseration and therapy at non-shrink rates.

Backpacking and hiking holds little attraction for the fast-laners and druggies. Too much effort. No artificial stimulation, booze, broads and easy highs. People who like nature, physical exercise, solitude, independence and resourcefulness walk to the beat of a different drummer than those in constant need of urban renewal.

The trail provides a time and a place to reflect on where life has gone and where it would be nice to make it go and a way to feel good naturally. At the same time it has some kind of beckoning attraction of its own, the lure of discovering what is around the next bend or just over the next peak. For me it provides the never-ending fascination of places and countryside never seen before and this is one of the primary reasons that people like to travel.

All in all I was completely satisfied with the experiences we had had on the A.T. and around it as well, since the side trips and other activities were all a part of it, too. It had been even more worthwhile than what I had originally envisioned when first I had read the article in the National Geographic that had induced me to give it a try. I was ready to come back and put my feet down on that inviting path into the woods when next we could get away.

12 Apr. Tray Mtn. to Unicoi Gap. 4.6 Miles.

Back to the A. T. again in mid-April of the following year. When we had awakened the day before we had found snow on the ground and it had provided an opportunity to locate one of our favorite campgrounds, Georgia Mountain Park at Hiawassee. The snow had melted enough to see the trail all right by the next day so Beauregard and I set out on a short break-in hike that same afternoon.

The A.T. crossed USFS 79 at Tray Gap and it was an exhilarating feeling to come back to it again. Shortly after Angie and Duffy had dropped us off they had had a dicey experience that I heard about later. They had forded a creek bed in the Blazer that had been deeper than what it looked. Water had come up to the floor boards because of the melting snow. If they had become stranded on that little-used forestry road it would have been a long walk for help.

When Beauregard and I hit the trail after being dropped off it was like coming back home again after a brief absence. It was a nice sunny day, too. We made good time until we trudged up the steep ascent to the top of Rocky Mtn.

On the top of Rocky Mtn. we admired the view of ever-successive ridges and we took a lunch break. Beauregard helped me with the sardines. After lunch we worked our way on down to Unicoi Gap and Ga. 75 where we had stopped last fall. It was a treat to see it again. I didn't like reversing back on the trail like that but it seemed the most practical way for Angie to meet us at a well-defined spot. I don't suppose it matters. It's sort of like walking backwards. You still do all of it just the same and you see the same scenery, its just that you don't have the sense of forward progress.

13 Apr. Tray Gap to Dicks Creek Gap. 12 Miles.

From a 7:40 a.m. start Beauregard trudged with me up Tray Mtn. There were fabulous views from the summit in a 360 degree direction. It is not often that you get to enjoy that experience. I wondered if it would somehow be possible to capture such a moment on film at sunrise. A telescopic lens would help but it wouldn't really do justice to the immensity of the different mountain ranges peeling away. The struggle up to the top always makes the reward of getting there worthwhile.

After Tray Mtn., at 4,430 ft., the guide advises that 'Beyond, trail is rough, rocky and steep.' By then I had learned to pay attention to these succinct little masterpieces of understatement. The new boots, a size too large, to accommodate double pairs of socks, wool and cotton, helped to carry me past this section all right. It included the shelter at Montray where I heard the voices of two late risers. Then it had worked up and down past two gaps to 'The Swag of the Blue Ridge' which was billed as the lowest gap in the area.

The trail next led around Dismal Mtn. and down to a very good spring at Sassafras Gap. After Addis Gap it started a bitch of an ascent for a mile up to a place called Kelly Knob, at 4,276 ft. the highest peak between Tray Mtn. and the N.C. line. Here we took a break for lunch with the usual sardine sharing routine.

That morning we had seen nine hikers on the trail.

These included one southbound loner, another loner from Alaska, who was hiking until the joints gave out, and an older woman with a couple who seemed to be related. The man had an artificial leg and I admired his perseverance. The others were another northbound couple and two hardy young hikers wearing shorts and tee shirts. One fawn had crossed the trail as well. I had a brief chat with the hiker from Alaska. He was retired. He had done the Florida trail, which was new to me, and he had a preference for wearing jeans. His observation, like mine, was that they were better for protection from yellow jackets, poison ivy, brambles and the sun. Shorts are lighter weight we agreed and pleasant enough when conditions are good but the jeans are better for all around protection.

About four and half miles of mostly down travel brought us to Dicks Creek Gap at U.S. 76. for a 4:00 o'clock Coors Light rendezvous. The last mile always seems the longest of the day.

15 & 16 Apr. Dicks Creek Gap to Bly Gap to Deep Gap. 15.8 Miles.

This was the first sure-enough solo campout experience. It started with an 8:40 a.m. departure from Dicks Creek Gap. It was a nice day and that section of the trail was pleasant enough but in mid-April it was cold with ice on the puddles here and there. The locals were terming it a late winter that year. There were no other hikers on the trail until Beauregard and I reached Bly Gap. Bly Gap was to be a sort of a hallmark because it was on the border into N. Carolina. I don't know what I was expecting exactly but I guess I thought there would be some sort of a sign indicating that we were leaving Georgia, maybe even 'Welcome to North Carolina' or something. Or, 'Hooray, you have just completed marching through Georgia on the A.T.' Nobody in either state seemed to be very excited about my accomplishment.

Bly Gap really was a kind of a miserable place for a

camp but it did have a good spring and it had been used before. In fact, there was even some litter and garbage that had been left at the remains of the fire pit. Three hikers were stretched out taking a break just above where I had planned to camp. One of them was a girl friend of the stockier of the group. Then a fourth hiker came up the trail. We visited for awhile and then they all decided to press on up the steep ascent to Muskrat Creek Shelter, some 3.2 miles away. I elected to stay and do my thing there where we were.

After getting the tent set up and more or less organized, Beauregard and I stretched out for a rest. Whatever reveries we were respectively indulging in were rudely interrupted by the ominous sound of dirt bikes. I couldn't believe it. Sure enough, though, up above us I could see a couple of teenagers with a girl friend on the back of the larger dirt bike. They got off and began to horse around and then one of them noticed the tent and he started to head his bike on down the slope toward us. Beauregard went into his 'Don't Tread on Me' bark, he doesn't like motorcycles anyway, and I crawled out to show myself. The biker changed his mind and shortly afterward he and his two friends left. I was sure that they were just having fun but it was kind of nerve-wracking all the same. One never knows these days. I thought we were miles from any kind of civilization. They had come up a side trail of some sort but I never could figure out how they managed to make it up there.

It was lonesome up at Bly Gap. It just didn't seem a friendly place. I watched the sun go down and around six I built a fire and I cooked some spaghetti for dinner. I hung the pack in a distant tree for protection from the b'ars, cleaned up and then I crawled into the tent with Beauregard right behind me. It was very cold outside but with a candle and the little fluorescent flashlight going and tucked into the sleeping bag it was sort of cozy in the tent. I started in on a John D. McDonald novel to take the edge off of my nerves. Beauregard growled a couple of times. I don't know exactly what produced the sense of apprehension I had but for some reason it was there all right. My intellect told me that there was nothing I couldn't handle, I have never had any fear of animals, or isolation, or the dark, or teenage dirt bikers, but I confess I had a difficult time listening to reason and I stayed up until three reading the novel by the bad light of the candle.

Around two o'clock Beauregard started to shiver. The ground under the tent floor was just too cold for him and a Labrador who hasn't grown a second coat of hair from sleeping outside doesn't have the protection that a dog with more hair would have. I worried about him becoming hypothermic and so I pulled him into the sleeping bag to get him warm. I worried about the candle catching the tent on fire, too, and so after Travis MaGee had accomplished whatever task John D. had assigned to him I blew it out and tried to go to sleep. I just lay there, though, trying to keep the bag around Beauregard to keep him from shivering and I kept thinking the wasted thoughts that pop up when you can't sleep. I did manage to doze off for a bit but the truth is that I didn't get much sleep that night. I had plenty of rest, though, and it was comfortable in the tent.

It was a real joy to have six o'clock roll around so that I could start moving again. It was freezing outside the tent with ice on the puddles still. The pack was all right, nobody had tried it on for size, or ripped it open looking for b'ar food. I had burned the rest of the litter that had been left there, including a half-empty carton of eggs that someone had left. I made some coffee and hot oatmeal, just the ticket for something to stick to the ribs. After an hour and a half's worth of chores and a mostly sleepless night it was a relief to get back on the trail again.

For the next mile and a half we trudged up the steepest section of the trail yet encountered. Straight up, my log says. Even the welcome sight of the sun coming up didn't help much. It took us two and a half hours to reach Muskrat shelter which was only 3.2 miles away. By the time we got there the others had already left. They were 'thru-hikers' but I would never know if they would be part of the 90% who enthusiastically set out from Springer Mtn. and gradually fall by the wayside somewhere between Fontana and Damascus, Va.

The rest of the 7.1 miles was not as steep after the shelter and much of it was very pleasant going until the rocky climb up and around an arduous piece of terrain called Yellow Mtn. I suspected that this long and circuitous detour of about two miles was caused by a land owner who wouldn't grant permission for the trail to cross his land. This last section was a bit difficult and dangerous with rocks and tree blowdowns to negotiate. It required a certain amount of precaution to keep from spraining an ankle or worse. At some places I had to turn Beauregard loose to keep from being pulled over at the crucial moment of stepping off of a rock. One spot was steep enough to have had steps carved into the earth itself with wood-shoring like a ladder. The trail was always well marked, though, with the ever-present white blazes carefully showing the way. 5 hours to do 7.1 miles!

In the 33 miles of hiking that week I figured that I had burned off some 7,800 calories, a fringe benefit while leaving Georgia behind. It was better than doing it with a restricted calorie diet, a form of torture that is less appealing.

21 Apr. Deep Gap to Beech Gap. 8.8 Miles.

In the campground we shifted over to the umbilical cord of a 'full hook-up' for the trailer so that we could use water without the nuisance of having to dump every 3 or 4 days. We did some sightseeing in the area and then I went back on the trail again.

Beauregard hiked with me and we made good time to Beech Gap where we could go down the 3 miles of the Beech Gap trail to USFS 67 for our rendezvous. This 5.8 miles of the A. T. was an easy walk over gentle terrain for a change. We made about 3 mph on it. We didn't meet any other hikers but we saw tracks for 4 or 5. We didn't see any wildlife.

The three miles downhill on the Beech Gap trail were

also very easy going with changing tree growth as the elevations lowered. Even though the trail was well marked and well maintained there was no sign of its having been used for a long time. Maybe it sees more activity in the summer. There was a nice stream down at USFS 67 where we had our lunch while waiting for our chauffeure.

22 Apr. Beech Gap to Betty's Creek Gap. 10 Miles.

Beauregard and I did this section going south as Betty's Creek Gap was easy to pick up from USFS 67 and it would be more fun doing the off-trail hike downhill, a repeat of yesterday. This was a lovely spring day. The polypro thermal undershirt came off in the first hour. Again, it was an easy trail with magnificent vistas on both sides of the ridge. The foliage was still pretty barren yet, except for the rhododendrum thickets, so you could still see through the woods. There were lots of springs and little streams. I had been drinking from the small springs and even the beginning streams where they were at the higher elevations with nothing much above them to trigger giardia problems. I suppose there was a remote threat of contamination but I hadn't seen any cattle and wildlife that high up and no people except on the A. T. itself. I didn't experience any problems from drinking the water that way.

Two other doggies were on the trail that day, the first that I had seen. One little trooper was carrying her own pack. There were more hikers out than I had seen before. Two men had a barking dog that Beauregard ignored. The other dog was with a young hiker I met at Carter Gap Shelter. He seemed to be a college drop-out from Boone, N. Carolina. He was at loose ends trying to get himself together again but he was sociable and Beauregard liked his companion, she was a female type, naturally. There were two more solos who were temporarily hiking together and a couple who had stopped by a stream. One of them was purifying water with a filter type pump that emptied into his canteen.

Another hiker that we met was a veteran who had done the whole A.T. He had done it in two week vacation stages each year with one final 700 mile push on retirement. He was responsible for maintenance of this section of the N.C. portion of the trail. It was an interesting visit. The reason the trail is so steep out of Bly Gap is because it is private land and it is the only route permissible. The big detour around Yellow Mtn. was laid out originally for the same reason as I had suspected but since then the A.T. has acquired it. They hesitate to reroute it, though, because they aren't permitted to use chain saws there as it is a dedicated Wilderness Area. Bureaucracy at work. He was p.o.'ed because horses had been ridden over a part of his trail. They do tend to wear it down a bit, I suppose, but I had seen no other horse tracks elsewhere and I felt defensive from all of my own time spent in the saddle as a youngster and during my ranching days.

There were three other hikers that we passed as well. You seem to meet the hikers going south but seldom do you see those who are going north. They are in the same holding pattern, unless they are faster or slower than you are or collapsed at a lunch break.

The log at Carter Gap Shelter complained of a skunk and a resident mouse at Standing Indian Shelter. Someone had seen a bobcat. There were reports of snow and lots of rain in the earlier entries. The menu for a previous night for one was 'noodles and something' with 'something and noodles' planned for the coming night. I recognized a 'Mister Rat' a/k/a with an elaborate sketch that I had seen last summer up near Nolichucky. 15 March was the earliest entry. About 70 or 80 had signed the log.

Something should be said at this point about the feeling of peace and contentment that comes from walking along through the woods. The awareness is usually there although it is easy to get caught up in the logistics of miles done and miles to do consideration. It is hard to lose sight of nature itself, though, with the beauty of a rhododendron glen or the refreshing ambiance of spring water running over rocks and moss or coming out of the side of a mountain. There is the intense quiet that often happens and then the glad sound of birds nearby or the cadence of a rushing stream that gradually becomes louder as you approach it. All of this is a welcome change from the harshness of man-made sounds that are sometimes heard from far below the crestline that the trail usually favors.

It is nice to finally see the sky filter through the trees at the end of a steep climb, signifying that the crest is due to be reached soon and that the anticipated reward for all of that effort is about to be enjoyed. Sometimes the crest turns out to be only a knob with more of the same up, up, up on the other side but the disappointment is quickly swallowed because the eternal optimist inside all of us says, 'Hey, Only One More to Go and That's It'.

There is something immensely satisfying about reaching a top. It produces a sense of justification for a well-earned break or a spot to have lunch and you get the feeling that you really are head and shoulders above everybody else in the world down below. It is one of the reasons why many of the most interesting campsites are found on the peaks and from up there you can enjoy a dramatic sunset and a friendly dawn breaking while you go about breakfast and trail-packing chores.

Something else that is equally satisfying is to reach a readily identifiable 'Gap'. It helps to have a marker that indicates its name and the mileage to the next shelter or the next gap coming up. It provides a welcome check on navigation along the trail. Some places are better than others about this. I would guess that it depends upon the enthusiasm and inclinations of the section group responsible for a given part of the trail. Some people resent signs of any kind, they feel that it takes away from the aspect of having a pristine wilderness as much as possible. Others figure it is nice for the hiker to be able to identify where he really is and to log his progress. Still others may have a hard time finding room for it in the budget.

26 Apr. Betty's Creek Gap to Wallace Gap. 9 Miles.

This was another easy bit of the trail. It passed over dead leaves and through open woods that had no foliage as yet. Beauregard tripped once or maybe it was because his back feet became tangled in a twig and he went down in a heap. He was embarrassed. Then I did the same thing. I stumbled on a root and I had a hard time trying to recover without a fall.

We reached Rock Gap Shelter for 1:00 p.m. The only hiker that we saw was passing on the main trail above the shelter and he didn't come down to visit. The log there was less philosophic than last year's logs in Georgia. Still, though, it was full of appreciation for this basic kind of life style. There was a good bit of crowing about 20 and 24 mile days, since these last three days had been a pretty straightforward section. There were reports on one medium-sized bear sighting, knee and ankle injuries and sore feet and there was the usual anticipation of pizza, showers, laundry and beer in Franklin, the next major town.

At Wallace Gap we were waiting for our ride when two of the hikers from yesterday caught up with us. One of them was a friendly 'all-the-wayer' who remembered Beauregard and greeted him enthusiastically. The other was a chap from New Zealand. He had come over especially to hike the A.T. He was about my vintage and he had read the article in the Nat'l. Geo., too. It had inspired him to come to the States and do a good slice of it. He planned to leap-frog up to Vermont after a few more miles. He had friends up there who wanted to hike with him. Aussies and Kiwis seem to get around more than anybody else I meet or maybe I just seem to remember them more because they seem to live so very far away.

WALK V

V. The Appalachian Trail from Wallace Gap to Fontana Dam.

(59.8 Miles)

My sister, Beulah Jean Lang, from Loomis, California, joined us for the next visit to the trail. She and her family are inveterate backpackers in the Sierras and elsewhere. We checked her into the nearby Fieldstone Inn, a very pleasant place on the lake there at Hiawassee not far from where we were camped. My sister has been saddled with the nickname 'Boonie' all of her life. It is because I had difficulty saying Beulah Jean when I was a toddler. I have been trying to make it up to her ever since. She has gone out of her way to help so many people throughout her life that we try to recognize it by also calling her Saint Boonie of Loomis. She is always cheerful, a good sport and a pleasure to be around.

<u>24 May. Wallace Gap to Wayah Gap. 9.1 Miles.</u>

Angie dropped Boonie, Beauregard and myself off at Wallace Gap for 10:00 a.m. in the rain. It was a storm that looked like an all day affair but Boonie was on a one week schedule and we were both aching to get on the trail. Once there again it was sort of like walking through the door of a favorite restaurant, you knew you were going to feel good as long as you were there.

It rained off and on for most of the day. Boonie was enthusiastic about the A.T., though. It was the first time that she had set foot on it. She found many wild flowers that were readily identifiable and it was interesting to learn the names of some I hadn't known. We had lunch in the shelter of a large rhododendron tree. I took the opportunity to dig out a dry shirt. It stanched the chill from the cold rain.

We met three young hikers who had started out shortly behind us. They were headed for the shelter at Siler's Bald. Two young men and a girl. They were friendly and handsome and they all wore shorts in spite of the rain.

We also became acquainted with another hiker who fell in with us. He was a young Doctor from L.S.U. in New Orleans. He had nine days that he'd managed to squeeze off and he hoped to make Fontana Dam in that time. He had already come 15 miles when he had caught up with us as we were leaving from lunch. He asked us to phone his sister in Chattanooga to verify that he was all right, which we later did. His wife didn't care much for his solo hiking. She worried about him out there with the bears and the bushwhackers and God knows what else. His life was dedication and long hours. He was doing AIDS research and I was glad that he had been able to manage a little time off.

My sister is married to an Orthopedic Surgeon who has devoted his life to helping people, too. Gil has been the Medical Director for the Western States 100 Mile Endurance Run for many years. The race is held in the Sierras each year in mountainous terrain. Just to succeed in finishing it is considered to be the ultimate in athletic achievement.

We made it into Wayah Gap for 3:15 p.m. Our young doctor friend left us to head on up the steep trail in the gathering mist and drizzle. The next shelter was 10 miles away so he would have a cold and lonely camp that night. We offered to have him join us for dinner but he declined. He was determined to keep his schedule.

25 May. Wayah Gap to Burningtown Gap. 8.9 Miles.

It was a misty, damp start for the 4 mile trudge up to Wayah Bald. Up there we met the same three young hikers from yesterday. They had spent a rainy afternoon and night at Siler's Bald Shelter and they had made a late start that morning. Two of the three were on their honeymoon. The groom had a degree in aeronautical engineering but he had changed his mind about his career and he would enter law school in the fall. They planned to make Harper's Ferry, the halfway mark for the A.T., by the end of summer.

The other young hiker in the trio was a college student between semesters or colleges, I wasn't quite sure which. His trail name was Brother Son. He had made a late start but he hoped to make the N.Y. state line in good enough time to hitchhike to Maine and then to work back down the A.T. before the bugs and cold became too bad up there. By doing it this way he could complete the whole trail near his home in New York. It was a pretty ambitious program. He had spent three days in Hiawassee with tendinitis. He had read the honeymooners entry in the log back at Rock Gap Shelter and he had gone all out to catch up with them. You could see that the honeymooners were fond of him but after all a honeymoon did require a measure of privacy. When he had suggested that they camp out somewhere beside the trail that night the comment was made that maybe he could do that by himself and that then they would join him in the morning. Well, you can't spend all of your time just hiking on a honeymoon.

This was another easy day and the sun came shining through the clouds in the afternoon to make it really pleasant.

2 Jun. Burningtown Gap to Tellico Gap. 5.2 Miles.

This was a short hike that is in sequence with the trail but not datewise since Angie and Duffy did it with Beauregard and me after Boonie had gone. We spotted our old Blazer that we had brought up for Boonie at Tellico Gap and we took the big Blazer to Burningtown Gap. The little tobacco farms are interesting when driving up to the A.T. in that area. There are some very picturesque places and I could see how it would be a pleasant way of life. Everyone had to have his own barn for drying and curing the tobacco leaves. I've been a non-smoker myself for many years now but I guess there will always be a market for it. If not, there is always moonshine, or potatoes, to consider. Pigs and chickens, too. Or Social Security and Welfare. It doesn't take much when you have your land and nature to help you out.

We saw two woodchucks on the way up. These are comical creatures and fun to watch as they go about their business by the side of the road. On the trail we discovered our first rhododendrons in bloom. I had been looking at them without color for so long it was a treat to see them blossom. They are like a big azalea only much fatter. Just a few had opened up so far but there were lots of mountain laurel and flaming azaleas that had bloomed as well.

We saw a great shelter at Cold Spring Gap. It had been built of logs that were old and weathered now. It had a nice fire pit and a good spring nearby. It was the best shelter that I had seen so far. The Honeymooners and Brother Son, their erstwhile tag-a-long, had stayed there. They were still keeping Indiana time.

We ate lunch at a campsite just after Copper Bald. It had a free-flowing spring and it was very wooded. Beauregard and Duffy caught some scents that made them anxious. I can't imagine what they were. We had smelled skunk back on the trail. Maybe that was it. The trail was rocky in parts with graded ups and downs but all in all it was an easy leg. It was good to have Angie and Duffy along for it.

27 May. Tellico Gap to Wesser. 7.7 Miles.

Bright sunshine, a lovely spring day. Vitamin E massages and moleskins helped a heel blister that was caused by the new boots. I wore high-top Nikies to give the new boots a rest. Beauregard and Boonie chugged along with me up the two mile ascent to Wesser Bald. Steep.

On the top of Wesser Bald are the remains of an old fire tower. It hangs over a horrendous abyss on the edge of a straight down precipice. Here we had an anxious moment with Beauregard. He was running free at the time. Boonie climbed the steep stairs that led to the midway platform which was still intact. She had wanted to admire the view. Quick as a wink Beauregard followed. He was wearing his pack. No telling what he had in mind. He has never been too keen on views before. He just wanted to participate, I guess. I had no idea about how we were going to get him down. And I have a serious problem with heights.

Reluctantly I climbed up the ladderlike steps to the platform while Boonie hung on to Beauregard who, naturally, couldn't see what all the fuss was about. I managed to remove his pack. Then Boonie climbed back down. I tried not to look at the drop-off to nowhere and somehow I got him turned around on the narrow ledge up there and pointed in the right direction. Step by miserable step we made it back down without either one of us going ass over teakettle.

Lunch was at a ridgetop on the way down to Wesser. There were views in every direction, even the Smokies in the distance. Beauregard ate the lunch that he had carried up in his pack. He was a good sport about being saddled up like a burro and he never complained about the rig he was wearing. I guess he figured it was all part of life's rich patina on the trail.

After lunch we came to a hiker who was slogging up toward us. When we asked him about a place mentioned in the guide that was called the 'Jump-Up' he said, "Oh, you'll know when you get there. Believe me, you'll know."

The Jump-Up was straight up and down rock. He was right. We climbed down it very carefully.

At the Jump-Up we met the other four members of the earlier hiker's group. They had come from Davenport across the Smokies and they were helpful about describing the shelter routine for that section. They had camped at Sassafras Gap on Cheoah the previous night. This is the big assault climb that every A.T. thru-hiker must face. The retired Eastman Kodak leader said, "This is what we do now." They were all friendly with grey hair and hiking shorts. They looked fit and they were enjoying themselves.

When finally we made it down to Wesser and the Nantahala River it was fun to watch the kayakers practice turning over so that they would be able to right themselves if they were knocked over in white water. One kayaker couldn't make it around, though. It looked like he was going to drown but his mate pushed his own kayak over to him and he grabbed the bow to pull himself up.

29 May. Wesser to Stecoah Gap (Everest expedition). 13.1 Miles.

This section of the A.T. is often described as the most difficult of the whole trail. With a climb of 3,000 ft. in about 7.7 miles the trail chugs straight up in several places. Of the several books that I have read about the thru-hikes of others this seems to be the consensus of opinion. It has been improved somewhat in recent years with more switchbacks but to get from Wesser to the top of Cheoah it is still demanding and slow going.

Boonie and Beauregard and I set out with full overnight packs around 10:00 a.m. from Wesser. Beauregard was carrying his bedroll, his food and his pie-pan dish in his saddle bags.

In a lovely glade we stopped to rest. A lone hiker with a daypack came down the trail. He stopped to visit. He was a member of the trail association who managed this section and he was out for a quick inspection hike. He gave water to Beauregard from his canteen by pouring it into his hand. He told us that he usually drank from the springs but that the water up at Sassafras, where we were going to camp, was now giving people dysentery problems and that we should boil it or use a purification pump. I had been drinking regularly from the springs and the high-up streams myself so this was welcome advice. Boonie had her pump and filter for Sassafras.

Our new friend told us that he had managed to get twelve volunteers together from his trail association, plus two forest service rangers, and that they had all pitched in to clean up the mess that was Cable Gap Shelter farther on up the trail. I could remember its being referred to in the Philosopher's Guide, a popular trail book, as 'The Ghetto'. He had built a bark trough for the spring there himself and he was justifiably proud of what they had all accomplished. I was looking forward to seeing it later on when I would reach that area.

About half way up we stopped at a spring for a drink and lunch. The water was clear and cold. It came out of lichen covered rocks beside the trail. Our site looked out over a glade of hardwood forest that was covered by many ferns because of the spring. It was an idyllic spot.

To take our minds off of the steepness of the trail Boonie described the backpack trip she had taken in Nepal with her daughter, Heidi. Just the two of them had gone together by themselves. They had flown to Katmandu and then to Nepal and then they had hired a sherpa guide and sherpa porters for a two week slog to where they could see Everest itself. Jesus! It had been a remarkable experience full of adventure.

When later I had mentioned the trip to my son, Bret, he had said that Heidi had confided to him that she had been anxious on many occasions for fear that the sherpas would rape them and dispose of their bodies off of the awesome precipices along which they had walked for much of the way. It would have been a convenient solution for body disposal, no one would ever find them in those bottomless canyons.

When we were almost to the top of Swim Bald we were astonished to see two hardy grey-beards who were riding mountain bicycles down the trail. They had driven a back road up as far as they could go and then they had left their car there. They had pushed their bikes on up to the top of Cheoah Bald itself. What a ride down they must have had. I hoped that their brakes were in good shape. The bikes were like my own but I doubt that I would have wanted to tackle something like that. Dropoffs on the trail could be fatal if the tires slipped or the brakes gave out. The rocky places would mean carrying the bike down them at times. It must have been a hell of a ride and all down hill.

When finally we pulled into Sassafras Gap around 4:30 p.m. it was with a sense of achievement that made up for the exhaustion it took to get there. I had looked at the map many times, wondering what it would be like to make it up Cheoah and wanting to do it because I figured after I had I would be able to negotiate anything else that the trail had in store for me elsewhere.

The shelter was not that clean or inviting and I found a better place to camp down below it. The spot was not far from the stream nearby. Boonie pumped water through her filter as I set up both tents, built a fire and hooked up the faithful little stove. Beauregard's bedroll, which was a spare ensolite pad, I set up next to mine in the two-man tent. It would be nice not to have him crowding into me. I fixed up the-one man tent next to the campfire for Boonie.

We cooked a trail dinner of dried beef stroganoff and noodles, just add hot water. We had chicken soup, fried toast and the balance of Angie's chocolate chip brownies. We sat around the campfire talking for awhile and then I joined Beauregard who had already put himself to bed. It was a beautiful moonlit night there in the little hollow at Sassafras Gap.

In the morning early I brought down our packs that I had hung in a distant tree and we made breakfast. Nobody had come to the shelter as I had thought they would. It was a Memorial Day weekend, too. It took us a long time to break camp. Boonie's filter was a bit clogged and it was a slow process filtering water through it. We were dependent on the water that we would take with us from Sassafras. The guide indicated that it was the only water between there and Stecoah

Gap, our destination. I enjoyed the anticipation of getting on the trail, though. I had still had a problem sleeping well at night. It was better than before but I couldn't seem to shake some vague feeling of apprehension that I couldn't quite put my finger on. Frustrating. It was a pretty campsite in the morning light and I wouldn't mind staying there again.

The top of Cheoah Bald was like some sort of a major conquest. I relished the steep climb up from Sassafras. It took us about an hour to do the final mile up to the top at 5,062 ft. For some reason it was sort of my own personal Everest and it was nice to have Boonie and Beauregard there to share it with me. We took the traditional photographs of each other standing next to the elevation marker.

The top of Cheoah Bald had a breathtaking view in every direction. There was evidence of its having been used as a campsite and it was easy to see why. In spite of the water lugging problem it would be a dramatic place to spend a night, especially with a moon and a clear sunrise.

The long trail down was almost as steep as the way up. There were a number of ascents over knobs, too, which added to the spice and complaints.

Boonie came to a spot where she wanted to stop to put on moleskin for the hot spots on her toes. I started to sit down on an old grey log by the side of the trail. I noticed what looked like a giant beetle where I was about to sit. Then it began to move and it had a long grey tail attached to it. It turned out to be the head of a small snake that leisurely slid on into a hole in the log. It was as surprised as I was.

The little grey snake reminded me of the three foot black snake that had been coiled in the middle of the trail yesterday. It had made ready to strike at Beauregard who seemed oblivious to it as usual. I had managed to pull him back in the nick of time. The snake was not about to move out of the way and it was too steep at that spot to go around him. I had been able to find a long stick that I used to gingerly move him off of the trail. Once moved he went on his way, slithering down the steep hillside. He must have been puckered about being so rudely disturbed in the midst of his morning sunbath.

I wasn't able to identify either of these two snakes. They didn't seem to have the triangular-shaped head of the poisonous snake so they were probably harmless. They were the only two snakes that I had seen thus far.

We met one other hiker. He had just graduated from college with a degree in Anthropology. He had taken the day off in Wesser on the day before. He had left Springer on May 20th and here he was ten days later all the way up and over Cheoah Bald. Ten days later! Over 16 miles a day averaged! He wasn't too sure what he wanted to do with his degree. He missed his apartment in Boston, his family and his new girl friend but he had planned this hike for a long time so you could see he held mixed emotions about it. He was really travelling light.

We reached Locust Cove Gap and collapsed for lunch. Beauregard helped us clean up the remnants of too ambitious a dinner meal. It was nice to know that Stecoah Gap was only 3.1 miles away.

On the way down Boonie entertained with bear stories. The one I liked the best was about the time when she had had her Campfire Girls Troop up in the Sierras near Yosemite. They had all been bedded down in their sleeping bags and fast asleep. A bear came by at first light. She happened to be the only one awake at the time. The bear reached up some nine feet and slashed open the bottom of their packs to extract some food. Disappointed at not getting more he came over to where Heidi was asleep. Poor Heidi. Buried deep in their bags the half dozen girls and Boonie's husband, Gil, were all unaware of the bear's presence. She decided it was best not to create pandemonium so she quietly reached for her camera. The bear began to look for food in Heidi's sleeping bag with Heidi still sleeping inside it. The flash from the camera startled him. He looked at Boonie and the camera and then he gave it up and headed back on up the hill from where he had come.

Overdue by twenty minutes we rolled into Stecoah Gap wondering if Angie would have waited. I don't like her waiting alone at trailheads so we have always had this arrangement where she is to leave and come back two or three hours later if we are not there when she arrives. She doesn't always listen to me, though, and sure enough there she was with an igloo full of beer, frozen yogurt and cold water!

Back at the camper we had a joint birthday celebration with a carrot cake that Angie had made. She had done a frosting map of the trail from Wallace Gap to Stecoah Gap! The next day we put Boonie on the plane in Asheville, No. Carolina. I know she enjoyed herself as much as we enjoyed having her.

3 Jun. Stecoah Gap to Yellow Creek Gap. 7.7 Miles.

The first two miles were very steep, as bad as Cheoah Bald, or worse, but with a lighter pack and being able to travel at my own pace it went a lot faster. Even Beauregard was panting by the time we finally reached the top for a lunch stop. I had to feed him his sardines and dog biscuits by hand.

This section of the trail was narrow and overgrown with grass in spots, almost as if it hadn't been used much. I had to check the blazes carefully to be sure we were really on the A.T.

The A.T.C. guide is seldom wrong but occasionally the trail has been changed since publication and it can't always be taken for granted. It is often at variance with the mileage on the posted signs, too. My observation has been that it is best to trust the blazes on the trees if there is any doubt. Even so, it is reassuring to identify the landmarks as they are mentioned in the guide and I like to check them against the corresponding mileage that is shown.

There was no one else on the trail that day, nor the day before either. It was my birthday, too, and it was a good way to enjoy it. I sat on a rock on a ridgecrest for a break and I remembered the birthday of the year before with Ann and David in London and the rhino cake that my daughter Kit had made for me shortly afterward at the Isle of Man where she was living at the time.

And I remembered the time that my birthday had fallen right in the middle of the Gulf of Mexico at a time when I had discovered water in the bilge of my old ketch and almost dead batteries as well. There was no way to make Mexico 200 miles to windward and the pumps wouldn't work without batteries or an engine. And how the best birthday present I ever had was when I managed to get the engine going with a screwdriver crossed over from the starter to the ground. And then the next two presents were finding and fixing the leak and then being able to repair the alternator as well. And how we all celebrated with a Bisquick birthday cake that my crew had made for me. That was a good birthday, too.

We pulled into Yellow Creek Gap six minutes ahead of schedule. Angie and Duffy arrived with a welcome can of Coor's Light and the good news that she had negotiated and bought a rare vanity collection she had had her eye on for the past several days.

4 Jun. Yellow Creek Gap to Fontana Dam. 8.1 Miles.

The old S-10 Blazer I took to Yellow Creek Gap so that Angie would only have to make one trip that day. I set off with a light pack and Beauregard for a little after ten. It was a steady climb uphill and then down to Cable Gap Shelter for about a mile.

Cable Gap Shelter had been called the worst shelter on the whole A.T. It was a pleasure to see what John Newton, 'Oliver Twist', and his friends had done. Originally the shelter had been built of logs and these had been retained. The floor had been redone, though, and the old wire bunks had been removed. A new rock firepit had been built. It was much like a real fireplace. The whole area had been spotlessly policed and the spring had been improved. The nearby campsites had been tidied up and even a little birdhouse had been constructed on a neighboring tree. Cable Gap Shelter is now one of the nicest shelters I have seen.

Two young boys were getting underway after having spent the night at the shelter. They were on a weekend hike to Wesser. It was nice to see it being put to good use. They were glad to see Beauregard.

In reading the log at Cable Gap I noticed an entry for the next day after our stay up at Sassafras Gap on Cheoah Bald:

'Visitors last night at Sassafras for about 9:00 p.m. Two bears appeared turning over logs for bugs. Stoked the fire and shone my light on them but they wouldn't go away until I started singing in a loud voice. Didn't know my singing was so bad.'

After slogging up the trail for half an hour, thinking about the log entries (Beth and Mark, the Honeymooners, and Bro. Son were up ahead somewhere, still on Indiana time) I noticed something was odd. I was walking without my faithful stick, the one I had carved my trail name into back at Hiawassee. It was a good hickory stick and it fit my hand just right. I hated to go back for it and to have to redo the climb that we had just made. It had just the right heft to it, though, and it was getting nicely worn where my hand had slid up and down it with each step.

Beauregard didn't like the idea of turning around but being the good sport that he always is he reluctantly headed back down the trail with me. I figured that it was worth the extra mile or two and it was a fine day anyway.

We stopped to lunch on a crest that seemed to be the top. There was a view of Fontana far below and the Smokies could be seen in the distance. How is it that flies and bees can assemble within a matter of minutes once you break out your lunch? Where do they come from and how do they spread the word so quickly? And the big black ants, too. They are Johnny on the spot when you break open the sardines. What do they do when you're not there to share your lunch with them?

On the way down we ran into a group of Boy Scouts, about six of them. They were really nice boys, well-mannered and friendly. We found the Scoutmaster and his two assistants with four other Scouts just below at a small stream. They were on a 50 mile sortie over to Wesser and then back by canoe. What a trip! It would be something they would remember all of their lives.

It was refreshing to meet people like John Newton and the scoutmasters, people who were not out for themselves but who were just happy to be doing something for others without any thought of personal gain. It is different from the norm with contacts in the business world.

Finally we trudged down the long decline toward Fontana Dam. It included some steep and treacherous sections until we reached the road. We crossed a parking lot and a little farther on we came to a spot that was just above the dam and there I indulged in a minor feeling of achievement. I had walked from Springer Mtn. to the Smokies and it had been a major leg of the trail! It had been 166 miles on the A.T. itself but a bit more with the side trails I had taken. Beauregard looked at me. 'Big deal,' he was probably thinking. 'The thing is 2,100 miles long.'

At Fontana there is an elegant shelter with two tiers of platforms for sleeping, picnic tables, rest rooms and drinking fountains. I can see now why they refer to it as the Fontana Hilton. It had a lovely view that overlooked the lake. Three hikers were there. They were dog lovers and they greeted Beauregard with enthusiasm.

Next to the Fontana Hilton is a set-up for the self-registry that is required for going thru the Smokies, which is a National Park. You fill out a little tag, drop the carbon copy in the box and then you are supposed to wire the original to your pack, as though you are a piece of freight in shipment. Thru-hikers, someone going through the Smokies plus 50 miles on either side, are permitted to just self-register and push off. You have 8 days and 7 nights to hike through. There is a $25 fine for a second night in a shelter. The idea seems to be to keep the traffic moving.

No pets, no firearms, no alcohol in the Park. Beauregard was not welcome. The U.S. Nat'l. Park Service doesn't care much for man's best friend. Bears, yes. Dogs, no. The fine for this violation is $500 and/or 6 months in jail. If Beauregard sets foot on this sacred soil or if I were caught drinking a beer they could lock us up for six months to make an example of us. Geez.

Angie and Duffy arrived and we piled into the big Blazer. I had my Coor's Light anyway to help celebrate the arrival at Fontana. It was a mighty good feeling.

Back at the camper, around a campfire, I thought about the A.T. experience now that we had done the leg from Springer Mtn. to Fontana Dam. It really had been fun. I had enjoyed the changing delights that had unfolded along a meandering trail: a cool stream or a flowing spring; a magnificent vista from a ridge top; the peace and solitude I had had where there wasn't any phone or mail to deal with and where I could think my own thoughts for a while, without interruption; the flowers and wildlife that had spiced up the trail here and there; the unexpected treat of meeting a stranger, someone I would never otherwise have known; the sense of anticipation that had always come from wondering what was around the next bend or over the next ridge; and the feeling of independence and freedom that always had happened once I had left the road and civilization behind.

Besides the trail itself there had been all of the fringe experiences that we wouldn't have otherwise had. And I knew I had wound up being in a lot better shape than what I had been in when I had set out. All in all the experience had been as worthwhile and pleasant an adventure as I could have hoped it to be.

Bibliography.

For trail guides and maps on the Appalachian Trail as well as other publications about it write to:

The Appalachian Trail Conference
P. O. Box 807
Harper's Ferry, W. Va. 25424
Or call and order at: (304) 535-6331

The Georgia - North Carolina section is Book No. 10. It will come with detailed maps showing shelters, roads, intersecting trails, streams, etc., and also elevation profiles for an indication of how much up and down is required together with mileage marked off for various areas and access roads that cross the trail.

In addition, the USDA Forest Service puts out a series of maps covering the A.T. These are usually for sale in camp equipment stores in the vicinity of the section in which you will be hiking or they may be obtained from the local USDA Forest Service office for the area in which you are interested. They are the same as the regular A.T. maps but they are more accurate for the location of the Nat'l. Forest Service roads that lead up to the trail in each area.

It only costs $25 to join the A.T.C. association. It is for a worthwhile cause and you receive copies of the Appalachian Trailway News, an interesting magazine that is full of articles about the A.T. You also receive an A.T. patch for sewing on your pack or your favorite shirt and a vehicle decal for your car. This decal is useful for those occasions when your car is parked at a remote spot on a back country road for an extended period of time. It indicates to the locals or the sheriff that the car belongs to an A. T. hiker and that it has not been abandoned.

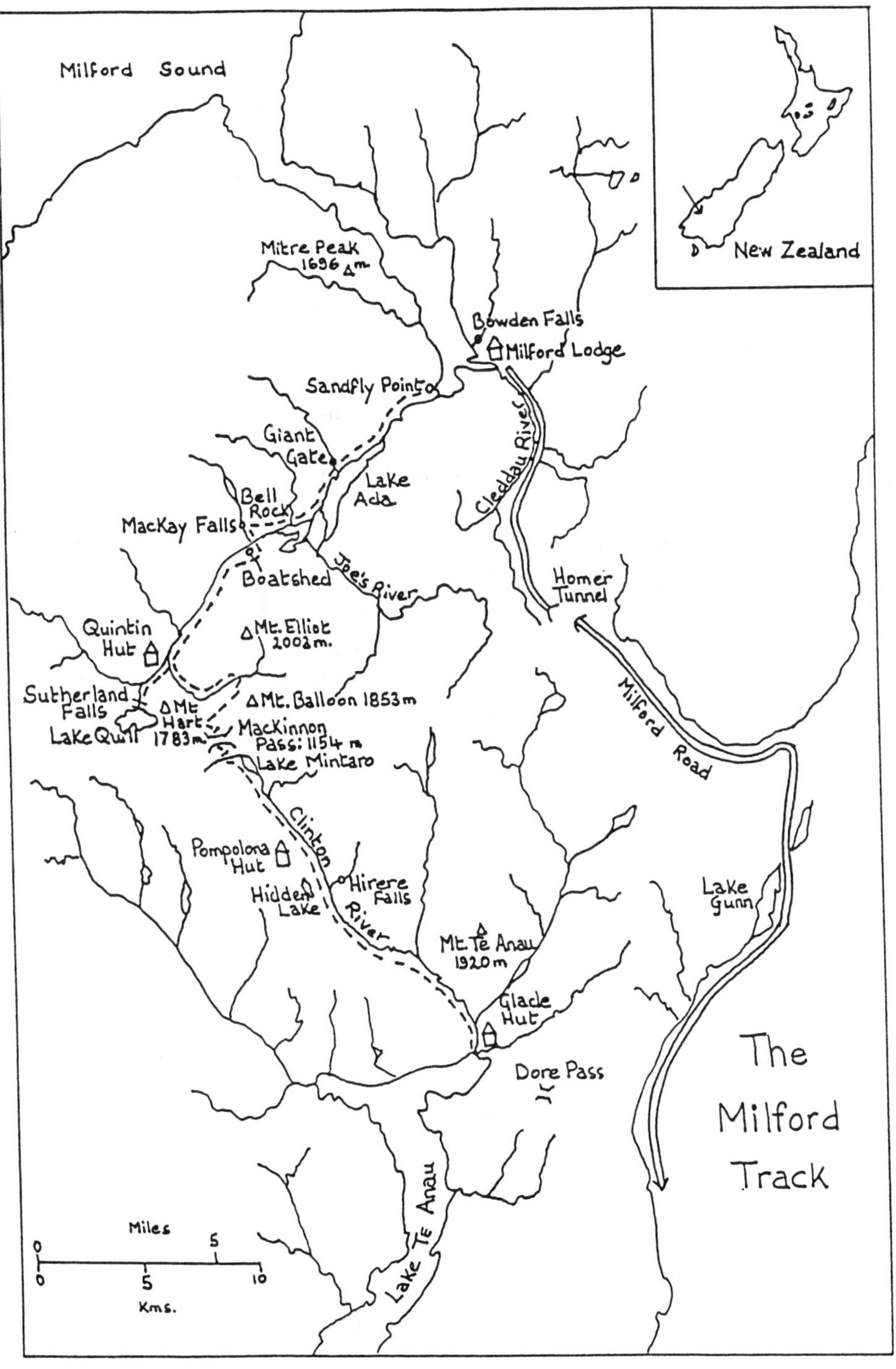
Milford Sound
New Zealand
Mitre Peak
1696 m.
Bowden Falls
Milford Lodge
Sandfly Point
Giant
Gate
Lake
Ada
Cleddau River
Bell
Rock
MacKay Falls
Boatshed
Joe's River
Homer
Tunnel
Quintin
Hut
Mt. Elliot
2002 m.
Milford Road
Sutherland
Falls
Mt
Hart
1783 m.
Mt. Balloon 1853 m
Lake Quill
MacKinnon
Pass: 1154 m
Lake Mintaro
Clinton
Pompolona
Hut
Hirere
Falls
Hidden
Lake
River
Lake
Gunn
Mt. Te Anau
1920 m
Glade
Hut
Dore Pass
The
Milford
Track
Miles
0
5
0
5
10
Kms.
Lake Te Anau

WALK VI

VI. The Milford Track

(36 Miles)

The Milford Track is billed as the 'Finest Walk in the World'. There are a good many things about it that are particularly unique to its location and the way that it is organized. Certainly it makes a memorable experience for anyone who undertakes it. Basically it is a 33.5 mile walk in the South Island of New Zealand with some of the world's most magnificent scenery. Accommodations are provided in the form of two types of huts, one catered, the other do-it-yourself, except for the fact that New Zealand shelters have virtually all of the conveniences of home. Stopovers include three overnights in the huts while on the track itself.

The rules for hiking the track call for a limit of 40 hikers per day under the auspices of the Tourist Hotel Corp. and an additional maximum of 40 hikers per day who stay in the park shelters. The two groups are scheduled so that they don't intermingle with one another. Since MacKinnon Pass is only accessible for about four to five months out of the year it is best to reserve a slot on the track well in advance of heading for New Zealand.

The start for the Milford Track for Angie and me was a two hour bus ride that went from Queenstown to Te Anau. The area was full of rolling grassy hills, streams and valleys with surrounding peaks, small frontier-like towns, sizeable farms and little or no traffic. The bus driver was a fount of information about the area.

At the Te Anau Hotel there was a staging room for trekkers, 'guided walkers' on one side, 'freedom walkers' across the way. Here we checked our luggage, except our packs. We checked into a villa arrangement that was even more reasonable than the apartment we had had in Queenstown.

We were hiking with the THC group and our briefing for the trek was at 6:30 p.m. There we began to size up the other members of the group. Roughly half of the trekkers seemed to be senior type citizens and the other half were of varied ages, male and female. All of them looked to be reasonably fit and regular walkers. The presentation was light and humorous and encouraging for anyone contemplating 33 1/2 miles in the rain, maybe, at this non-refundable stage of the project. The idea was to walk light and to be prepared for cold weather, heavy wind and probable rain.

White wine and crudities were offered after the briefing. We were also issued maps, a towel, and the same clever bed sheet arrangement that we had had on the Routeburn Track which we had done previously. Slickers and packs were available for those who had not brought their own. We wondered what we had managed to get ourselves into with this group of people who were then all strangers to one another. I suspect that all of the rest of them were probably thinking the same thing.

Earlier that day we had noted that winds over a hundred miles an hour had descended upon the coast below Wellington which was not far away. Usually it is sunny about one day in four. This mountain range acts as a barrier to the edge of the Roaring Forties from time to time and this is what produces so much wind and precipitation. It is also the reason for the numerous streams and waterfalls. The trees and vegetation thrive in these rain forest conditions.

Glade Hut. 3/4 Mile.

The next day we dutifully assembled for a group photograph and we purchased a couple of hand-made walking sticks from the outfitting shop where we checked our goods. We met our 'guide', Fred, who would walk with us and count noses at the end of the day so that no one would turn up missing. That done we loaded into a bus that would take us up to the boat dock. After a short ride we boarded an ancient steamer that had been converted to diesel. The old boat chugged for two hours up Te Anau lake. The lake was mostly shrouded in cloud and rain. It was a substantial 62 miles long and 1,200 feet deep. Every now and then it became possible to catch a glimpse of huge peaks and awesome waterfalls that pounded down to the shoreline. It was impossible to imagine anyplace else that could have been more forbidding and impenetrable.

At the landing we unloaded and hiked the short three-quarters of a mile up to Glade House. Here coffee and tea were waiting and the first scramble for a desirable bunk (younger hikers on top, please), men in one bunkhouse, women in the other. The central dining room was an unpretentious affair with a welcome fire at one end. People became gradually acquainted and everyone was friendly.

After an ample dinner, no booze unless you brought your own, the group was rallied around and encouraged to enter into a series of old time parlor games under the affable hut manager's direction. These were surprisingly well received and turned out to be a good way for people to meet one another. Name tags were helpful.

On the wall of the hut the nationalities in the group of 29 had been posted:

Australia	8
U.S.	9
U.K.	2
Canada	1
Japan	1
No. N.Z.	4
So. N.Z.	3
Germany	1

Pompolona Hut. 10 Miles.

The next morning when we set out we could see fresh snow on the surrounding peaks. This was the 2nd of Feb., too, New Zealand's summer. It was all above tree line, though, and not a problem where we were. Angie said that from now on whenever she sprinkled a cake with powdered sugar it would remind her of these mountains.

The path through the bush beside the Clinton river was as near to perfection as any path could be made. It was groomed to about three feet wide and manicured with a gravel-bed and stone-lined sides. It bordered the clear water and from the long swing bridge that we first crossed I spotted a trout some two feet long. Farther along I saw, too, a large eel. The path led through forest covered with moss. Dense ferns grew beneath the trees in subsequent sections.

Markers were placed every mile along the trail. Distance covered was shown in miles and kilometers. This provided encouragement and reassurance as well as logistic information that was hard to come by. Distances on the Milford Track seemed to be kept a virtual secret until you actually showed up for the briefing. The PR sheets were always careful not to reveal the actual mileage involved, presumably not to discourage prospective trekkers.

Walking up the valley was easy going for several miles. Then the track began a gradual climb that was interspersed with running streamlets, sometimes bridged and sometimes navigated by crossing on the best stones available. On either side of the precipitous canyon numerous waterfalls cascaded down.

Contrary to expectations the sun was shining during the whole day that we made this walk.

At Clinton Hut we looked at the independent walkers' accommodations. Here there were bunks with mattresses, butane cooking rings, sinks, tables, a pot-bellied stove, toilets and a nice view of the river from the veranda.

A Kea bird was methodically pulling off the rubber insulation strip around the top windows of the hut. The Kea looks like a huge green parrot. He is an outrageous thief and charlatan with a can-opener beak. He looks like a huge hawk in flight and he gracefully rides the thermals whenever he feels like going for a spin.

Hiking along a wet bit of track we were surprised to find an aluminum row boat that was chained to a tree beside the path. We later learned that this boat was for ferry purposes when the trail became flooded in that particular spot. It was also used by staff now and then for fishing in the lake-like section nearby.

After about 8 miles we came to Hirere Falls Hut around noon. There the coffee and soup were going and we stopped for the lunch that we had been issued and carried up from Glade Hut. It was a peaceful spot beside a clear stream where four paradise ducks nonchalantly cruised. The male sported a magnificent white head.

Waterfalls became more numerous after lunch, stream crossings, too. They were so numerous that we soon became accustomed to them. Finally we saw MacKinnon Pass in the distance. It was covered with fresh snow and the weather report on Clinton Hut's blackboard said that gale force nor'westerlies were on the way!

At the last mile before Pompolona hut it became necessary to ford a fast-moving stream over large boulders. A rope had been strung across it between two trees on either bank. Angie and most of the other walkers elected to just wade across it in ankle deep water holding onto the rope. I had managed to find some rocks upstream, though, that would keep my feet dry. Then I noticed the group's old German friend struggling along even farther upstream. He was looking for an ideal place to pick his way across. There really wasn't a spot that was any better.

The old man was in his late seventies and he spoke no English. Conversation was mostly confined to sign language and what few words of German that could be dredged up by the rest of us. I had worried about him. I rock-hopped back across and I went on up to where he was. I motioned for him to follow me and I led him back down to the spot that I had used. It was touch and go. For a moment I thought I was going to lose him as he teetered precipitously over the raging torrent on a slippery rock. Somehow I managed to hold onto him and he maintained his balance long enough to get to the other side. I wondered how he would do going across MacKinnon Pass the next day but he was quite determined and enjoying the whole adventure.

When we reached Pompolona Hut after the 10 miles up there from Glade Hut it turned out to be a series of corrugated tin cabins that were nicely done and joined by walkways. A player piano was in the lounge and beside it were a choice of scrolls for many old tunes. A hot shower felt good and then we had a bake in the sun.

One of the group, Bill, was a Professor of Medicine from Edmonton, Canada. He was somewhere in his seventies and he had sprained an ankle on a piece of tussock grass. He had managed to make his way on up to the hut at Pompolona, though. I had carried his handheld bag that contained his camera and assorted goods the last couple of miles for him and I had saved him a lower bunk beneath me. He had a conference with the hut manager about the ankle and he opted out by helicopter. He had a fondness for the poems of Robert Service and he memorized a new one each year. He did a well-delivered rendition of Dangerous Dan McGrew for me.

MacKinnon Pass and Quintin Hut. 10 Miles.

The start for the big slog up to MacKinnon Pass began a little before eight a.m. The trail was well switchbacked but rocky. The 5 1/2 miles up to the top were relieved at the last of the eleven switchbacks by the appearance of a large and friendly bird who strolled down the trail as though he owned it. He seemed to be wondering what we were doing by using it without his permission. We were unable to identify him. What came to mind was a cross between a Kea and a Kiwi. Whatever he was he refused to yield an inch of the track and we both had to step aside while he continued his paseo.

On top of the pass we paid homage to Quintin MacKinnon who had taken six weeks of unbearable hardship to reach it in 1888. He and Ernest Mitchell had steadfastly hacked their way through the same bush that had now taken us a leisurely day and a half to cover. At the time we were blessed with sunshine and ample breaks in the clouds. It was one of the most formidable and hostile environments I had ever seen. It was possible to view the dense valley up which we had come and to see down the other side where we were slated to go. The track itself was like a lifeline through hell. All around us jagged peaks jutted skyward, rocky, snow-covered in parts and completely impassable without the pass.

We crossed over to 12 second rock, so named because that is how long it takes you to hit bottom if you tumble over the edge. It had no guard rail. Nearby several Kea birds watched for a careless hiker to leave his pack unattended long enough for its contents to be decimated with their razor sharp beaks. Overhead others rode the thermals like hang gliders. One launched himself out over the edge and he rose like a shot out of a cannon as he hit the roaring updraft.

The views in every direction were awesome. We had been blessed with no rain and although it was very cold, with the remnants of snow still on the ground, no gale was blowing and the clouds had graciously opened to permit awareness of the jagged alps on levels rising above our own at 3700 ft.

Two days later we would have reason to remember the pass. A 33 yr. old Japanese hiker would leave his pack at Mintaro Hut around noon. He would leave on his own with climbing gear to tackle nearby Mt. Hart. He would last be seen around 3:30 p.m. by other track walkers as he began his ascent. Even though he was known to have been an experienced climber his body would be retrieved on the following day by helicopter. He would have fallen about 400 ft. down the steep face of the mountain. It would be hoped that he would have died instantly and not from the 20 inches of rain and bitter cold that night.

A short way up to the right of the pass we stopped at an emergency shelter for lunch. Inside a couple of butane heaters were going and it was warm and cozy. Juice, hot coffee and soup were available. The soup was labelled 'Creme de Kea' in typical Kiwi humor. The hut guide said that they closed down the pass whenever the winds exceeded 80 knots.

The way down to Quintin Hut was a 3500 ft. drop in some five miles over a rocky trail. It had ample switchbacks, though, and it was not brutally steep, just enough to be hard on knees and toes if one's boots were not well broken in. The trail was well-maintained with appropriate footbridges. These had been thoughtfully chickenwire-meshed for safety against slippage. Cable safety rails had been stretched along the outside edge of the drop-offs, too, so that the trail had been made relatively safe in the bad spots.

A memorable rocky stretch about halfway down featured a sign that had been posted suggesting that it would be prudent not to stop in the vicinity because of the danger of avalanche. A glance upward revealed a huge slab of rocky mountainside that appeared to be making up its mind exactly when to cut loose. The debris over which the trail passed was from some previous regurgitation. There was no way around it, though, and like a school of sardines taking refuge in the safety of time and numbers one hoped that the mountain would not choose those few minutes that it took to get across for its moment to strike.

On the overall walk the individual pace was usually set by the woman for couples travelling together since she generally led the way, ladies first gents. This pecking order usually held true for most of the time throughout the walk. Angie's pace enabled us to usually stay up with the frontrunners. Some of the time it seemed to become competitive but great pains were taken in passing or being passed to try not to give this impression. The dubious reward for being a frontrunner was a little better choice of bunk for the night and a first shower.

Sutherland Falls. 2 1/2 Miles.

The hike up to Sutherland Falls was an optional side walk after reaching Quintin Hut. It was made easier in spite of the day's prior walk since one could leave the pack at the hut. Rain gear was desirable. The trail up to the falls was fairly easy and it only took me about a half hour to negotiate the incline that led up to them. The falls are the fourth largest in the world and the Milford Track hike is the only way that they can be seen. They fall a spectacular 1904 ft. from Lake Quill.

The falls were named by the luck of a tossed coin. The two explorers, Sutherland and MacKay, happened on an earlier waterfall which each had wanted to name after himself. MacKay won the toss. Later they discovered the infinitely more important falls that fell to Sutherland by way of default. They were truly spectacular and worth the extra effort to get to them. For those who didn't want to strap on the extras miles for the day there was a long-distance view of them from the regular trail itself on the following day.

Back at Quintin Hut the other hikers trickled in little by little. One of the walkers had made a penned sign with an arrow that pointed toward a second bunk room. The sign said 'Snorers Only'! The non-snorers' side filled quickly, where I had located, and on reflection I sensed that reverse psychology was at work since most people don't know if they are snorers or not anyway. I shifted to the snorers side where only four of us spent the night. It was the first comfortable night's sleep I had had on the walk.

One of my roommates on the 'snorers only' side was a likeable Ob/Gy doctor from Long Beach, Calif. Bill, his wife Joan and his eldest son Pete, were doing the track together.

They were a family of seven and the doctor organized his practice so that he could have a goodly share of adventures each year. He ran the Long Beach marathon every year. He was 64, lean, easy-going and always pleasant. His white hair and full white mustache in a tanned, craggy face made you think of a daguerreotype photo of a revered sheriff in the days of the wild west.

Bill's son, Pete, was equally remarkable. He had an engaging smile and a down-to-earth candor in talking about himself that was always likeable. He was a bachelor who lived in a small town near Mt. Shasta in northern California. He owned a couple of successful lumberyards. He loved sports. He had wind-surfed, skied and hiked the mountains around where he lived for as long as he had been there. Now he was into rock climbing.

Rock climbing has always terrified me. Pete said that he had always had a problem with heights, too, but in order to conquer this fear he had decided to try climbing. He described his first struggles at learning the sport. He had gone up a 350 ft. rock face with an older but experienced partner. Up near the top they had reached what is termed the 'crux' of the climb, the most difficult obstacle in every climb. His partner had fallen four times in trying to get up and over the overhang that stood in the way. Each time he had been saved by the carefully placed clamps that are wedged into cracks to support belaying ropes. Then he had told Pete that he was pooped and that he could go no farther.

Pete said that even though he was completely terrified he elected to try with the clamps rather than rapel some 300 ft. down the rock face, something that he had never done before either. He succeeded and they were able to then get to the top. He said that he had been so charged up for three days afterward that he couldn't sleep or do anything else for thinking about it.

Our old German friend, Goetz, finally made it down to the hut. He bunked in on my side of the dormitory. That night at dinner he was awarded a Milford Track visor with built-in sunglasses for being the oldest tramper this year. He was 79. He complained to me about the fact that he was not used to carrying a pack on his back during his walks in Germany.

Goetz had been a German prisoner of war on the Russian front and his hands shook badly. He said that it was the result of forced labor in the snow but he pointed out that his legs were all right. Always cheerful he was an inspiration to the rest of us and when later we all left Milford Sound and it became apparent that he planned to stay there for another day or two everyone disembarked from the bus to shake his hand and say goodbye.

There was a light drizzle coming down when we left Quintin Hut on the final 13 1/2 mile leg of the track. The pressure is on at that point because there is a 4:00 o'clock boat departure time from Sandfly Point. If you push it a bit it is possible to make the three o'clock boat for the independent walkers. With an eight o'clock start there is not much time for lolly-gagging around along the way.

Soon the rain stopped and we were treated to a distant view of Sutherland Falls. With so many extraordinary falls constantly on display throughout the walk it is difficult to single out any particular one as being the most spectacular but the Sutherland Falls were as impressive as any I have seen anyplace else in the world.

We were first across the long swing bridge with Angela setting a blistering pace again. She is a good mudder on the flat, especially in the home stretch when downwind from shops in the distance.

After another rocky descent named 'Gentle Annie' the footpath leveled out through rainforest and the walking was easy but wet as it took us through muddy stream crossings from time to time. Soon we reached the independent walkers' Dumpling Hut. We were the first of the group to arrive and we took advantage of the facilities.

Once again the N.Z. trail shelter was far superior to anything I have seen in the States. It had three-decker bunks with good mattresses, butane cooker rings, a sink and faucets, toilets, a wood-burning stove with plenty of cut wood, info on the weather chalked on the blackboard and wide tables and benches, a veritable back-packer's palace.

The next to arrive at Dumpling Hut was Lynn. She was an attractive late-twenty-year-old travelling by herself from Wellington, N.Z. She was hard to get to know at first but a strong walker and a warm person underneath the independence. Behind her was Libby. She and Raewynn had been friends for some nine years having married two lawyers who had been best friends themselves. They were on their own with a pass from home. Libby was descended from a Maori grandmother who had lived to the age of 112. Raewynn looked like a young Ingrid Bergman. Both were New Zealanders, enthusiastic and always cheerful. They were well-liked by everyone in the group.

Boatshed was next at the 26th milepost. This was a tea stop with the affable caretaker, Bob, who lived there and who furnished his own well-brewed tea. Located beside the track on the edge of the river it was also accessible by outboard from Milford Sound. An impressive collection of old liquor bottles gathered dust on the rafters. The little house had a kitchen, a bedroom and a common room with two long tables and benches. It had a nice view of the water and it was easy to see that it would be a comfortable place to live.

Alan was the first to slip away from the Boatshed break. He was a Brit, retired from Cunard and living in Auckland. He had already hiked the Track 18 months before and seemed determined to be the first to finish. He, too, was pleasant and full of gentle English humor.

Two old friends of Alan's were Fred and Dorothy, also retired and Brits, living outside London. They had been with Cunard, too, and Fred was a sailor with sea stories to swap. Both were keen walkers and always full of consideration for others.

When we reached MacKay Falls after leaving Boatshed

we felt a bit sorry for poor old MacKay's win of the toss. Anywhere else they would have been quite respectable falls but not in Fiordland Nat'l. Park. Next to them was Bell Rock, a curiosity shaped by centuries of rushing water that had worn it inside to resemble a giant bell without a clapper.

The next long section had been provided with an extensive series of board walkways above a swamplike area. Here we caught up with the last of the independent walkers who had stopped to admire a rare blue duck occasionally sighted there.

After crossing a couple of suspension bridges we climbed up a long rocky ledge that required care in negotiating. Off to the right was a nice lagoon and then a white water river that could be a challenge. John, an American from Wisconsin, caught up with us. He had had some difficulty on the descent from MacKinnon Pass because of his bifocals. He had taken advantage of the offer to fly packs out at Quintin Hut, though, and now he was chugging right along. He was, in fact, ahead of his son, Skip, with whom he was travelling.

Skip was a boatbuilder from Massachusetts. He made fiberglass catboats in 15', 18' and 22' sizes. They were finely built and they would be a joy to sail. He, too, was affable and he was pleased to be making this trip with his dad.

Beyond the rocky cutting that formed the ledge the trail became easy walking once again. The milepost markers lent encouragement and around one o'clock we reached the magic number 30. Just beyond we crossed a suspension bridge over crystal clear water that flowed down the falls from Giant Gate. Here a natural gate-like half-moon effect had been carved out of the rock at the head of the waterfall. We stopped for a quick lunch with the welcome realization that we could probably manage the last 3 1/2 miles to Sandfly Point in time enough to make the 3:00 o'clock boat.

Colin and Jan were already at Giant Gate. Usually early birds they were part of a group of three Aussie couples, all friends, who were walking the track together. Brian was the

Mgr. of a large coal mine operation in northern Australia. He and his wife Sue were pleasant and enjoying the outing as a change from where they lived.

Of the three Aussie couples travelling together big John was a candidate for a Reader's Digest most unforgettable character. He was a big man, an Olympic shot putter and discus thrower who trained for veterans' competition with a 400 lb. bench press routine. His handshake was like an automobile compactor and his humorous quips were just as strong and loud. Underneath the Crocodile Dundee type of exterior, though, he was a gentle man. He and his wife Wendy had been primary school teachers and later he had become a regional superintendent of schools. Now retired early they were embarked on the venture of being an Amway Distributor in their home town of Albany near Perth.

And finally, mile 33.5 and Sandfly Point! In time for the three o'clock boat, too. The sandflies tried to live up to their reputation but they were not as bad as we had expected, not even as bad as we had often experienced living on the boat in the Cayman Islands. A local product, Dimple, or any other type of repellent will keep them at bay. I never received any bites on the whole trip but Angie collected a dozen or so itchy reminders. They were a small price to pay, though, when one considers that they are the only animal or insect of any detriment in this part of the world.

Ten of our group made it in time for the earlier boat. The last was Barbara, together with her husband Owen. Barbara had enjoyed the comparative luxury of the THC facilities while Owen had hiked with his mate in the independent group. He had checked back to help her and to be with her frequently. They were Kiwis from Christchurch and both amiable. Owen was rugged and used to tramping all over New Zealand. I remember when I had first seen him storming down the track on his way back to walk with Barbara up over MacKinnon Pass. I had figured him to be a mountain ranger of some type. He was the sort of mate you would choose for back-up if you were trying to take a short-cut across a crocodile infested river bank.

The boat trip on Milford Sound was pleasant and a welcome sit-down treat. We were even transferred the short distance from the landing to the THC Milford Sound Hotel by bus. Nothing could have felt better than the hot soak in the tub and the clean clothes that had been sent up from Te Anau for the group banquet.

After gathering in the bar for a welcome series of lagers the group was presented individually with attractively designed certificates by the hotel manager. The remaining members of the group not yet mentioned were: Gayle, a single young woman who was an attorney working for the Dep't. of Labor in Washington. Redheaded and friendly she was a good sport. Angie had introduced her to a piece of Second Skin that helped with a blister. Then there was Yutaka, a young Japanese X-Ray technician from just outside of Tokyo. He carried a tripod on the walk and this he used to take an infinite number of pictures, mostly of himself I was told, with a self-timer against varied backgrounds. He was likeable and appreciative and he good-naturedly struggled with his limited English vocabulary in conversations with others.

The remaining couple in the group was Jonathan and Gillian. He was originally a Kiwi himself but for many years he had been a professor at a university in Syracuse, New Jersey. He was looking forward to a research project at Oxford after the Track and this was also a pilgrimage to his old home country. He had an academic frame of mind and his conversation tended to head in that direction whenever possible. It was interesting to watch them read a book as after one would read a page he would tear it out and hand it to the other who in turn would then throw it away when finished.

The last of the two members of the group who were travelling together were Les and his son Robert. They were Aussies from the outskirts of Melbourne. Les was retired and he was walking with an artificial hip joint. He came through with flying colors. Robert was a baker and he was accustomed to different hours. His normal day generally began at midnight and Les was forever riding herd on him to make sure that he made it to bed on time so that he wouldn't oversleep in the morning.

The remaining member of the group was an attractive brunette from the vicinity of Charleston, N.C. Thirty and independent Dana was an anesthesiologist nurse with an interest in travel, adventure and men. She put in 60 to 70 hour weeks so that she could store up for long vacations. This was to be a three month affair and after the walk she was scheduled to join a boat on the Great Barrier Reef near Cairns.

She liked being the magnet that she was. She hiked in cut-offs and black long-johns with her hair often in a streaming pony tail. She and Pete had latched on to one another and they had often been in the lead. She was amusing but some of the group worried about what was going to come out next at times. Dana good-naturedly referred to herself as a 'gas-passer'. She had been composing a poem on the walk and I could remember her struggling with it on rest stops. In the middle of dinner she rose from her place and recited the poem. It was about the walk and it was funny and well-done and it endeared her to the group.

A good deal of speculation took place about who would end up with Dana on the night of the banquet. We were hoping that it would be Pete but the question was resolved when Fred, our short but muscular young guide, had picked her up bodily over his shoulder and carried her out from the bar. He was accompanied by another mate and the trio marched off in what had to be as dramatic an exit as any that could have been scripted.

When Angie apologized to the waitress for the rowdiness of our group she replied that we had been the most animated lot that they had seen all year.

The next day the package included a boat trip out on Milford Sound for a cruise among sheer rock walls and extraordinary waterfalls. Dolphins and seals swam alongside and mighty Mitre Mt. towered overhead. Another buffet lunch followed that would have been worthy of Harrods and then the bus took the group back to Te Anau where it had all begun.

The five days had been a memorable walking experience, not difficult and full of variety. We had been blessed with good weather and all of the members of the little expedition had been compatible and helpful to one another with never a complaint or a cross word. The Milford Track may well have reason for claiming to be the finest walk in the world. When you add it all together, the accommodations, the food, some of the most dramatic terrain to be seen anywhere, well-organized and maintained, it is hard to compete with it.

Bibliography.

The way to book for the walk is by writing the Tourist Hotel Corporation, P.O. Box 185, Te Anau, or by calling: THC (0229) 7411, N.Z. Ask for the Milford Track Dep't.

The best book on the various walks in New Zealand, including the Milford Track and the Routeburn is:

'Tramping in New Zealand', by Jim DuFresne. It can be obtained by writing the publisher: Lonely Planet Publications, Embarcadero West, 112 Linden St., Oakland, CA 94607 USA. Lonely Planet has a number of other guidebooks for other parts of the world that are interesting to consider as well.

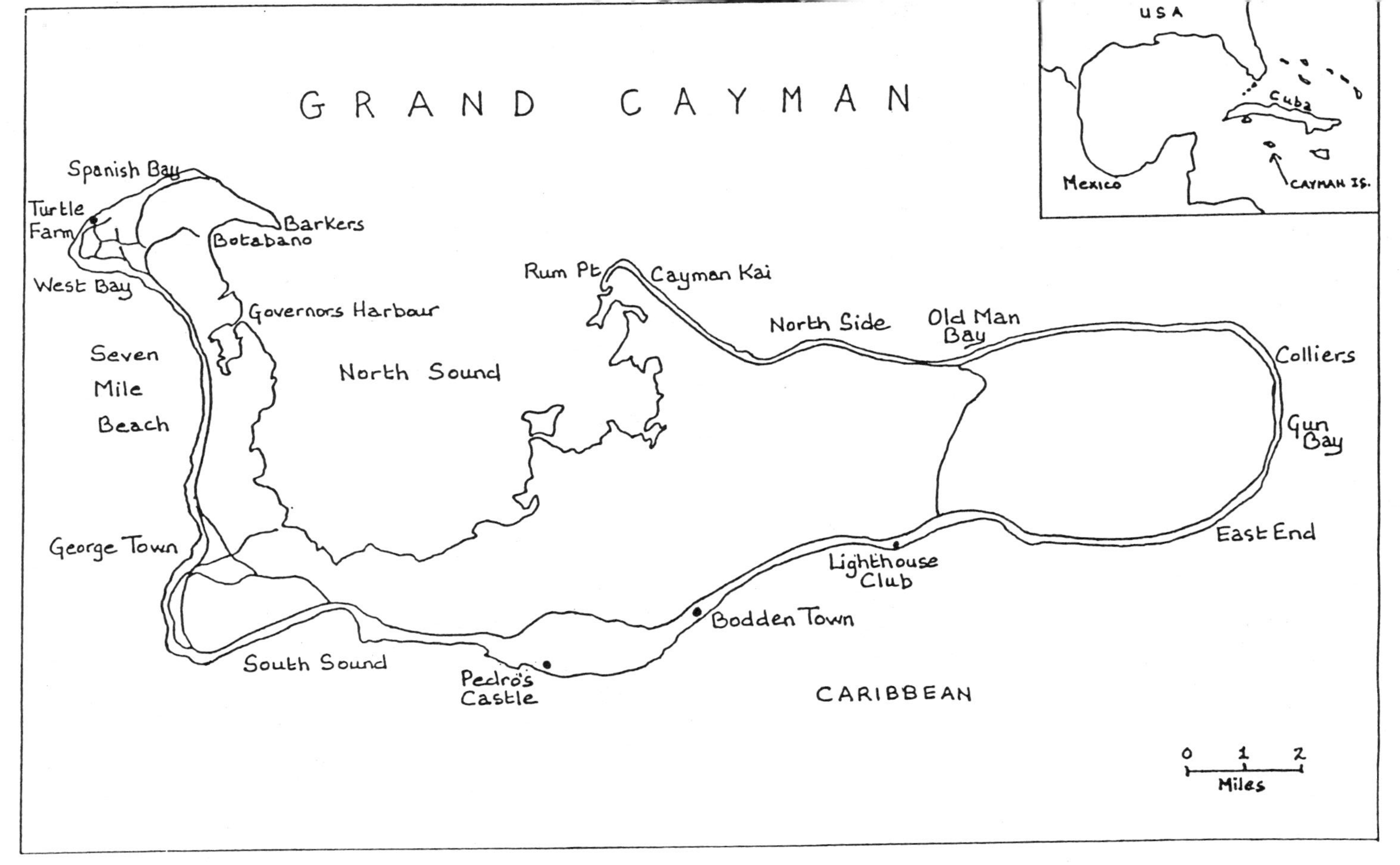
GRAND CAYMAN
USA
Mexico
Cuba
CAYMAN IS.
Spanish Bay
Turtle Farm
Barkers
Botabano
West Bay
Rum Pt
Cayman Kai
Governors Harbour
Seven Mile Beach
North Sound
North Side
Old Man Bay
Colliers
Gun Bay
George Town
East End
Lighthouse Club
Bodden Town
South Sound
Pedro's Castle
CARIBBEAN
0 1 2
Miles

Narrow Boats Moored Along the Thames.

The True Source of the River Thames.

The Village of Torla at Ordesa in the Pyrenees.

Hiking the A. T.

Wild Azaleas Feast for Bumble Bee on the A.T.

The Author's Ketch, Vagrant Gipsy.

Sassafras Gap on the A. T.

Switchbacked Trail, MacKinnon Pass, Milford Track, N.Z.

Beauregard Crosses Cheoah Bald.

Rowing Shells on the Thames.

Stone Wall Pass-thru, (Mind the Bulls), Coast to Coast.

Young Rider and Her Pony at Reeth, Coast to Coast.

Underwater Shot of the Shark That Attacked Brian, Cayman Is.

Milford Track Hikers Fording a Torrent by Rope.

Swing Bridge on the Routeburn Track, N.Z.

Sutherland Falls, 4th Highest, Milford Track.

WALK VII

VII. Around the Shores of Grand Cayman.

(52 Miles).

Many years ago I designed and built a 53' ketch out of wood. I built the Vagrant Gipsy in Belize and finished her up in New Orleans. I had her for 25,000 miles and 18 years and she was a member of the family. For five of those years I kept her in the Cayman Islands where we lived aboard her during the many times that we came to visit.

Some two years after we had left Cayman with the boat, and after she had been sold to friends who would take good care of her, we returned to the islands. We had been invited to stay in the condo of Cayman friends while they went home to Toronto to visit family for Christmas. It was an opportunity to do something I had long thought of doing, namely to walk the perimeter of Grand Cayman.

When first I sailed into Cayman it was a friendly place, the water was gin clear and nobody took themselves too seriously. Over the years I had come to know every foot of its beaches, coves and reefs and I had snorkeled, scuba-dived, speared fish and sailed its waters many times. We had our favorite picnic spots, our places to gather conch, catch lobster, look for grouper, places to jog undisturbed, places to beachcomb, and all of the island restaurants were like old friends. But I had never walked all the way around it and I thought that maybe a log of the experience might be of interest to others, too.

The first day of the walk started from George Town itself after doing chores there in the morning. It wasn't much of a walk from there to Trevor and Elaine's place on Seven

Mile Beach but it was such a good feeling to be back on that white sand with its clear water lapping at the edges that it was hard to keep from just plopping into the gentle surf. Naturally that's what happened, as it always had.

In the clear water I spotted a large tarpon. At first I thought he was a barracuda, that would have been more probable. The barracuda is an entertaining fish. They are amazingly efficient and quick and very curious. It can be a bit unnerving to have them come up close and work their jaws with those rows of sharp teeth but they are only checking you out (hey, brother, big fish here, mon, come see...). I have never had a bad experience with one myself and their unsavory reputation is undeserved.

By way of illustration about barracudas, I had once speared a fish near an island off the coast of Belize. My son, Brian, was a youngster then and he and another young friend had been swimming ahead of me in deep water. I had left the fish on the end of the spear when suddenly I saw both boys swimming for all they were worth in the direction of the island. Right behind them was a six foot barracuda. I managed to get between this huge fish and the boys and I let my spear with the still wriggling fish on its end trail below. The barra looked me over, I was about his same size, and then he went down to check the struggling fish. I felt sure that he would go for the impaled fish and leave us alone but he did neither. He just followed us right on in to shallow water. He never went for a bite out of any one of us or the speared fish, though. It was something that he could have easily done any time that he had taken the notion.

Over the years I have swum amongst barracuda many times, often with over a dozen at a time around me. I have never had one zoom in for a quick slice. I have even shot some but this is not wise, of course, because the only barracuda attack that I know about occurred that way. A diver had put his spear into a three footer out in deep water on the leeward side of Grand Cayman. That barracuda came back with spear and all and he grabbed the leg of the diver. The diver lost part of his leg before he was able to grab the spear and get him off. He then tossed his gun away and the barracuda followed it toward the bottom. But that is the only incident I know about and I long ago gave up worrying about them. The rule is always the same for ol' 'cuda just as it is for any other fish, if you don't bother him he won't bother you.

Along Seven Mile Beach to the town of West Bay. 6 Miles.

At 5:00 a.m. the next morning the revelers next door were just getting in and they provided the incentive to walk Seven Mile Beach to the town of West Bay. The first light was from a full moon that made it light as day when I set out.

The walk along Seven Mile Beach that morning showed the progress in accommodations for Grand Cayman. There had been many changes over the years that we had known it. The beach was the same, though, five miles of clean white sand and clear water. Most of the hotels and condos had been tastefully done and I adjusted to them. The sand of the beach shifts throughout the year. This was something that I especially remembered as I passed by the old Coral Reef apartments. We used to stay there in the days before I brought the Vagrant Gipsy to the island. In the summer there would be lots of sand right out to the first little reef. Then in the winter the sand had somehow gone elsewhere so that the surf came up almost to the edge of the thatched hut where we used to assemble at sundown.

The regulars of the six-pack one-bedroom apartments that was the old Coral Reef used to religiously watch for the green flash out on the horizon each evening. The green flash is reputed to appear in that elusive little second when the sun drops into the sea. I saw it once, I was sure I saw it, but maybe it was just because I had been drinking a different brand of rum at the time. We all tried hard, every evening. We were dedicated green flash watchers. We shared stories and conviviality before and after, too, and those were good days.

Parts of the Seven Mile Beach have firm sand, good for jogging, and parts of it run to soft sand, the trudging kind. Part of it, not much, is under overhanging sea grapes and across a bit of coral, called iron shore in Cayman. All of it is next to the most inviting water in the world.

Near the end of Seven Mile Beach I came to my favorite reef that extends out from shore with some interesting coral formations in deeper water. It is always a rewarding reef to swim on. Beyond and farther out is a favorite dive spot, Trinity Caves. This is a huge coral formation with a series of interconnecting caves, the deepest of which opens out onto the famous Cayman wall at about 115 feet. The wall drops off to about 6,000 feet, straight down.

In the sleepy little town of West Bay I was lucky enough to catch the 'bus' that was headed back for Georgetown. Its driver was none other than a local calypso guitarist for 'Barefoot' and the boys at the Holiday Inn. 'Smiley' dropped me back at the Cayman Sands before anyone else was up. Walking Seven Mile Beach had been as much of a pleasure as always.

Botabano to West Bay. About 7 miles.

Botabano is a boat landing on the North Sound. It has a bar and pizza restaurant that we used to frequent when we were feeling in a local mood. It was also on the regular route that I used to take when I went jogging with Beauregard and Duffy along the dikes of the mosquito canals. Angie dropped me off on the far side of a new cut that flowed into an aspiring housing development.

Since I had earlier walked around the beach at Barker's on a brief sightseeing visit with Angie, I took a shortcut down one of the many canals to pick up over on the north side where I had left off. I knew most of the canals fairly well. They cut through dense areas of jungle and mangrove swamps in an effort to let salt water flow freely through the area. Mosquitoes can't breed in salt water and this has cured what used to be a serious bug problem. The canal I chose was one that I hadn't visited in a long time.

After a while I came to an area where the maintenance crews had been working. They had elected to cut this dike in two for some strange reason. The water was black and hostile and it was impossible to see what was lurking on the bottom. It was a long way back around, though, so reluctantly I stripped off all of my clothes and put them in the pack. I waded chest high through the muck and dark water carrying the pack high overhead. It was a relief to climb out on the other side.

When I reached the north side beach where I had previously left off I turned and headed west. The reef off this part of the island was one of my favorites for looking for lobster and grouper. I knew the hole of a wary 40 pounder out there who lived straight out from where I then walked. I could never get close enough to him for a shot and then I had become fond of him and lost interest in spearing him.

A family of tourists were out doing some early beachcombing. Beachcombing on the windward side of the island always provides a generous amount of things to pick through. Oddly enough the most frequent item is usually a lone flip-flop sandal. Pieces of boat wreckage, weathered driftwood, coconuts, old bottles, sea shells and what have you wash up from time to time. They make the quiet waters of the reef-protected beach worth exploring.

By the time I had made it along the sand beach to the Papagallo Condo development, the first bit of civilization on that side of the island, it started to rain. I waited the squall out in the shelter of a condo patio. The north reef ends there and the sea bends around to the leeward side of the shoreline. Just beyond, at the Spanish Bay Reef club, the beach turns to iron shore. I walked the road for a while. Just past the house on the far side of the resort I turned down a path and through a tunnel of sea grape trees. This brought me out to sand beach again.

When the sand beach turned to iron shore once more I took the road off to the left past a cemetery. I went by a native house where a puppy played in the yard. He hadn't quite acquired the confidence to bark until long after I had gone down the road. Then he had carefully weighed his sense of obligations and done his best. After winding down a side road to see if I could get back to the beach I asked two girls playing with a ball for directions. They told me how to get there and that when I came to another road off the beach I should take it because otherwise I would just go on forever. I was sure I didn't want to do that so I took their advice and eventually I found myself in familiar territory at the turtle farm.

The turtle farm was forced out of business when the U.S. wouldn't allow them to sell any of their products in the States. They had been trying to do something about propagating the endangered green turtle. The effect of the ban was to halt the good progress they were making because of the lack of revenue. The Cayman Gov't. finally took it over on a reduced scale and hopefully it will survive until the U.S. reconsiders the problem.

The walk down the West Bay road revealed a number of new homes that had been built during my absence from the island. Prosperity had finally come to Cayman. For a long, long time the menfolk used to go to sea for a living and it was a sleepy island with few amenities. When Pindling took over in the Bahamas some of the Bay Street crowd shifted to Cayman and since then it has never looked back. Here is a place with zero unemployment, no taxes, easy living and a casual government that does its best to treat everyone fairly. It is also afforded the security of being a British Crown Colony.

Back along the beach, just before the meeting place, I passed a couple of teenage Westbayers tucked back into the bushes on a flattened cardboard box. It was a secret bedroom hideaway that was a convenient spot for young love. I tried to discretely look the other way so as not to spoil their concentration.

This section from Botabano around Barkers and back to West Bay is about seven miles. Allowing a little extra time for the sand of the beach sections and a little beachcombing it should take around four hours. The remoteness and local Caymanian houses and the prevailing trade wind breezes make it a pleasant change from the resort scene of Seven Mile Beach.

Bodden Town to George Town. 12 miles.

Bodden Town is still the old Cayman, the way it used to be before offshore banking, captive insurance, scuba diving and tourism hit the island. It is the largest community on the south side. I elected to walk back to George Town from there in order to save Angie the nuisance of having to come out to meet me in the five o'clock traffic.

There is a little side road that angles back to the right as you first come into Bodden Town. I headed down this road knowing that it spilled out onto beach that soon became iron shore.

Iron shore has the nickname for a reason. It is old coral or volcanic rock on the edge of the sea that has been weathered by the waves and wind and marine life in such a fashion that all that remains is the jagged edge of the harder core. It is punishing to your Nikes and murder on bare feet or a hand stretched out for support. To be a beachcomber, though, and to see the places where no one else goes, or to walk around the island, it is necessary to put up with it now and then. Besides, it beats walking the main road with Caymanian and tourist drivers being what they are. A Caymanian driver thinks nothing of stopping in the middle of the road to gossip with a friend along the way. The tourist has the problem of remembering to drive on the left side of the road. Between them they can make a trip in the car an exciting adventure, especially on Saturday night when demon rum can enter the picture.

When I reached the iron shore part of the beach I worked back into the dense bush hoping to find some kind of a path. No luck. Every step had to be taken with care so it was slow going. After about a mile of it I came to a little beach in front of a condo development. There I followed a tract road through Beach Bay Estates, a development that had been laid out with more optimism than judgement.

The road soon petered out and I found myself back on iron shore again. This time it was easier going. I walked along the ridge of an old coconut plantation that had seen better days. A cool sea breeze was blowing but even so the hot sun produced a burning thirst. I had to hit the canteen I was carrying more frequently than usual.

Finally I was elated to pick up a dirt road that I knew fairly well. It passed a quarry where a friend of mine worked. He had looked after the boat for me when we were off the island. Then the road came to Pedro's Castle, a local landmark and one of the oldest buildings on the island. It was originally a residence whose owner, Pedro, tried to build it to resemble a small castle. It has changed hands several times over the years. It used to be a place we would sometimes go for a drink or a meal. I went inside looking for a cool drink.

Inside the bar I discovered that it had become a native place with a pool table and the usual quota of indolent drunks passing the time of day. One of them had reached the spouting-off-mean stage. In the past I have had some interesting times in a native bar but it can backfire, too. I had a long way to go and I didn't feel like a beer and sloppy conversation. The bar maid didn't have any iced tea and I didn't think a coke or a seven-up would quench my thirst so I pushed off.

Down the road I turned off onto another back road just before I reached the main highway. This took me past some well-done homes that had been recently built in the area. Finally, when I could avoid it no longer I was forced to do a stretch on the shoulder of the main road. This was a case of stepping out of range when a truck or a speedhead came by on a straight stretch. Caymanian drivers often interpret any straight piece of road that is over fifty feet in length as a speedway invitation.

Around one o'clock I stopped for lunch at a little stretch of beach near Spott's Bay. I found a casuarina tree for shade. I killed most of the last of my water there, something I knew I was going to regret.

After lunch I continued down a back road that bordered the sea. My thirst was becoming a problem until I came to a little grocery store at Prospect Bay. I went in and polished off two bottles of something that pretended to be Gatorade.

When I made it to South Sound, at its beginning, just at the turn off, I went behind the roots of a blown over casuaurina tree and pulled off all of my clothes. I plopped down in the clear water that lapped through the mangrove trees. What a luxury!

On the way past Pirate's Lair I stopped at the home of a friend hoping to fill my canteen but no one was home. Continuing on down South Sound I finally reached the Crow's Nest, a favorite restaurant. The cook took pity on me and she gave me two tall glasses of ice water. She couldn't believe I had walked all the way from Bodden Town. She thought I was crazy.

South Sound is the most desirable part of the island for a residence these days. It has a protective reef, lots of lovely casaurinas and coconut trees and an ample breeze that is not as strong as it is on the windward side. The area is not too far from town but away from the tourist areas and the traffic is bearable.

Angie found me slogging along about a block away from our rendezvous in town. Needless to say I didn't refuse a lift. It was five o'clock and time to get ready for the green flash.

Bodden Town to Gun Cay Village. 10 Miles.

This area is a taste of what old Cayman used to be like, before it become popular with the tourism industry and

After a good early start I walked along the beach of Bodden Town. It was interesting there, like crossing the back yards of a succession of old beach houses from yesteryear. The bleached and worn reef boats were pulled up beyond the high water mark and here and there laundry fluttered in the cool breeze.

For the next seven miles I was able to stay on sand most of the way. Occasionally there was the odd bit of iron shore to struggle over but nothing too difficult. I passed behind some very pleasant homes that overlooked the water. One of them was an old style Caymanian cottage that I had almost bought a few years back. I had agonized over it for a long time. It had a wrap around veranda, a pretty sand beach and an off-lying reef for protected snorkeling and spearfishing.

A long-legged egret kept me company for a good while. Just as I would almost reach him he would fly off to then land up the beach a short distance away. We kept this game going until finally he grabbed a little white crab that was scurrying down the beach. I stopped and waited for him to consume his prey. He flipped him around in his beak for a while and then with a gulp he sent him down the hatch, claws and all.

A couple of green parrots screeched at me. It was hard to distinguish them against the green leaves of the sea grape tree where they roosted. The green parrot is seldom seen. The black parrots are quite common and similar to the ching-ching birds that become such little beggars when they sense a bread scrap handout can be promoted.

Memories came filtering up when I passed by the old Lighthouse Club at Breakers. Many were the luncheons we had enjoyed next to the surf there over the years. When Miss Peggy became the new proprietor we went to try the new Sunday buffet as a gesture of support. In going through the line Angie and Kit had both selected a touch of shrimp salad and a small regular salad for their tiny salad bowl. They were told that they could choose one but not both of them together! Miss Peggy was determined to show a profit, none of this double-dipping.

The place continues with new management and good food and it makes a delightful stop on a trip around the island.

This time I carried an extra container of water in my pack so that I would have no problem with becoming thirsty. It became fairly hot whenever I had to leave the beach itself with its cooling tradewind breeze, especially in the noonday sun. I made it to Cayman Diving Lodge for mid-afternoon. It was right across from the East End reef and I remembered bringing the Vagrant Gipsy in through a break in the reef there once. It was a nice anchorage once you managed to thread your way through the coral heads that lurked in the channel. Nearby was the rusting remains of an old freighter that had gone aground years before. It had long since broken in two.

Gun Cay Village To Old Man Bay. 10 Miles.

The next day I managed another early start from Cayman Diving Lodge. In walking through East End, my favorite village on the island, I passed a memorable Sunday church scene. The congregation numbered about thirty inside the white-washed church beside the road. They were singing a hymn at the time. The ladies were dressed in their Sunday-go-to-meeting best and the men wore suits and ties despite the tropic heat. The windows were open and many a curious eye watched as the Crazy with the straw hat, the pack and the sun-bleached walking stick trudged on by.

That morning I walked the beach again for most of the way. This part of Cayman is still unspoiled. It is far enough away from George Town so that most of the residents don't want the long commute and too far away from the action on Seven Mile Beach for the tourists. The long reef stretches all the way around the northeast point of the island and it is the least visited area for small boat activity or reef swimming.

For lunch I sat down at a favorite picnic spot near the end of Collier's Bay. I had once scrounged some drift wood from the beach long ago and it had served as a crude bench and table beneath some sea grape trees. It looked as though it had been used by others many times but everything was still in place. In fact, my two sons, Bret and Brian, had come down for a short visit over Christmas and we had all picnicked there only the week before. It looked out to sea, across the outlying reef where I had almost lost both of them to a shark attack that day.

Bret and Brian went over the coral reef with their snorkels to swim out to look down in the deep at the wall. Angie and I were swimming inside the reef looking for conch. After they had been gone a long time we became concerned and climbed up on the beach to look for them. We couldn't see a trace of them anywhere!

Because of the sea then running I thought that maybe we just couldn't see them in the five foot swells. They were both strong swimmers and certified scuba divers but I also knew that a hard current emptied out of the nearby cut from Collier's Bay. If you couldn't fight it the next stop was Mexico 350 miles away.

With a father's screaming anxiety I churned out to the reef to look for them. After threading through the pounding surf over staghorn coral and swimming out for a closer look I still couldn't find them. I came back petrified. It was Christmas Day.

In frantically walking up the beach I finally spotted them headed towards us. Both of them were whitefaced and in shock.

Brian had cut his leg without realizing it when he crossed through the coral. He had been broadcasting a small trail of blood on the swim out to the wall.

Two large sharks had been cruising about 75 feet down. Bret had seen them when he free dived down to around 50 feet. He had watched the closest head for Brian with open jaws. We have been around sharks before over the years but we have never had one home in on anybody with his mouth open wide.

Brian suddenly discovered the shark just as he was

about to grab him. He had been carrying Angie's underwater camera and he yanked it up to take a picture. (He explained later that at the time he had figured it would have been the only way that Dad would have known what had happened to them. The sharks probably wouldn't have eaten the camera and it might have been found on the bottom.)

By this time the shark was only five feet away. Angie's camera makes a loud metallic click underwater and when the shutter went off the foreign sound somehow penetrated the limbic process in that primeval brain. The shark veered off and then Brian lunged at him in one last act of desperation.

The shark retreated and by then Bret had managed to get back to the surface from his dive. He had swum on over to Brian. Somehow the sharks thought better of attacking the two of them and they gradually backed off.

They had next faced the problem of swimming back in against the current. When they had finally made it back to shore it had been far up the beach and they were both exhausted.

When the roll of film from Angie's camera had been developed the picture of the shark was on it. Bret had later had it enlarged and mounted on his wall. To this day I can't look at it.

After lunch I gathered myself up and crossed over to the Queen's Highway which runs along the coast on that remote end of the island. Before the road had been built I had taken a hike one day along the jagged iron shore that is at its worst there and I had followed along a treacherous path on the bluff that ran next to the water. It bordered some four miles of uninhabitable jungle but parts of the track passed exquisite little sandy coves. We had later found that the close-in reef was full of marine life seldom fished. We had scrambled down to some of these coves from time to time and we had enjoyed the peace and solitude that they provided.

That day I walked the new road. It was hot most of the time because it was screened from the northeast trades by jungle. The dense vegetation that grows over this jagged area of coral sometimes includes a dangerous plant called Maiden Plum. The leaves are elongated, dark green and shiny. It should be avoided like the plague. If you simply brush against it with bare skin its poison can penetrate the skin itself. It then works its way into the blood stream. Your skin soon begins to swell and become painful. It can take a long time for its effect to work its way out of your body. It is best to wear long sleeves and pants and to be constantly on the lookout for it when walking in or near the jungle in that area.

Trudging along the road in the noonday sun I thought about a book I had just read that had been given to me as a Christmas present by Trevor. It concerned an Englishman named John Merrill. He is probably the world's most dedicated walker. He professes to doing an average of 25 miles a day with never a day off, never a companion (who could keep up with him?), and usually carrying a pack that weighs from 45 to 60 lbs. He does this for months at a time, usually over six months of the year. For example, he walked the Appalachian Trail in 90 days and the Pacific Crest Trail, albeit somewhat detoured but 2,700 miles, in 118 days. His 'round Britain walk of 7,000 miles kept him going for 10 months.

What is difficult for me to fathom is John Merrill's single-mindedness or compulsiveness about everyday mileage and his dedication to it. It is a career for him, though, and he hopes to be, I believe, the individual to have walked the most miles throughout history. I suspect that he already is. No less difficult is his method of accomplishment. He drinks no water during the day. He has never carried a canteen and he does not stop to rest. He does not stop for lunch, except for five minutes when he removes his rucksack to read his map and eat a couple of candy bars. He eats candy bars underway, too, as many as nine a day. I would imagine that they give him energy while indulging a sweet tooth.

After about a mile along the Queen's Highway I came to a familiar sandy path off to the right that leads down to the beach through the treacherous bush and iron shore. This path is bordered by a short wall that is faced with coral stones. It leads to a section of beach that offers the best beachcombing on the whole island. In all the times that we have picnicked or visited there we have never seen another soul on this beach. I passed another driftwood table that I had also made back in the sea grapes. It was still undisturbed and free from any litter so I assumed it had remained undiscovered.

The shore became a bit rocky just beyond the picnic spot and I took to the road once more. Soon I came to a small pavilion that housed a bronze plaque with the inscription: 'This Highway was opened by HER MAJESTY QUEEN ELIZABETH II on February 16, 1983'.

Shortly afterward I passed another beach house that I had also once considered buying. It was vacant and badly neglected now. This side of the island is one of the most peaceful and unspoiled of the different shoreline areas. Finally I pulled into Old Man Bay just as Angie arrived with the car.

Later that evening I stopped by the house of my old Caymanian friend Jeff. He was not at home but I related the shark incident to Phoebe, his wife, and her sister, Louise. They had lived in Cayman all of their lives and they responded by telling me about an event that had occurred to their brother when he had been on a turtling schooner down at Old Providence off of the turtle beds at 'Far Tortuga'. It made my blood run cold.

Phoebe's brother had been sitting out on the bowsprit of the old sailing vessel as it lay at anchor. His cousin had gone over the side to look for fresh fish. His flippers had splashed up in the air as he made his dive. Suddenly a long dark shape went by and then it came back. He saw his cousin come up out of the water toward the ladder on the side of the boat. His hands were on the ladder when the dark shape hit hard and his cousin went back down in the water with it. Then the head of a huge shark surfaced with its jaws completely around the waist of his cousin. The shark shook its head vigorously and the upper trunk was severed at the waist. The top portion of the body fell off into the water. Then the water became roiled as the shark fed below.

Immediately afterward, according to Phoebe and her sister, the crew went ashore and they killed a cow. They hung the carcass over the side of the boat. When this same shark came back to feed on the cow they shot it with a rifle several times and they dragged it on board. When they cut the huge fish open they found their shipmate in pieces inside of its stomach. The pieces were still quivering.

Old Man Bay to Rum Point. 7 Miles.

The final section of the walk around the island took me from Old Man Bay on the following day to Rum Point. It was mostly along the road that borders the beach. The beach is a bit too coral strewn for comfortable walking. The road led beside the sleepy island homes that perched up on the top of the beach, many of them with coconut palms as they faced into the constant trades.

Presently the road passed the local bar called Apollo Eleven. The proprietor's name was listed on the required notice above the door: A.B. McDoom, Licensed to Sell Intoxicating Liquors. (so as to eliminate any doubt as to what he was all about). It is named after the NASA moon flight and ever since then its patrons have been flying high at McDoom's place on a regular basis.

Next I came to a graveyard scene where half a dozen men were sadly digging a new grave in the tidy little cemetery beside the beach. Perhaps it was for the hit and run victim who had been killed the night before. Just beyond was the beach house that had belonged to a couple we knew who had built their home on the beach entirely with their own hands. They had lived in a tiny pump house while working on it and the house had turned out quite well.

Eventually I came to the entrance sign for the island's well-known resort development Cayman Kai, 'The Delightful

Community by the Sea'. This project has been carefully done over the years next to the island's shallow banks inside the North Sound reef. The clear water and clean sand bottom is as pretty as any of the banks one crosses in the Bahamas or the Turks and Caicos. I was shocked to see that the beach bar where we used to sit to eat our turtleburgers had been completely swept away by the hurricane earlier in the year.

Finally I pulled into Rum Point and I flopped down on the beach with the happy knowledge that I had completed the walk around the perimeter of the island. The old bar that is located there was not open because of the Sunday law so I contented myself with the remains of the canteen, really the best drink of them all.

To really encircle the island would take a remaining five mile swim across North Sound. I had thought about it, just take a rest midway across at a little sand bar there and another at a small coral outcrop called Fisherman's Rock, but I didn't get around to it so I guess I didn't really do the whole perimeter.

Cayman is a good island for easy walking. It has the best of just about everything, too, so it makes a nice place to combine a walking holiday with swimming, diving and water sports. Maps of the island are readily available everywhere once you get there. The best map of the island comes in two parts. It is 1:25,000 and it can abe obtained from the Land Registrar's Office in George Town for a nominal charge.

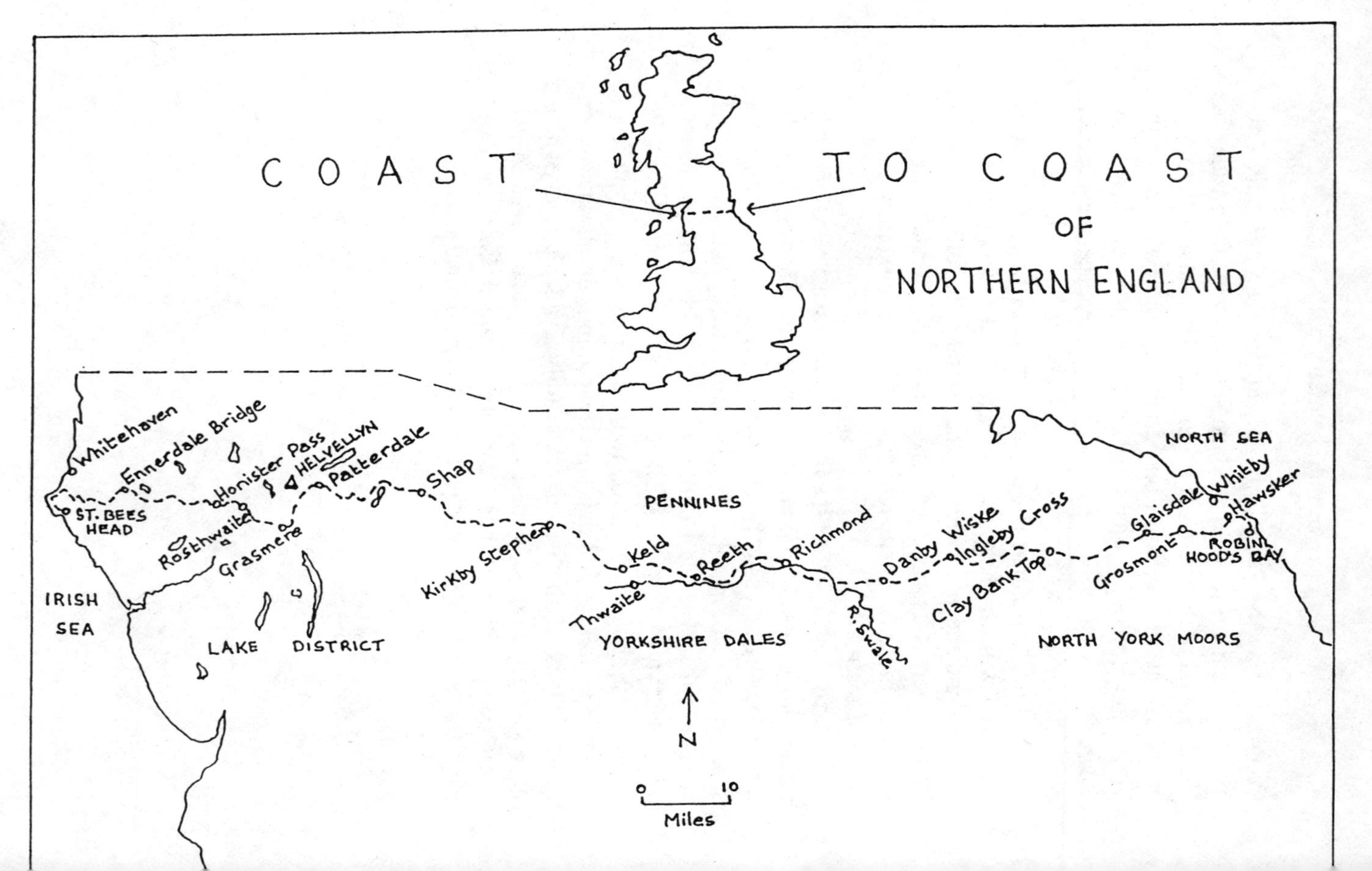
COAST TO COAST
OF
NORTHERN ENGLAND
Whitehaven
Ennerdale Bridge
Honister Pass
HELVELLYN
Patterdale
Shap
ST. BEES HEAD
Rosthwaite
Grasmere
IRISH SEA
LAKE DISTRICT
Kirkby Stephen
PENNINES
Keld
Thwaite
Reeth
Richmond
YORKSHIRE DALES
R. Swale
Danby Wiske
Ingleby Cross
Clay Bank Top
Grosmont
Glaisdale
Whitby
Hawsker
ROBIN HOOD'S BAY
NORTH SEA
NORTH YORK MOORS
N
0
10
Miles

WALK VIII

VIII. The Coast to Coast Walk of England.

St. Bees Head to Keld.

99.5 Miles

In browsing through the London Map Centre book store I had found a book called 'The National Trust Book of Long Walks'. This book gave an account of the ten most popular long distance walks in England and Scotland. All of them were over 80 miles in length and they pretty well sampled the whole of Great Britain. Some long walks had been excluded I noticed, including my Thames walk, but by and large they were what appeared to be the most favored of the lot.

The Pennine Way seemed to be the best known and the most frequently travelled of these U. K. walks. It is 270 miles long and it has become almost as crowded as the M4 motorway. Some 4,000 or more hikers manage to complete it each year. A. Wainwright, himself, the father of the Coast to Coast Walk and England's most revered walker, put together a guide for it. Wainwright was less than kind about the Pennine Way. It was one of the reasons that prompted him to develop The Coast to Coast Walk.

The Coast to Coast Walk has the strongest appeal from the standpoint of variety and motivation. It cuts across the north of England, below Scotland, and it travels through 3 national parks, including the famous Lake District and the moors of the Yorkshire Dales. It is a relatively new walk and as such it is not subject to as much traffic as the others. It crosses the area made famous by James Herriot, the popular country vet of 'All Creatures Great and Small' and its objective is appealing, too.

It stretches 192 miles from one coast to the other.

Also on sale at the book store in London was a small book that would be easy to carry with you. It chronicled the route of the Coast to Coast Walk and it was done by Wainwright himself, in his own meticulous hand. It included a multitude of well-done pen and ink drawings, diagrams and pithy comments and observations. The book itself is an absolute treasure and fun to read in its own right. In addition, I later found another book on the walk that is much larger with exceptional photographs of many scenes along the walk. It, too, has Wainwright's provocative narrative running through it but with a little less of his original brand of humor that is so delightful in the earlier chronicle.

The choice then became fairly easy for another U.K. walk to do. I opted for the Coast to Coast Walk.

The Lake District becomes increasingly popular each summer but fortunately more and more farms and homes seem to succumb to the lure of bed and breakfast money. Their doors are opened to non-reservation travelers and this makes it possible to do a trip there without a set schedule, something that might otherwise be cause for concern.

Angie and I found a delightful old inn, The King's Arms, above a pub in Keswick. It was handy for a base to start the Coast to Coast walk from West to East. For some unfathomable English reason Keswick is pronounced 'Kessick.'

The inn had a vacancy on the third floor. It was a walk-up-no-porter situation but it had the luxury of a shower, w.c. and wash basin 'en suite', meaning not down the hall. There were fire extinguishers and fire doors every fifteen feet in the King's Arms but this was no different than any other inn in England. Doing over a building in keeping with the local building codes must be a landlord's nightmare.

'The Loose Box' (translation, 'horse stall') was the inn's companion restaurant. The spaghetti and pizza were very good, especially with the excuse of carbohydrate loading for the morning's start at St. Bees Head.

St. Bee's Head to Ennerdale Bridge. 14 1/2 Miles.

We went inside the old Priory Church in St. Bees and it was impressive to realize that it was 700 years old. The workmanship throughout was surprisingly intricate and sound for being so ancient. The red granite entrance and the doors were remarkable and well-preserved.

On the beach at St. Bees I made a 10:30 a.m. start at the beginning of the Coast to Coast Walk. The trail worked up the cliff edge of St. Bees Head. It was a steep climb that turned into a pleasant walk along the edge of fields with long views out to sea. The footpath passed a lighthouse and then headed for the little village of Sandwith. It soon petered out or I missed it because of the many cowpaths that also used the field. In negotiating a pasture with some friendly cows a heavy-set man hailed me. It looked as though he might have wanted to take me to task for crossing private property but, no, he just wanted to help with directions.

The path to the next little town of Moor Row was a bit tricky with gates to cross and a faint trail that again petered out altogether. I stopped to have lunch beneath a tree on the way. No other hikers passed by. The trail had apparently become lost in pasture grass and it became necessary to climb a barbed wire fence and a hedge row in order to get onto the A595 highway that then put me on the proper lane to Moor Row.

On the hill down from the town of Moor Row a sign had been nailed to a tree beside the public footpath. It was a pitch for an enterprising grocery, Farren's Store, in the next town of Cleator Moor. The sign was an invitation to sign a register for the Coast to Coast Walk. It noted that 650 walkers had signed it the year before.

Just beyond the tree with the sign a spry old man was walking along another path that joined the public footpath. He was big in spite of his age and we stopped to talk. He said that he would walk along with me for awhile. Part of the pleasure in doing a long distance walk is the chance meeting with someone along the way. Old Tom was a retired lorry driver from the little village of Moor Row and he was out for his afternoon walk. He was proud of the local cricket team whose playing field we passed and he observed that the 'beck' we crossed, (stream), was good for young salmon. He had many interesting stories about the area and he accompanied me as far as Cleator. There he posed for his picture to be taken in front of a favorite pub. I sent him a copy of it some weeks later.

The walk on up to Ennerdale Bridge was full of rural scenes. At one point three sheep had managed to sneak out from under the fence. I put them back in where they belonged and then I tried to mend the fence where they had slipped through. Chances were that they would soon be back out again whenever they took the notion. The grass is always greener....

Angie met me at Ennerdale Bridge and that was the start of the walk. That night we went to a travelling theater in Keswick. We were astounded to realize that the whole affair, box office, seats, stage, dressing rooms and gallery all folded up and into a caravan like a carnival. Apparently this theater arrangement went from town to town. As soon as they had exhausted their audience potential or the bookings became a bit slim they simply folded up and moved on. We saw a well-done rendition of Woody Allen's old play, 'Play It Again Sam', and it had been very well performed.

Ennerdale Bridge to Honister Pass. 12 Miles

Ennerdale Bridge was the departure point for the next day's start. The walk followed a paved country lane that passed through a forest on the way to Ennerdale Water (translation, lake). At the bridge over the stream that emptied out of the lake a father and his two young sons had stopped to adjust their packs. We became acquainted and it turned out that they were out for a hike from St. Bees to Patterdale. They carried light packs and they had planned to stay in the hostels along the way. They owned a Bed and Breakfast house in Richmond.

The walk along the south edge of the lake was some 2 1/2 miles of easy going with maybe a dozen other walkers out for a hike as well. One hardy jogger passed by. He was going hell bent for leather down a rocky section of the path at a spot known as ‘Robin Hood’s Chair’. How he managed to keep from twisting an ankle at that pace was beyond me.

After the lake the path crossed pastures and the river Liza. It then followed a forest road up the valley which bordered the pretty river. It passed through densely planted trees that were being logged in several places. On either side of the narrow valley high escarpments raised perpendicularly to the upper fells.

At the end of the five miles from the lake the footpath reached an isolated youth hostel, the Black Sail Hut. The place was locked up and empty. A sign in the window said ‘vacancies for tonight: 6 males and 1 female’. I couldn’t keep from wondering whether a seventh male would get to sleep in the female dormitory in that extra bed there, assuming that the lone female failed to show. Timing in life can often mean everything.

The hostel sat on the edge of a huge basin surrounded by high peaks. The terrain was barren and treeless but rich in grass and streams. Sheep seemed to graze everywhere. It was a lonely place and I assumed that the keeper was the young biker that I had seen going down the forest road on my way up. Other hostels closed from 10:00 a.m. to 1:00 p.m. each day I had noticed and if this was the case then I was sure that he had well earned his break.

The doorway of the Black Sail Hut offered some shelter from the wind that was blowing hard and cold. I settled down and made my lunch. Two sheep came moseying over for a handout. They were persistent and reproachful when they found I had nothing I could share with them. I brought out the thermal underwear and a sweater and I put them on under the faithful old Gortex jacket. Then the mittens and the familiar watch cap kept hands and head warm and off I went into the teeth of a modest gale to experience fell-walking in the English tradition.

Wainwright had an alternative route for 'supermen' that led over Red Pike and High Stile, an abrupt crag nearby and I resisted the temptation to see if I could qualify. Instead I climbed arduously up some 700 feet of straight-up rock path that was labeled the route for 'non-supermen'! Switchbacks were not a part of this trail's vocabulary. The wind was at my back and strong enough to give me a lift from time to time whenever I held my arms out to the sides to form a sort of giant sail.

Up on top I quickly forgot about the climb, as one always does, and I marveled at the magnificent view that stretched before me. I could see the Buttermere valley far below with its two famous lakes and behind me was Ennerdale lake along which I had walked earlier that morning. The area where I was looked like a sort of mesa with sheep grazing on the mountain grass. Over in the distance I could see the workings of a slate quarry and suddenly I began to see other hikers around and the loneliness of the fells evaporated.

The one and a half mile descent to Honister Pass was again without benefit of switchbacks but it was not quite as bad. Part of it followed the old tramway track to the quarry. Below, at the hostel located at Honister Pass, Angie was waiting and I tried to describe that first experience of walking the 'fells' of the Lake District.

Honister Pass to Grasmere. 12 Miles.

English weather was determined not to disappoint me so that when I set out from Honister Pass on the following day it was raining with a heavy cloud cover overhead. I later learned that the Borrowdale Fells, through which I would pass, had a reputation for being the wettest place in all of England. And wet it was that day.

After working my way down to the quaint little village of Rosthwaite, with a good many gate openings, and then up the valley past Stonethwaite, most of it next to a very old stone wall, I began to climb again. Soon I came to a raging torrent of a stream that swept across the footpath. I could see that four other hikers had found a way across it well above. I climbed on up there and managed to get across with the help of a tree limb on one fork and a large rock on the other. Then I began to notice the other cascades up ahead. They looked unusually boisterous because of all of the rain that morning. They bounded down both sides of the surrounding peaks to join the now impassable Greenup Gill which joined the raging Langstrath Beck which, in turn, flowed into the Stonethwaite Beck, all of which would seem to spell flash-flood back in the States.

A little farther on up the trail I came to four hikers with packs on their backs and rain suits in bright colors. They were debating whether to continue because they said another party had turned back after reaching the next torrent that swept over the trail. One of the members in that party had broken his leg the previous year by slipping on a rock in a similar situation and he had decided not to risk a repeat experience. I offered the suggestion that we take a look at it.

When I reached the stream in question, up above, the flow across the footpath was intimidating. A slip could have sent me tumbling in the current down a slope of rocks on the off side of the trail. It was not likely to do me in but it could have produced a nasty injury from the mishap, enough to dampen enthusiasm for continued progress. I found a place, though, where I was able to jump across to a large rock in the middle of the deluge. I was committed to continuing across then but I managed to make another successful leap to the other side. The others were undecided and I could see that they did not want any advice from me so I pushed on up the trail.

There were a number of other cascades that crossed the trail as it made its way on up out of the valley. None of them were quite as bad, though. They were just wet and I had waterproofed my boots before I had left the States. The rain let up, too.

When I gratefully reached what I thought was the top I looked around and saw a large basin that circled in front of me. This was after some 1,200 feet and two miles of soggy climbing. I decided to stop and enjoy a drink of water and an orange. It was then that I realized that where I had yet to go was up the side of a nearby precipice called Lining Crag. What was more disheartening was that the rocky path or what looked to be the path had become a cascading streambed itself. I gloomily peeled the orange and wondered what it would be like up on top once I managed to get up there.

Just as I had finished the orange the father and his two young sons from Richmond appeared. Shortly afterward the four other hikers who had stopped at the second torrent came up to the false top, too. All of us looked at the foreboding scramble up the side of the crag. We set out with one of the two boys leading the way. I followed but then his father passed me. None of us were quite sure where we were headed but eventually we reached the top of Lining Crag and carried beyond.

The others stopped for lunch at the top of the crag and the father and I pushed off with his two sons in tow. A little later one of the boys stepped in a knee-deep bog. He was just ahead of me. I was careful not to follow him in. We continued to climb more gradually on the top of a barren grassy plain. Finally we came to an old fence line that was no longer intact. This was known as Greenup Edge and it seemed to be the crest of the route. There was little evidence of a trail. Shortly afterward the father selected a large rock and his two sons settled down beside him. He waved me on making it apparent that he didn't want me to join them for lunch. At first I was taken aback but when I thought about it I could understand that it was probably because he was doing a hike with his two sons on a sort of mini-vacation, probably the most important of the whole year, since school would start soon. I felt certain that he wanted to savor every moment of it, especially with his wife back home looking after the B & B.

Far below me I could see a broad plain that had a rim in the distance and beyond that was the green valley with trees and houses that I assumed was Grasmere. I brought out the compass and verified it. I began to see other hikers, too, in the distance.

After working on down across the plain with its usual contingent of grazing sheep I dropped on over the rim. I stopped for lunch in the lee of a large rock there. The wind had been blowing fairly hard all morning but it was not as strong as it was yesterday. I would have welcomed Beauregard's company.

The father and his two sons passed me by again as I was getting ready to leave. The tortoise and the hare. I was the tortoise.

After I became more confident about the rain's having let up I took off the flapping poncho and made my way down the rocky trail toward Grasmere. I passed the little family group one last time as they were having a snack break and I didn't see them again. The tortoise did make it to Grasmere first, just as all tortoises are supposed to do.

Grasmere to Patterdale. 8 Miles.

At 8:20 a.m. I left Grasmere the next day. It was a sunny day with scattered clouds overhead. I walked down the narrow lane and crossed the busy highway to Windermere. It had been ten years since we stayed down there at Miller Howe to enjoy John Tovey's famous cooking. The gourmet's gourmet. I guess the three days that we spent there were among the most memorable of our dining experiences. Even the box lunches were full of exotic treats like roast pheasant, home-made croissants, chocolate mousse tarts, fresh fruits and vintage wine.

On the other side of the highway a gravel track led through gates over a stream and up the side of the mountain toward Grisedale Tarn (a small lake). After about an hour and twenty minutes I reached what I thought must surely be the tarn. Nope. A false basin. Ten minutes later I made it up a steep slope and there before me was a jewel of a little lake surrounded by Peaks on three sides. I sat down on a rock next to a large cairn (a pile of man-made rocks to signify a path marker) and studied the map.

As I was reading the map I was startled to see a young hiker standing next to me. He was from Essex, near London, and he had come up on the train. We walked down around the tarn together. He was going to Patterdale, too, but he was taking the Helvellyn route. We separated there where the trail forked and I can remember him saying the scenery wasn't really all that important to him because he just loved walking.

There are two alternative routes to choose from there at Grisedale Tarn. The left one climbs up some 1,300' to Helvellyn Peak and then drops down to a sharp ridge called The Striding Edge. This effort involves a couple of extra miles of hard climb and some degree of risk apparently. The day before an item that had been buried on page three had appeared in the local paper. It had not been good for the tourist industry or not unusual enough to warrant more than the one paragraph I guess but it had reported that a woman had fallen to her death from the crest of the Striding Edge.

The other alternative route climbs up some 1,000' to St. Sunday Crag on the right side and then it drops on down to the head of the valley where it joins the other two.

All of these routes have marvelous views with the two side routes having farther fields of vision of course. It was tempting to waltz along The Striding Edge but the prospect of possibly tumbling down the side of Helvellyn that was there in front of me at the time did not seem too appealing.

A large number of intrepid hikers were out and about on the way down alongside Grisedale Beck. A blond labrador came by. He looked a lot like Beauregard. He was the first dog I had seen off the lead. I guess the big worry was the possibility that they might get after the sheep. He didn't seem to be interested in them, though, so I guess that was why he was allowed to run free. The trail passed an old stone hut named Ruthwaite Lodge. Its sign read 'erected 1884, rebuilt 1887'. Probably a fly-by-night contractor and his replacement had done it right the second time.

The footpath next went through a series of immaculately kept gates and pastures and wooded areas with stone walls and tidy stone buildings. Mostly sheep with a few cattle and four goats made up the farm there at the edge of the valley. Then a paved lane deposited me at the meeting place, Grisedale Bridge, in Patterdale. I was an hour and a half ahead of schedule. It had been an easy walk with dramatic peaks and a gentle valley to enjoy.

Patterdale to Shap. 20 Miles, unplanned.

Subconsciously I must have been thinking that I would like the experience of becoming lost in the fog on a mountaintop in the cold and rain with the problem of finding a way down. This turned out to be that day.

The early start at Patterdale was overcast but not raining or ominous. It became a pleasant trudge uphill toward Angletarn Pikes. On the way up fabulous views were everywhere, including Ullswater (lake), Patterdale and the distant Helvellyn Peak where I'd walked the day before. I felt strong and good after a day off and then the easy 8 miles.

It became necessary to pay close attention to the dominant trail. Many divergent paths branched off for different hikes in the area. Wainwright's admonitions were clear enough here, though, and it was possible to sort out the correct way with the use of compass, the ordnance map and his friendly words of encouragement. I noticed a couple who had taken a wrong turn and who were in the process of working back to the trail that I had taken. The weather looked nasty over in the west and it was headed my way.

On the trail below Angletarn Pikes I passed a section that went along a precipitous slope that dropped down for about a thousand feet to the valley below. It idly occurred to me that if you happened to be reading your map as you passed by and you inadvertently made a misstep off to the right because of it there was nothing to break your fall until you hit bottom. Then I remembered reading another item on page three of the local paper again. It, too, had mentioned the fact that a 58 year old man had fallen to his death there at Angletarn Pikes. Now I could understand how it probably happened. The footpath was deceptively reassuring, like a tourist guide across the river Styx. It earned my respect and close attention.

The path soon rounded a bend and its ominous threat was quickly replaced by the view of an inviting little tarn nestled in a basin. Half a dozen tents were pitched near its shore. No trees or wood were around for a campfire at night and it looked a cold and windy place to stay but life inside the tent would be all the more cozy because of it.

Then the weather began to engulf me as the route climbed a peak called The Knott. When I rounded this steep section of the trail rain and cloud suddenly enveloped me. I broke out the poncho and snapped it into place. And right there was where I somehow missed Wainwright's turn-off to the east.

Visibility became nil. Just before that it had been possible to catch a quick glimpse of the distant Hawsewater reservoir far below in the distance. This was where the route would eventually pass. It was due east but the heading on the compass showed 140 degrees, or southeast.

Instinctively I knew that something was wrong. I had been following a heavily travelled footpath next to a stone wall. Just then two joggers in running shorts came barreling down the hill behind me. They stopped and took a break in the lee of the stone wall. I had heard about fell-running but I would never have expected to see anyone doing it way up there. I went over to them and I asked if they knew whether the trail followed the wall, as it seemed to do, or if it cut through it at that point and followed the remains of an old Roman road which headed up and off to the right. They said that they were locals and that the trail continued up the hill beside the wall. They were not familiar with the Coast to Coast Walk. We talked some more and then they continued on up along the wall. Thus reassured I followed in the same direction.

In retrospect where I first went wrong was in not identifying The Knott carefully enough. I didn't realize that the peak to my left was Kidsty Peak at 2,560', billed as the highest point on the Coast to Coast walk. I mistook the peak ahead, High Street, at 2,718', as being the clue for a left turn. The take-off trail that I missed actually headed back north-northeast and it had no cairn or marker to identify it. Plus which the footprints in the boggy parts were more plentiful in the direction in which I was headed. I had no way of knowing that it was, in fact, a more frequently hiked footpath than the Coast to Coast take-off trail. If there had been no fog I probably would have readily seen where the trail branched off to the east. It was a big goof not to have kept better oriented and another not to have double-checked the well-meaning but wrong advice of the two runners. They knew where they were going. I should have taken some kind of a bearing or two with the compass in spite of the fog and given myself a position fix.

Up the stone wall I went feeling vaguely disappointed not to be heading due east yet. As I neared the top of High Street I came to what looked like a trail off to the east. It was, in fact, but when I examined it carefully it seemed to be seldom used. This was actually a second opportunity to go down the mountain across some rough crags but in the fog I couldn't make out how much of a trail it really was. It looked like it could also have been a sheep track and it had no cairn beside it for a marker.

The third mistake I made occurred when I reached the top of High Street peak. I found an ordnance marker there and I failed to notice that it was shown on Wainwright's sketch or to notice where it was on the ordnance map. I continued to blindly follow what was obviously a main footpath with its multitude of footprints in the boggy parts. I kept telling myself that it would soon turn to the east.

Suddenly the trail did turn toward the east and I was elated. Here was the Coast to Coast easting that would lead me out of this mess for sure! Right? Wrong! Then I saw a solitary hiker come up out of the gloom. We said hello. So sure was I that I knew where I was that I didn't even bother to check it out with him.

After a while the trail became rocky and difficult to follow. Every so often, though, a pile of rocks, the traditional cairn, showed the way. Suddenly I came to a very large cairn and here the ground was nothing but rocks or thick grass which refused to reveal a footprint of any kind. I looked at my compass and headed east down a steep slope in the direction that the trail had been headed. I ranged back and forth hoping to find the trail or a footprint. Nothing. I remembered then that Wainwright had mentioned that the trail became indistinct after awhile and I had already had that experience before. Then I thought, the hell with it, I'll just do it cross-country with the compass, sooner or later I'll reach the huge Hawsewater reservoir and I'll pick up the trail there.

Soon I came to a bluff and then heavy rocks. The sheep around me were not about to give directions. I asked myself how is it possible for an old sailor like myself to get himself lost up here on this steep 'fell' when I have a perfectly good map and a compass? I really felt silly and terribly annoyed with myself.

Reluctantly I had to admit that the idea of working down that mountain in the fog was stupid and that it could easily become disastrous. Plus which I'd never make the distant rendezvous and Angie would be worried sick. I took a reciprocal course and hoped that I could find the large cairn again in all of that gloom.

After cruising up and up and back and forth I finally spotted the big cairn once more. As I made for it I noticed two hikers who briefly appeared and just as quickly disappeared in the mist. These apparitions had come from the south. I discovered then that the trail had swung to the right there and I happily picked it up again. Apparently a very large cairn is akin to a double-blaze on the Appalachian Trail. It signifies a change of direction.

For the next mile I stuck to the footpath like a leech. Suddenly I came to a sort of a pass, or gap as it is called on the A.T. A high stone wall had been built there to serve as a windbreak shelter. I huddled down behind it for a rest and a drink of water, my first for the morning. By now it was almost one o'clock and I dug out a croissant sandwich, too. I had noticed a cross trail going north and south there and now I had a sure enough bearing that I could sink my teeth into. I perused the ordnance map and to my complete amazement I discovered that I had wound up over two miles southeast of where I was supposed to have actually made the turn-off. My ego had become severely shattered.

As I was finishing the sandwich the two hikers came down the same trail that I had been following. The heavier of them was having trouble with both of his knees. They had had to turn back. "Twenty-six years old," he wryly observed, "and I'm a physical wreck." They confirmed where we were at that moment since they were going back to Kentmere and they had come up on the south trail right there.

The rain had stopped, the fog lifted and I could see where I now had to go to get down off of the mountain. Things began to look rosier. There was a little tarn called Smallwater down below and beyond that was the south end of the Hawsewater reservoir, my then big objective. The place on the map said Nan Bield Pass and I felt like kissing it so glad I was to once again know exactly where I was in that environment.

The path down to Hawsewater was rocky and steep but it sported a few half-hearted switchbacks of the English variety. I was able to take off the flapping poncho and the hiking felt good in spite of the realization that I had managed to add four miles to the day.

When finally I reached the reservoir I decided to save a little time by doing the next four miles alongside it on the eastern side. Now my problem was to reach the meeting place on time. It was a spot on the map that we had agreed upon but neither of us had actually checked it out beforehand. By now it was 2:00 o'clock and I had seven or eight miles to go before 4:30 p.m.

About halfway along the reservoir I came to a remote hotel. It was out in the middle of nowhere. Apparently the hotel had been built there as compensation by the company that had dammed the valley of Mardale to form the reservoir. They had completely submerged all of the farms and homes and the previous hotel that had formerly occupied a spot on the valley floor. In fact the water was down low enough, because of the summer's drought, so that it was possible to see the old stone walls and lanes and crumbled remains of the buildings themselves. It produced an eerie, ghostly feeling.

A sign on the hotel said 'Afternoon tea'. I looked at my watch. It was now 2:50 p.m. I had been walking steadily for almost six and a half hours. Maybe it was time for a tea break. I felt in the mood for some encouragement. With one of those what-the-hell moments of exhilaration I went into the vacant lobby. A solitary waitress appeared from out of the kitchen. She wasn't the least bit perturbed about my boots and pack. She took my order and I flopped down gratefully on a velvet chair. A nearby blonde labrador named Candy looked up at me out of one raised eye. She good-naturedly wagged her tail a couple of times without changing her sprawl.

After two scones, three cups of tea and a glass of ice water I was pumped up again and I headed toward the rendezvous with an improved stride.

Two hours later some of the hikers seen earlier that morning began to appear on a trail down below the short-cut I had taken to save time. I by-passed them in my concern to make it on time to the Shap Abbey bridge where we had agreed to meet.

At the ruins of Shap Abbey it was a relief to crash down on the grass next to the bridge at a few minutes before five, not too late for the E.T.A. No Angie, though. Some 40 hikers straggled slowly by on their way up the road toward the village of Shap, this section's stopping point for those using accommodations along the route. All of them had to be Coast to Coast walkers as there would be no other reason for them to be hiking there. They came in twos and threes and singles with a variety of gear, some heavy, some light. The lab that I had seen a couple of days ago was there and also an irish setter, both on leads now. All of them looked weary but pleased with themselves.

At around five-thirty I had begun to worry. I headed up the road for Shap. I knew that Angie would have to come through there. At six o'clock I knew something had happened. I decided to try to phone the hotel to see if an accident had been reported or if she was ill or something had gone wrong.

As I was trying to get the phone to answer at the hotel in Keswick I was overjoyed to see the familiar little white Ford pull up beside my red phone booth. As luck would have it Angie had stopped at that particular spot to try to figure out how to get to Shap Abbey. She was going to ask a hiker passing by the phone booth for directions when she recognized one of my legs in the faded jeans that had been holding open the door. We repaired to a nearby pub and she described the bad road that she had been forced to use, the hay truck she had followed and the ordeal she had undergone in trying to find lodging before a major holiday that was coming up that weekend. The bottom line, though, was that she had rented a newly available cottage on a farm near Richmond. It was a perfect ending to a 20 mile day and the humiliating experience of getting myself lost in the fog at the highest point of the Coast to Coast walk. A couple of pints, or was it four, helped us to celebrate the turning point in what had been a difficult day.

<u>Shap to Kirkby Stephen. 20 Miles, planned.</u>

Because of the move we spent a rest day in a traditional English hotel in the small village of Clifton. It was difficult to figure out how they managed to fill the fifty rooms and the large dining area in such a remote place until that night when two large buses pulled into the parking area. They were crammed to the gills with O.A.P.'s (old age pensioners) in what appeared to be a package tour for the older set.

Our hotel room was about fifty feet from the railway tracks and at first we were just grateful to have a place to stay at the beginning of the busy 'Bank Holiday' weekend. Our cottage would not become available until the following day. That night, though, the incredibly efficient British Rail System sent a train whizzing down those tracks about every three to five minutes. Just as I'd start to doze off, zoom-zoom, and the windows would reverberate.

The next morning it was easy to get an early start for the long hike to Kirkby Stephen. It was a respite from the noise of the trains. Angie dropped me off at Shap for 7:15 a.m.

The route followed down a lane, across three fields and up and over the busy M6 motorway on a footbridge. Then came the moors with fields of heather and frequent checking with the compass. It became a toss-up as to whether the path had been defined by generations of sheep or by the shoes of itinerant coast-to-coast walkers. Often it just petered out altogether and then the compass or Wainwright's odd landmarks here and there would furnish the clues. One of the highlights of that part of the walk was a huge cairn which was reputed to be Robin Hood's grave, though not too seriously methinks.

Around 10:30 a.m. the town of Orton came into view. As luck would have it a pub was open there and it was possible to stop for tea. The affable proprietress brought forth a steaming pot of it on a tray with a plate full of biscuits (cookies) alongside. She said that she had coast-to-coast walkers who would drop by from time to time but that they seldom arrived before twelve or one o'clock. "You're early," she said. The trains had done me a favor.

After Orton the course followed a farm lane through the settlement of Raisbeck. Just beyond, a farm owner was putting nine cows and their calves into a nearby pasture. He had been herding them with his Land Rover. He said that his family had owned the place for over two hundred years but that he had no sons to pass it on to. His daughter had just given him a grandson, though, so there was still hope. He was urbane and knowledgeable and it was difficult to cast him in the role of a farmer.

Across the way was a well-cultivated pasture with a very high fence. Inside the fence was a large herd of red deer. These deer were sold for venison to Harrods in London. Nowadays the public wants more lean meat and venison has less fat.

Walking across a huge field that went on for a couple of miles it was surprising to see a farmer come barreling across the moor on a Suzuki four-wheeled trail-buggy. He nodded as he went bouncing past. He was probably out checking his sheep or looking for strays and Suzuki's don't eat hay.

The route passed on down another country lane to an estate known as Brownber. It was comprised of a number of interesting farm and estate buildings, quite large, and one of them was marked 1604 A.D. They were surrounded by lots of trees. The little road that I took passed through a quaint tunnel beneath a dismantled railroad. It opened into a field full of sheep on the other side. The sheep came charging over when they suddenly discovered a stranger in their pasture. Then they followed in one huge drove like the Pied Piper of Hamlin. They were disappointed when the gate was closed and they finally realized that they were not going to be fed.

After manoeuvering up a narrow lane that dissipated into a track and then a path the route eventually crossed over a very old footbridge that is known as Smardale Bridge. Now for the first time someone had taken the trouble to paint 'C to C' on the gate. Soon afterward a rickety stile crossed over a barbed-wire fence. Someone else had thoughtfully wrapped the top strand of barbed-wire with a fertilizer sack and tied it in place. Could the good samaritan have been someone whose own crossing had been marred by an unfortunate assault on his dangly bits?

The 'C to C' encouragement then became evidenced at strategic spots from time to time. Even so it became necessary to use the compass a lot because of the multitude of conflicting sheep trails in the two miles of open moor that the route crossed.

The course finally led over a stone wall on a stile. This emptied out onto a little-used lane that joined another lane nearby and this was the location we had chosen for a readily identifiable meeting place. My arrival turned out to be an hour and a half early and there would have been plenty of time to do the other two miles on into Kirkby Stephen itself. This would have made a twenty-two mile day but walking the moors is not as demanding as walking in the mountains.

Years ago we had stayed at a hotel in Kirkby Stephen and it was possible to remember having taken a walk along the same path that the C to C now used. Even more deja vu was the fact that it was probably about the same time that Wainwright himself had been there, too, as he laid out this walk for posterity and for my then undreamed of later enjoyment.

While waiting for the welcome sight of the white Ford at the five o'clock rendezvous time the other hikers slogged on by. They included a solo hiker, a couple and a threesome. All of them seemed a bit weary but pleased to be nearing journey's end for the day. These were the only eastbound hikers seen all day. Two westbound walkers had been passed earlier on and then a group of four around three o'clock. For the rest of the day, though, there had been no one else out on the moors except the ubiquitous sheep. It had been like another day in the life of a Basque shepherd.

Kirkby Stephen to Keld. 13 Miles.

Kirkby Stephen is pronounced 'Ker...bee Steven', the second 'k' is just for show, the ph has been trampled into a 'v', and the double-barreled name makes it sound like a more important town. I left the little Waitby junction with a good early start.

The route crossed some pastures and went through an underpass beneath railway tracks. It then went through a lush green field that led to a group of large farm buildings. Inside the gate a huge flock of sheep came charging toward me again. It was a strange feeling to suddenly be converged upon like some celebrity about to endure an autograph session amongst his fans. They followed doggedly right on down to the other gate out of their pasture, too. Sorry, gang, no autographs today. Nothing to feed you, either.

It was a Sunday morning and there was no activity at the Green Rigg farm through which Wainwright's sketch led the Coast-to-Coaster. A black lab was on guard at his little dog house. He was on a chain, like a Spanish dog, and I could see that his heart wasn't really in it. He knew that he couldn't do any good as long as he was on that chain. He barked but he didn't bother to get up or to come out of his house. It was difficult to understand how the farm could be amenable to hikers tramping through their principle work area but that is where the route went. It was enough to restore one's faith in the potential for generosity in mankind. And this farm was not alone on the Coast to Coast walk. Perhaps it has something to do with the British sense of fairness.

After walking down a tree-lined lane the edge of town soon appeared and just beyond it was the main road. Here there was a choice of routes to take. I opted for the Nateby-Keld way along a back country road. Heavy clouds with rain were hanging over the dales and it looked like they held the possibility of producing a day in the fog and mist following a compass course out on the moors. The same country could be enjoyed on the tarmac with just as much quiet and solitude.

The walk to Keld was a pleasant sample of the Yorkshire Dales of Herriot country. After an easy climb up a long hill for about 2 1/2 miles, out from the town of Nateby, the route was on the flat or back downhill. Long vistas were everywhere. Not a bush or a tree grew on the Dales, nothing but grass in various shapes and sizes, mostly well-grazed by the ever-present sheep who were now widely scattered in the distance. Strangely enough, it was not a lonely place.

Along the way it was possible to look down or across to the different 'gills' and 'becks' that eventually emptied into the River Swale. The Dales were gently rolling hills that were favorable for the formation of these little streams. I stopped at a stone sheep barn and had lunch in its lee. The wind was cold and rain was imminent.

After lunch the poncho came out for protection from a light drizzle for a short while. There is something cozy about the shelter inside the hood and folds of a poncho. There was an interesting stone bridge that crossed the river and shortly afterward the road passed the Wain Wrath Force. These were water falls and several people had stopped to admire them. As they were only some three to four feet in height it was difficult to properly share in the excitement.

The rest of the way down the length of the valley to Keld was a treat to cover because now small farms began to line the banks of the river as it wound on down between them.

In Keld, the rendezvous, a crafts sale was being held by a couple who had spent the winter making various little items for sale. The exhibit seemed to attract the Sunday drivers. It also attracted a number of hikers because here at Keld the Pennine Way crossed the Coast to Coast Walk. It was enough of a crowd for another flat in the village to open its doors for tea and cakes. I went on in and had a welcome mug of tea for only 35 pence. I talked with a friendly couple who said that the walking was easy from here on out. I told them that I was glad to hear that because I was into Walking Easy.

WALK IX

IX. The Second Half of the Coast to Coast Walk.

Keld to Robin Hood's Bay.

99.5 Miles

As Wainwright jubilantly points out Keld is HALFWAY there!

Keld to Reeth. 12 Miles.

It was bright sunshine in a clear sky for an 8:24 a.m. start at the little square in Keld. No one seemed to be stirring around much but the delicious aroma of bacon gave promise that others would soon be out to enjoy what was a British holiday. The footpath sign had an arrow pointing downhill with the town of Muker indicated below it.

Soon another signpost appeared marking the well-known Pennine Way. The path headed on down towards the river from there. Before using a footbridge across the Swale river it became necessary to make a decision. To the right it looked possible to make one's way along the river and so enjoy the pleasant valley through which it ran. To the left Wainwright's route led up onto the moors and it would pass a succession of ruins of the many abandoned lead mines in the area. For someone living in the area the moors route would probably be a treat but for me the little river was too inviting to resist.

The muddy path along the river ran beside some waterfalls, 'forces', that is, and pools beneath abrupt limestone cliffs on either side. Then the trail came to an impassable bluff. Here it became necessary to shift into goat gear and the wisdom of selecting this route began to appear questionable. The path climbed steeply along a perpendicular facing, up and over rocks and in and out of trees and low-hanging limbs. It was muddy, too, and a slip could tumble you on down to the rocks of the river below. It was nothing spectacular, like the incident at Ordesa in the Pyrenees, or the Rio Cares adventure in the Picos de Europa, just enough to do you in right there in the gentle Yorkshire Dales.

Eventually the path came to a fork that led upward through a break in a stone wall. Suddenly the fork joined up with a proper, stabilized trail. It was the Pennine Way itself as it made a bend down through the valley toward Keld. What a pleasure it was to set foot on it.

For the next two miles, on the Pennine Way footpath, more or less, down through a flat grassy bottom beside the river, I experienced the kind of ecstacy that you sometimes get on a long-distance walk when you are in the right place at the right time. There was no one around and it was an absolutely perfect morning, sunny, crisp and clear. It was early enough, too, so that the pheasant and rabbits were still out doing breakfast. The little river was babbling alongside and the grass was all green and fresh, like a putting green on a golf course. It was a jewel of a piece of time when there was nowhere else I'd rather be or anything else I'd rather be doing than what I was doing right then and there at that moment.

Then another option presented itself when a footbridge made a crossing of the river. The Pennine Way was about to head south across the narrow road that would be full of holiday traffic and it would be possible to avoid that problem by travelling along a little used track on the other side of the picturesque Swale valley. I passed that way on down to the tidy little town of Gunnerside and then it became possible to once again cross a one-lane bridge on the main road to the other side of the river. Over there on the south side a long dirt track was easy for walking. It sometimes bordered the river and it sometimes climbed up to look down on it. It petered into a path at one point and became a paved road for a short distance at another but all the while it was a delight to walk.

The route went next to the yard of a handsome estate. In the yard was a shiny Rolls Royce. I wondered if the owner would have been interested in hearing about my old 1939 Rolls, the one that used to belong to the Shah of Iran that I kept for so many years and which met its downhill demise when I foolishly took it to the island of Eleuthera in the Bahamas and kept it there for a couple of years. And the time that a would-be scoffer came up at a service station and said, "I hear these are supposed to be quiet running cars. How about turning the engine on so I can hear it?"

"It's on," I said. And it was.

After a late lunch break on a grassy bank beside the river I continued towards an ancient cable footbridge that doubtfully recrossed the river. It held together while I reached the other side which was the town of Reeth, the end of that day's walk. I can remember thinking that so far this may well have been the best day's walk on the whole Coast to Coast footpath. It had certainly been a perfect day for it, the walking had been easy and interesting and there was still a lot more of it to look forward to before reaching Robin Hood's Bay.

In Reeth there was a British Telecom phone booth perched in an unlikely spot up from the main cobblestoned walk of the interesting town. These phone booths have a habit of suddenly materializing in the most bizarre places. Yesterday one had appeared on a lonely stretch of road out on the moors. The British Telecom system for calling the States is one of the most gratifying experiences I've ever had with any foreign telephone company. By simply dialing 0800-89-001 an A.T.& T. operator comes on the line in the States.

At two o'clock it was an hour early for rendezvous but so was mon chauffeur and off we went. The charming and well-appointed house that Angie had found was out from Richmond, all by itself. It belonged to the dairy farm owners who lived down the lane. We were to be their first tenants.

Reeth to Richmond. 10 Miles.

The next day I was back at Reeth for an early takeoff. I passed down the main road to a fork that led to a lesser-used lane toward Marske. After that I turned off onto a still paved road toward a place called Marrick Priory.

The day was overcast with heavy clouds but no rain. Even so it was nice to see the river Swale down below and to take in the green pastures of the valley. Just outside Reeth a large field was in the process of being organized for an agricultural show. We had decided to take the day off from hiking to attend it.

The Marrick Priory was established in the 12th century for Benedictine nuns. Now, though, it is an adventure centre, whatever that means, and it seems to be in operation. It featured a minibus with a long roof rack of the kind that indicates group outings to some kind of wilderness. It is a far cry from the cloistered lives of the nuns. Just beyond the old Priory an unusual path took off uphill. It was laced with flagstone steps all the way to the top. Then the route led down a lane and through several gates. One of these had come off its bottom hinge and I stopped to fix it, something I knew that I had to learn to resist doing if I wanted to make it to Robin Hood's Bay anytime in the foreseeable future.

At the end of the lane the route went through a cluster of houses that were known as Marrick itself. On the far side a fork in the road appeared and it seemed that the proper way to go was to the right of the two. Wrong! The next mile was consequently devoted to freewheeling in and out and over and around various stonewalled pastures until it became possible to identify a house described in Wainwright's narrative that was far in the distance below. One pasture contained three docile-looking bulls who looked disdainfully in my direction with a bored expression of 'There goes another one of 'em, screwed up as usual.'

The little house down in the dale, all by itself and next

to a tiny brook, had been tastefully restored. It had a lovely courtyard with flowers in the garden and a set of stone stairs leading up to a loft that looked like a studio. It was all the more remarkable because of the absence of a road to it, only a footpath.

After crossing the brook on a shaky footbridge it became necessary to religiously follow instructions since there was no path, only grass in open fields. This policy carried the route past several more fields and part of a large farm until it eventually connected with a paved road that passed through the town of Marske.

Beyond Marske the route was off again across more pastures, stiles and over a stream on a well-made footbridge. It then led uphill and onto a farm road. Suddenly I was engulfed by a herd of cows who were being called to lunch by two farmers who had just loaded hay into a couple of circular feed troughs. It seemed strange to see them being fed in the middle of summer but the land did look overgrazed and they had had a mild winter with a probable surplus of hay and a summer drought of sorts. A farm gets bent by weather from time to time and the soil on the hill there was less fertile than down below.

The farm road led through the Applegarth Farm where a border collie came over to check me out. He circled behind me and I felt a nudge on the leg as I was saying Good Morning to his owner. Oddly enough I would see this very same dog in action at the sheep trials the next day. The road continued through some gates and then downgraded itself into a dirt track.

The view from the dirt track was captivating. It was possible to see the River Swale down below. It had grown to considerable size since yesterday and the day before when passing by its beginning. Large trees bordered it and off to the right a tightly-packed caravan site had been located beside the river. I stopped to admire the view and to have lunch.

Lunch is something that always seems to become worth looking forward to around mid-morning and I often try to do something interesting with it. That day's lunch was a couple of

Baps that I had made with the remains of Angie's Coq au Vin from last night's dinner. It also included the rest of a sea-shell pasta salad I had made, a Scotch pancake and a scone. When I'm logging miles during the day I don't have any problem rationalizing the extra calories, another little fringe benefit of long-distance walking.

The dirt track wound through some woods and then it emptied out from a gate onto tarmac. Suddenly the historic little city of Richmond could be seen below. What a lovely sight it was. Richmond was probably the most classic of the cities that we saw in the north of England. With its cobblestoned streets, ancient inns and restaurants, its handsome stores and statues it produced a sort of medieval feeling. I halfway expected to see a knight on a white horse come riding up asking for directions to the castle. A real castle actually did exist in the town, built in the late 11th century, but the white horse turned out to be a rented Ford with Angie at the wheel.

Richmond to Harlsey Grove Farm. 20 Miles.

In order to attend the Agricultural Show at Reeth I took a day off from hiking. This was the 78th annual show, which meant that it had been continuous each year since 1911. The experience was one of the most reassuring and touching events that could be encountered in a world full of violent news. Here were several hundred participants from the Swale River valley area who were competing good-naturedly with one another in productive, wholesome, down-to-earth activities. And here, too, was an orderly, interested and appreciative crowd of visitors of a like number who had come to sample and admire an example of how people can bring satisfaction and basic meaning into their everyday family lives.

In a large tent prizes had been awarded for various categories of entries. Flowers and vegetables were on display, including a pair of leeks as big as a man's leg. Also included were cleverly carved walking sticks and sheep crooks, lace tatting and crocheting, oils and water colors, flower arrangements, all kinds of tea snacks, pies, pastries, home made wines, pressed flowers, butter and cheeses, jams and marmalades, breads and cakes, different types of arts and crafts and cleverly decorated mugs and thimbles and photography and all of these categories and entrants were actually listed by name in the general program.

One of my favorites was a little lady who was proudly sitting by her six winning eggs, one of which had had to be broken open in a saucer, which it was, with its beady yolk eye staring up at us from beside its winning ribbon.

Another favorite was the handwriting contest, especially the category for the six and seven year olds who had entered their best effort in copying a poem by Spike Milligan called 'A Baby Sardine':

'A baby sardine saw her first submarine.
She was scared and stared through a peephole.
Oh, come, come, come said the sardine's mum,
It's only a tin full of people.'

Outside in the main paddock a day long series of horse judging activities took place. To see the children riding their ponies over jumps and doing dressage, the huge draft horses being paraded around and the affection that these horses received from their riders and owners and the families that encouraged them was really heartwarming.

Endless pens of sheep were judged and a fell run could be watched as the runners raced up the hillside and then back down again. And a highlight event of the day was a five man parachute team who jumped from a plane overhead and managed to land in the center of the main ring of the fair.

My favorite event, though, was the sheep dog trials across the road. To see a dog bring three skittish sheep across an open field entirely on the whistle command of his owner and to then gingerly herd them into a small pen that was set-up in the middle of the field, this is the ultimate test in dog obedience demonstrations. The race is against the clock, of course, and the sheep invariably have other ideas.

The farmer and the dog I had met at the Applegarth farm the day before took their turn, too. Unfortunately they had drawn three sheep who absolutely refused to enter the pen in the time allotted. Crestfallen, the farmer had been forced to abort his trial. He still had a pat for his dog, though. It was a touching sight because I knew how much it must have meant to him. His son, with whom I had been watching and talking, just shrugged his shoulders and walked away from me toward their pick-up. My heart ached for both of them and equally as much for their brave little dog, too.

The agricultural show was a glimpse at a rewarding lifestyle where the age-old virtues and values of rural life continue to carry on as they have for centuries past. It had a tendency to make me consider getting a small spread, a few cows, a flock of sheep and a good sheep dog or two, a modern-day, glass-enclosed, cab-over tractor and a farm mortgage for incentive and join in the fun.

The next morning it became possible to get a good early start from Richmond because the farm cottage where we were staying was not far from where I had left off. I blew it, though. This is getting to be embarrassing to reveal, after the other wrong turns already mentioned, but the fact is that the main bridge where I started, with its convenient little sign indicating the C to C marker on the other side, was actually the wrong bridge. I followed the markers back a half mile until the trail reached the other bridge, called the Richmond bridge no less, although less used. Then it became apparent that I had to double back the half mile that I had already walked. It was not a good way to start a twenty mile day. Oh well, it was a nice day and I tried to be philosophical about it. I looked forward to seeing more of the river Swale and some interesting farms along the way.

The route became better marked after leaving Richmond

because of the work that has been done by the North Yorkshire County Council. No mention of this was made in Wainwright's guide so it must be a fairly recent improvement. They had done a fine job of indicating the trail direction by placing distinctive little yellow arrows on green backgrounds at strategic spots. They had also erected weathered sign markers that had been neatly carved out of wood to say 'Coast to Coast'. These were placed at road junctions or trail departures from the road. The folks of the N.Y.C.C. who are responsible are entitled to the gratitude of all Coast to Coasters.

Because of the N.Y.C.C. markers the route became easier to follow as it worked its way for eight miles along the Swale river bank, across pastures, through farm yards and over many stiles. For the most part an identifiable path could be seen, too, where other walkers had trod before.

No other hikers passed by in either direction all morning. I crossed a pasture with some bulls grazing in it. One of them was pawing the ground and snorting, obviously concerned about something. I hoped that I hadn't offended him. He started moving in my direction and I gave him a wide berth but he didn't seem interested in me. Instead he snorted his way on over to the fence just after I had managed to get around him. I think he was trying to impress a heifer in the next pasture.

The country was mostly flat or gently rolling hills, all farmed. I stopped for lunch by a creek. The sky was lightly cloudy and clear blue in the patches. It was possible to see the distant moors where they jutted up on the horizon some fifteen miles away. I knew that the next day would see me up there on the top of them.

At Bolton-on-Swale a monument had been erected in St. Mary's courtyard by public contribution in 1743. It was to commemorate the life of Henry Jenkins who had been born in 1500 and who had died in 1670. Right. 169 years of age. The extent of his progeny must have been mind-boggling and it is hard not to wonder how he had achieved such a long life.

At Ellerton Hill the route followed back country lanes

for the next twelve miles. These had little or no traffic on them and they made for easy, trouble-free walking.

In passing the White Swan pub in Danby Wiske I went in and ordered an orange drink. The proprietor brought forth a visitor's register for those who had stopped on their Coast to Coast walk. He asked me to make my entry. I counted the names. From June 24th to August 31st there had been, including myself, 814 people who had signed the book. This was for both directions, of course, so I think it is fair to speculate that 1,200 or so a year drop by and possibly there are another two or three hundred who don't succumb to the pub's temptation. How many of them actually complete the entire 192 miles of the walk is open to conjecture but those who have made it to this spot from the usual west to east route have now done 131 miles of it and it would seem fair to conclude that they would go on to finish it. Those going in the opposite direction seem to be in the minority although I did see several entries who had been headed that way.

If you interpolate the entries in the register and then make allowances for little activity outside the summer months as well as the probability that some of the Danby Wiske walkers would eventually drop out for various reasons, lack of sufficient time, problems with the feet, the knees, finding accommodations, the weather, or something else, then I would feel comfortable with an estimate of around a thousand a year for those who were then managing to walk the whole route. All of this is based on the visit to the pub, an oasis in a long, dry section that would be hard to resist and the perusal of its register. This is not much of a crowd when you scatter them over 192 miles and several months. One entry's comment called the Coast to Coast walk the longest pub crawl in all of England.

Harlsey Grove Farm to Clay Bank. 16 Miles.

This was a pleasant walk from an early start with plenty of sunshine. It passed down back country lanes for four miles to Ingleby Cross. Just before the handsome Sydale Lodge estate I noticed a farmer who was driving his tractor with a load of muck to spread on the pasture. He inadvertently knocked his gate down. I stopped and helped him to put it back together again. It was a heavy metal gate and I'm sure he was glad for the extra hand but even so it is hard not to wonder if farmers don't grow tired of having walkers cross their land or having them pass alongside it. They seldom seem to mind having you there, though. Farming is generally a pretty lonely life. Perhaps it is a relief just to see someone now and then. Many of these farms do have public right of way across them, too. It is difficult to determine, though, because 'Trespassers Welcome' signs somehow never seem to be displayed.

After Ingleby Cross and after the surge of adrenalin in getting across the busy A19 highway the route at last began to climb toward the North York Moors. I had been looking at them with anticipation all the way from our cottage at Richmond where they could be seen from 25 miles away.

About a mile up the hill that led to the moors the track passed above a small inn called Park House. Thinking it might be possible to promote a cup of tea or coffee I walked down and rang the bell. No one answered. Not even a dog responded. Cars, kayaks, tents, packs and groceries, even a rescue squad ambulance, all were in evidence but not a soul was around anywhere. In the window of a small building I saw Coast to Coast T shirts and patches for sale. They were nicely done and I would have liked to have had one of each. I couldn't hang around, though, so I resumed plodding on up the hill.

Soon afterward the route reached a sharp turn and a junction track. A signpost said 'Cleveland Way'. The Coast to Coast joins this path for some 16 miles. It is a well-travelled and popular long-distance walk of 100 miles. It includes long stretches of the moors and the seacoast. It was the second official long-distance walk that was opened after the Pennine Way. Another walk, the Lyke Wake walk, also uses part of this same path. The latter is a 40 mile effort that is supposed to be done in 24 hours or less, for which one receives a certificate and a badge. The path is immediately indicative of much traffic but once up on top it doesn't matter.

When the route finally crested out it was immediately surrounded by magnificent views in every direction. As far as you could see for 180 degrees the gentle valley stretched with checkerboard farms and villages. Back the other way the lonely moors paraded with lavender heather everywhere and the bluff edge itself could be seen as it fell off abruptly to the floor of the valley below. It was truly a dramatic sight.

Working along the well-trod path of the heather-covered moors it was startling to hear the strange cluck and the now and then sudden appearance of a grouse. They would usually wait until I came to within ten or twenty feet of them before they decided to rise and flutter off. It was a bird-hunter's paradise but I felt sure that they must be protected by the National Trust's restrictions.

According to Wainwright's narrative a sign was reputed to be mounted on a gate near Beacon Hill. Apparently it had been purloined but it would have read:

Be ye man or be ye woman
Be ye going or be ye comin'
Be ye soon or be ye late
Be ye sure to shut this gate.

After a dip down between two extensive bluffs the path came to a pleasant stream called Scugdale beck where I stopped for lunch. Then the route passed another isolated phone booth in the middle of nowhere, a sight which always seems so incongruous, and it went up a six-foot wide, finely-graveled path to a series of steep earthen steps. I know that steps are meant to be helpful and to preserve the trail, and a lot of effort goes into building them, these had wood risers, but I always find them cumbersome. It is easier to shift into goat gear, take smaller steps and more time, without breaking pace, and to just steadily climb on up the slope, no matter how steep it is. Steps break your rhythm and they are harder on one's knees, particularly if they are higher than the normal 7 to 8 inches, which they usually are on a footpath. Going downhill the same thing is true, unless it is slippery or perpendicular and then they can provide a measure of protection against a slip on your fanny. Switchbacks are usually preferable.

At the top of the next hill it was interesting to see a long, cleared runway that led down a pronounced slope. A glider club owns the hangar at the top end and apparently they launch themselves without a tow-plane by travelling down the slope and out over the edge where they can ride the thermals of the long bluff. Not too distant is an R.A.F. training base and the sleek Harrier jets go screaming in and out of the area on a regular basis. Hopefully they know one another's habits well enough to avoid a problem of savage proportions.

The trail worked its way down and up some badly eroded spots until it reached a pinnacle known as Cringle End. None of these are tongue-hanging climbs like one often finds on the Appalachian Trail. They are only a matter of a few hundred feet. At the top a nicely made stone bench had been located along with a view indicator that was a memorial to an Alec Falconer (1884-1968) whose a/k/a trail name was 'Rambler'.

At Clay Bank car park I succumbed to the luxury of drinking the last of my canteen's water, save a few drops for reserve, while waiting for Angie. Water did not seem to be a problem when hiking the Coast to Coast, even in August. I perspired but it was never very hot and I was usually cooled by the wind. Up on the moors and peaks it often blows fairly hard. I found that I drank a sufficient amount at lunch and then at the end of the hike. Seldom in between. Springs and creeks appeared from time to time but they were questionable because of the ever-present sheep. I did drink once from a high-up streamlet that was so inviting I couldn't resist it but that was the only time I felt the need. Then, too, a pub often presented a welcome opportunity for refreshment, the ultimate watering trough.

The good news at pick-up time was that after scouting hard for a suitable place where we could do our own housekeeping, Angie had found a quaint little stone cottage right in the village where the Coast to Coast officially ends, Robin Hood's Bay.

Clay Bank Top to Glaisdale. 19 Miles.

The next day the route continued up an incline to get back up onto the moors. There were high clouds with little wind. The heather was a bright lavender and it stretched for miles.

After a while the Coast to Coast took advantage of an old railway bed that had been constructed in 1861. It had been built to carry down the iron ore as it was mined in the area. These mines have shown evidence of having been worked for as long as two thousand years. In 1929, though, their operation became unprofitable. The railway had then been dismantled and the level cinder bed that remained became an ideal trail for walking. In three pleasant hours of good time, mostly on the railroad bed, The Lion's Inn at Blakey came into view, a distance of 9 miles.

The Lion's Inn was a refreshing oasis, the only building in this entire section. It was a welcome contrast to the bleakness of the moors. A good road passed beside it and the route took advantage of it for a couple of miles before turning off onto a track towards the northeast. At the Lion's Inn I went in and had a pot of tea. It was roomy and cozy inside and popular with the Sunday drivers on an outing. The food looked good but I had my sandwiches so I headed out the door in search of a sheltered spot somewhere out on the moors.

The route left the road and headed down a path to the east that eventually joined another road briefly. Then it took off toward Glaisdale on a cart track. On the path I found a nice bench in the lee of a stone hut for a lunch stop. A friendly goat came over in an attempt to solicit for a sandwich. The cart track worked its way on down through the town of Glaisedale where it had become an honest road and I reached the meeting place at the local train stop in the late afternoon.

During the day I had met and talked to a number of walkers but oddly enough none of them were doing the Coast to Coast. This was a bit puzzling because my horseback calculations seemed to indicate that it would be reasonable to expect some ten or so a day. Maybe early September is too late for vacationing walkers on the Coast to Coast. Anyway, a number of people were out enjoying the moors, including one 'rambler' hiking club of about thirty men and women who were all talking a mile a minute as they sauntered past. The men were in the front group, the women were in the rear group. Also, a small boy on his new bicycle had accompanied me down the steep hills of the little town of Glaisdale. He was testing his brakes on the hills with feet out to the sides, just in case. We had both agreed that the brakes were in fine shape.

The Coast to Coast had not been marked since Ingleby Cross. No signs or arrows of any kind had been encountered for some 32 miles. It had become necessary to carefully dig the route out of Wainwright's illustrations, although this had not been hard to do. The problem for me had been that it was sometimes easy to become a bit preoccupied with one's thoughts at times and this tended to occasionally result in an overlooked landmark.

All in all, the day's walk had been easy. The heather and the frequent whir of the grouse had made it interesting. The usual sheep had been more widely scattered. Some of them had been comical at times as they scratched their backs on markers or the eroded banks at the edge of the trail. This had been my next to last day of the Coast to Coast walk and I had found myself feeling sad to see it come to an end. It had become a way of life that I was reluctant to abandon.

Glaisdale to Robin Hood's Bay. 19 Miles.

Last leg. In retrospect it occurs to me that I can't remember not seeing sheep virtually everywhere along the whole walk. It is not surprising, though, since there are over 43 million of the little creatures in Britain, according to the most recent count. A problem with them on the moors, though, is that they eat away at the heather and over the last 40 years they have decimated some 30% of the heather in the Yorkshire Dales. In the Lake District they have done away with over 70% of it. This means less grouse, too, since they survive in, on and beneath the heather. In the North York National Park I saw all three of them seeming to get along well together but perhaps they are more regulated there. It would be a shame to see the heather go by default. Environmentalists, the public and the authorities are aware of the problem and they are trying to do something about it. The U. K. is more concerned about the greenhouse effect, conservation, the environment and the preservation of tradition than the States or any other country in the world.

The last day began with a start at the railway stop in Glaisdale. The course went down a short hill for a glance at the picturesque Beggar's Bridge across a delightful stream, the River Esk. Here the first sign appeared that acknowledged the Coast to Coast walk once again. It pointed up a steep hill with earth steps.

For the next three and a half miles the well-worn path wound along the River Esk through the East Arnecliff Woods. This section was so much like the Appalachian Trail that it made me homesick for the old white blazes. In addition, many stone slabs had been strategically placed on the ancient trail. These had been ground down in their centers by centuries of foot traffic so that you felt as though you were walking through history.

The route passed through an old toll road beside the magnificent Eaton Manor Estate. The rates were still posted at the quaint toll house along the way. These prices varied between a horse and wagon, a rider on horseback, or pedestrians and the like. A special discount rate was offered for a hearse, the logic being, probably, that the dead are not too keen on paying much for their last ride.

A sign on the fence at the Eaton Manor Estate was indicative of an apparent problem with regard to the theft of high-blooded horses. It warned that, 'Our horses all have freeze-dried tatoos and are readily identifiable by the police'.

At Grosmont there is a collection of steam trains and a railroad museum. The station was charming and one dining car had its tables set with linen and silver in readiness for the dinner run that weekend. The trains operate every hour during midday and as I went by I had thought that it would be a fun trip to make. (We did, in fact, make this trip the following year after walking the West Highland Way in Scotland and it was a memorable experience).

Next came a steep slog up a 1:3 grade until the guide said to leave the road and to take to the heather again. It became difficult to find an obvious path but the sheep trails eventually carried along up to a crest called Flat Howe tumulus. Here it was possible, at long last, to see the North Sea in the distance. Down the other side a predominant trail through the heather coincided with my compass bearing and it led on down to a bottom that held a cluster of houses known as Little Beck.

After crossing a delightful little stream another trail promised to go to Falling Foss. Here again heavy forest and a well-travelled footpath looked down on an interesting gorge where flowed the stream known as May Beck. This section was also reminiscent of the Appalachian Trail and it, too, contributed toward making this final leg one of my favorite sections of the whole walk.

The trail passed a huge rock that had been completely carved out on the inside to make a circular little room with a carved bench around one wall. The legend above its portal said, 'The Hermitage, 1790 A.D.' I thought about having my lunch in there but it was a bit gloomy and it seemed sacrilegious as well.

Just beyond the Hermitage I came to the falls known as Falling Foss. They dropped down to an inviting pool about fifty feet below. Nearby a couple were pondering their ordnance map that was laid out on the ground in front of them. They were obviously Coast to Coasters who were just starting their walk from east to west. I wallowed in the brief moment of satisfaction that one gets when answering questions about a trip completed when the other party is embarking on that same adventure. They were from Leicester and they had already booked themselves in a series of youth hostels along the way. This is okay, of course, but it does marry one to a set schedule that doesn't provide for eventualities. You could twist it around with a lot of phoning, I suppose, if you needed or wanted to take a day off, but I think most people simply head out and hope for the best.

As a practical approach to the problem of accommodations along the walk it may be of interest to someone contemplating the walk without benefit of a willing mate or friend for shuttle service to know that I never observed a lack of lodging available. There always seemed to be plenty of Bed and Breakfast vacancy signs hanging in the windows wherever I passed. Some of them probably had bathrooms down the hall with garrulous landladies but they would usually be clean and comfortable I am sure.

A perfectly shaped tree for a backrest was growing out over the edge of a stream. It made a good spot for a welcome lunch break. Then the path went up a hill on tarmac before it headed back out onto the heather again. At the little town of Hawkser, pronounced without the interloping 'k', I could feel the walk coming to a close.

On the way to the cliff edge, where the Coast to Coast briefly rejoins the Cleveland Way, an abandoned railroad track took off in the direction of Robin Hood's Bay. It was too good to resist. It was like the Ironstone Railway bed back on the moors near Blakey. I could look down on the Cleveland Way with all of its stiles to climb over and its eroded ruts to follow. I confess I felt a bit guilty. I hoped that Wainwright would have forgiven me but he had promised the traditional pint of lager at the old Bay Hotel at trail's end and its image was like a mirage in front of me as I walked along the old railroad bed. I knew that it would take me there a lot sooner. My feet just wouldn't move on down to that prescribed cliff edge path.

The Cleveland Way and the railroad bed eventually joined one another and with a mixture of reluctance to see the walk come to an end, tempered by the realization that, By God, I had actually walked the whole 192 miles across England, I started down the steep hill toward Robin Hood's Bay.

The little cottage that Angie had so fortuitously rented was located in the heart of the village halfway down the hill. It was on the actual route itself. I stopped and knocked on the door so that Angie could join me in the final wee moment of triumph. We walked on down to the sea. It was low tide, naturally, and we had to continue walking on out to it. At the big moment I had my picture taken with both feet standing in the North Sea, as tradition demands you see. Then we repaired to the great old pub at The Bay Hotel which overlooks the bay and the fishing boat ramp.

At the bar I ordered a pint of lager for each of us, the pint that tradition also demands should be consumed at that time. As a matter of fact it tasted so good and I was so dry that it went down in one gulp. And when Angie wasn't looking I drained half of her glass as well. Then it seemed only fitting to have another one in memory of Wainwright. After all, he was the one who got me there, and a jolly good job he did of it, too.

Arthur Wainwright.

The actual task of laying out the Coast to Coast walk, checking the numerous rights of way, researching interesting bits of history for inclusion in the narrative and doing the guide itself took Wainwright something over a year to do. It is remarkable that he was able to do it in only a year.

The guide book is small in size only. It has been reduced to about 6" x 4" so that it is easy to carry. Inside its covers one finds that it is meticulously done in perfect longhand printing. Incredibly it includes some 205 pen and ink sketches, all perfectly drawn, and 104 detailed pen and ink maps showing the route step by step throughout the 192 miles. Many of these pen and ink drawings are suitable for enlargement and framing. The narrative itself includes many interesting anecdotes and various items of gossip and history about each section as you go along. It also makes an effort to furnish advice about accommodations and alternative routes, depending on the weather, the state of the blisters, time, etc. It offers encouragement and prodding in a good-natured way and above all it offers boundless enthusiasm for the countryside itself.

To delve into the 195 pages of this little book is an inspirational experience. It is well written enough to be a classic piece of contemporary reading in itself. It is hard to keep from breaking out the boots and heading for St. Bees Head once you start to get into it.

Wainwright did a great many other guide books, mountain drawing books and sketchbooks over some thirty years. His publisher is: Westmorland Gazette, Kendal, Westmorland, England. He was a champion for conservation and naturalism and it is easy to see why he was England's best-loved and most well-known long-distance walker.

Guides for the Coast to Coast Walk.

These can be ordered from:

Stanfords Travel Bookshop
12/14 Long Acre, London WC2E 9LP, U.K.,
Tel: 071-836-1915

or:

The International Map Centre
22-24 Caxton St.
London SWH1 0QU
Tel: 071-222-4945

- A Coast to Coast Walk by A. Wainwright, published by Westmorland Gazette, Kendal, Westmorland, England. (This is essential, of course).
- The following maps (in order of use, these are essential, too):

Ordnance Survey Landranger Maps:
No. 89 West Cumbria
No. 90 Penrith, Keswick area
No. 91 Appleby-in-Westmorland area
No. 98 Wensleydale
No. 92 Barnard Castle
No. 99 Northallerton, Ripon
Ordnance Survey Tourist Map:
No. 2 North York Moors

- Wainwright's Coast to Coast Walk with photographs by Derry Brabbs; published by Michael Joseph, Ltd., 27 Wright's Lane, London W8 5TZ, England.

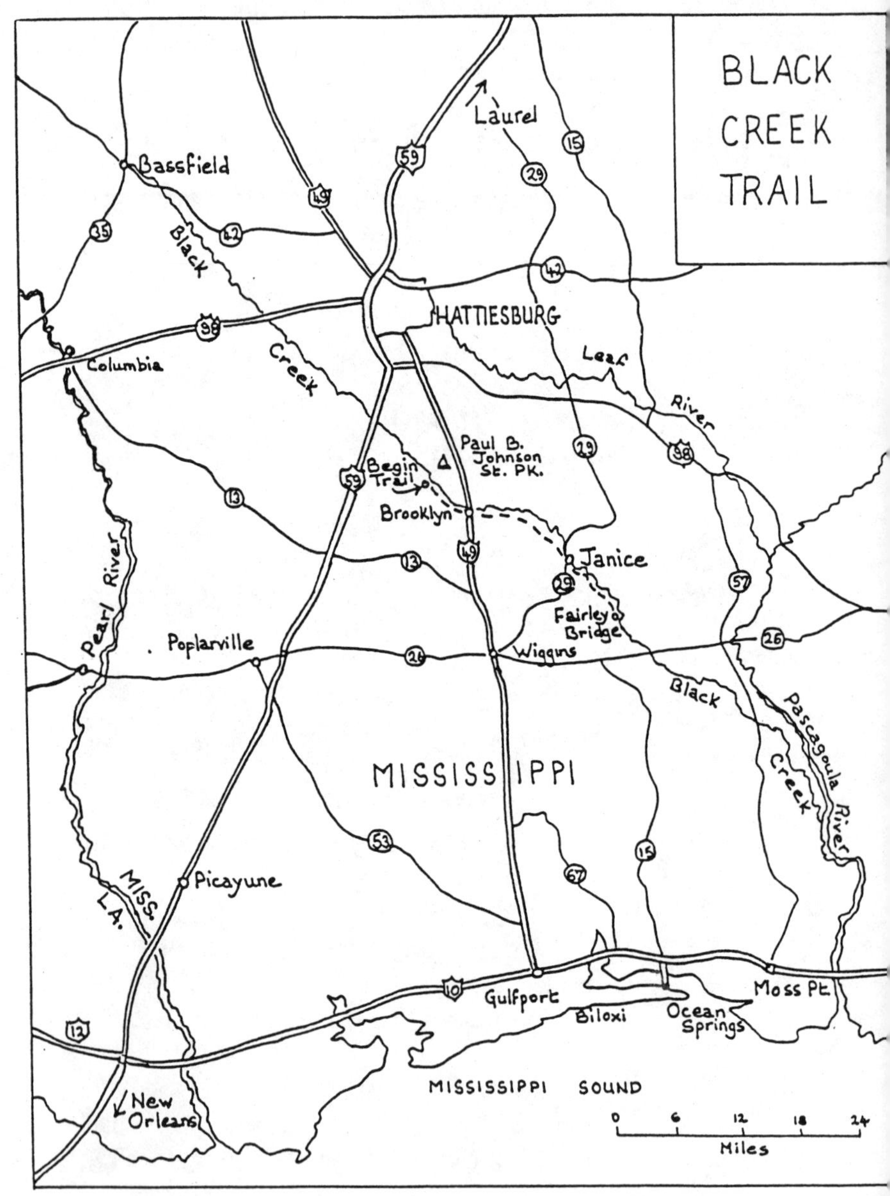
BLACK CREEK TRAIL
Laurel
Bassfield
Black
Creek
HATTIESBURG
Leaf
River
Columbia
Paul B. Johnson St. PK.
Begin Trail
Brooklyn
Janice
Fairley Bridge
Pearl River
Poplarville
Wiggins
Black
Creek
Pascagoula River
MISSISSIPPI
Picayune
MISS
LA.
Gulfport
Biloxi
Ocean Springs
Moss Pt.
New Orleans
MISSISSIPPI SOUND
0
6
12
18
24
Miles

WALK X

X. The Black Creek Trail of Mississippi

(41 Miles)

Black Creek Trail is an easy, safe walk maintained under the direction of the National Forest Service. There are enough road crossings to make for a series of three to four hour hikes, or longer, while camping at Flint Creek Campground near Wiggins, Miss., or Paul B. Johnson State Park near Brooklyn, Miss. It can also be done from a motel stay at Hattiesburg, only twenty miles away, or even the golden Gulf Coast of Gulfport/Biloxi for that matter. It is good for backpacking, too, with numerous sand bars or pine needle bluffs for pitching a tent. There are many streams with clear water that flow into Black Creek along the way. These can be used for a water supply taking the usual precautions of boiling or filtering.

Black Creek itself flows for over one hundred miles to the Pascagoula River in Alabama. It is ideal for summertime skinny-dipping, canoeing or camping. The sand bars are usually without human footprints or any sign of civilization. The trail beside it is hikeable year round.

In giving a log of my own experiences with the trail I can start on a recent day in late March when the two labs and I began it at the northwest end at a place called Big Creek Landing. This is not hard to find as it is marked by the forest service and it is reached by turning off just after crossing Black Creek on Highway 49 when coming from the north. Just continue down the paved road there toward the west until you find the indicated turnoff.

At the time we were camped in the faithful Prowler on the edge of the lake at Paul B. Johnson State Park, a delightful spot. Old friends had joined us with their recent acquisition of a new Winnebago Chieftain RV. Angie ferried me as usual to the trail head.

Beauregard and Ben and I left Big Creek landing at 10:00 a.m. They were thrilled to be running free. The trail ran along the south bank of Black Creek. It was well marked with white A. T. type blazes generously applied. They were frequent enough to stay out of trouble on the twists and turns and the fallen leaves that often tend to partially cover the trail. Black Creek had numerous white sandy beaches from time to time. The river was moderately full with a good canoe current of around two knots or so. The water was darkish brown becoming lighter and clear at the edges.

After about a mile and a half the trail left the river and headed southeast up into the piney woods that are so typical and inviting in this part of Mississippi. It crossed three roads and then hit a gravel road that had no trail markers. This was very confusing at the time. I coursed up and down the road but I could not find any continuation where the trail had crossed the road. Finally, I decided to follow the road itself toward the northeast and eventually a blaze appeared indicating that the road had now become the trail. I guess the initial markers had somehow become confiscated by someone with a difficult sense of humor or a teenage sign collection. If you do this hike yourself just remember to take a left when you hit this particular road. After about a quarter of a mile the trail then took off from the road toward the northeast, on the same side of the road that it had entered, an unexpected direction.

The road eventually emptied out onto the dual lanes of the busy Hwy 49 at the same place that the trail did. With the dogs both on tight leashes we managed to get across the southbound traffic lanes and then between a break in the northbound traffic we reached the other side of no man's land. Just beyond the highway some wooden steps led down to the railroad tracks. No train was in sight at the time and we made it across and up into the welcome safety of the woods once more.

For the next two miles we hiked across mostly pine needles with the exception of a soggy bottom or two where deer tracks were noticeable. We crossed a gravel road in the first part of this section but it was the only sign of civilization anywhere. The trail had passed a parking area set out by the national forest people but it was empty and it showed no sign of use.

At 1:30 p.m. we reached the Ashe Nursery Road where we hiked on up to the nearby bridge with the dogs on the lead. We must have presented a curious sight to the occasional passing motorist, a blond lab on one side and a black one on the other, a destitute hobo with his worldly goods on his back and two friendly dogs for companions. We went beneath the bridge to the bank of Black Creek which was the agreed upon rendezvous. The labs went for a swim and then we shared a sardine lunch together. We stretched out on the grass to enjoy the sun of a perfect day.

No one else had been out on the trail that day and I had seen no tracks or signs of its having been used by anyone recently. The trail was easy to follow and it was easy walking on the flat or up and down its gentle slopes.

The next leg was another trip on the following weekend when our friends the Terrys joined us again at the Paul B. Johnson State Park. It was after lunch before I was able to squeeze in a hike and this time we drove past the Black Creek bridge where we had stopped before. This is just on the other side of the slumbering little town of Brooklyn on the Ashe Nursery Road. Just before Ashe Lake, about a mile or so farther on, there is a well-maintained gravel road that crosses the paved highway and here one takes a left. We finally located a dirt road going to the left again that was labelled 319G. This little road crossed the trail and Angie dropped me off again with both labs keen to go pounding into the woods as usual.

The trail was inviting as it led through mature forest and across a small stream. After about forty minutes of walking back toward the west we crossed a sand bottom creek with gin-clear water on a well-built footbridge. Shortly afterward we came to the bank of Black Creek itself. Somewhere in the forest could be heard the tattoo of a serious woodpecker. He must have been huge for his staccato beat sounded like a .50 caliber machine gun resounding in the distance.

The trail was well-marked and easy to follow for the most part. Occasionally, though, high water had muddied the blazes and inundated the sandy parts with river debris. Sometimes it became a little tricky locating any semblance of a trail but then it would invariably pick up again and become obvious as it climbed out of the low-lying portions. It always followed along in the general direction of the twisting Black Creek river bed so it was not difficult to surmise where it was headed.

At times the trail passed ideal camp sites along the way and sometimes it produced sweeping vistas of the river itself in both directions from the vantage point of a high bluff on the edge. After an hour and a half the trail left the river and it climbed into a cutover field that had become densely overgrown for a while only to turn back to rejoin the edge of the river again.

Two hours from leaving the 319G road the trail emptied out onto another gravel road. We turned right and walked down this until it, in turn, came to a paved road known as Anderson Loop Rd. Just beyond this road the trail took off into the woods once more. I stopped and picked a couple of sprigs of mountain laurel in full bloom. They would brighten up the camp and provide a measure of good will, hopefully, for being gone from chores. It is a blossom seen frequently along the Appalachian Trail in Georgia, North Carolina and Tennessee but not quite this early.

Then the same old Ashe Nursery Road appeared which we had reached on our first leg before. We went back to the river again and the dogs had a good swim. Duffy and Angie found us all right, although we were a bit late for the rendezvous, about twenty minutes. Distances are hard to figure along the banks of the river because of its many curves.

This was a three hour walk with no one seen and the only evidence of anyone having used the trail before us were two sets of mountain bike tracks and a lone set of boot tracks. No snakes, no deer, nothing but wilderness and tranquility.

The next day we left from the 319G dropoff again, this time headed east. All three dogs were in attendance this time, Duffy having decided that he would leave his two friends, Boats and Betsy, back at the campground for the day. Betsy is a Peke-a-poo and a proper vamp, especially in the eyes of a West Highland Terrier.

This day held some special anticipation because it meant that we would join up with the rest of the trail which we had walked many times before. There is a long footbridge across a primeval swamp that has always been a stopping point. The last time I reached this footbridge with Angie it was over a foot underwater. Now it would be coming up from the other side and it would have to be crossed, water or no water.

About a half hour into the walk the dogs and I were surprised to see a couple of back-packers coming our way. They were a nice young couple who had camped out on a sandbar beside the river the night before. They were headed for Brooklyn where they had left their car when someone had been good enough to give them a shuttle from town.

Also on the trail were two other noticeable sets of tracks, one coming and the other going. The trail was getting some recent use here. I was the fifth person to use it since whenever the last rain had obliterated tracks.

After another ten minutes or so the trail wound alongside a cypress swamp. Here the mosquitoes came to call and the dogs went wading. I found a huge feather on the trail. It was over a foot long. I couldn't help wondering what sort of a giant bird had lost it and whether he missed it as part of his aerodynamic configuration. Even more perplexing was how he happened to lose it, it was too important a feather to be given up casually.

Shortly afterward the trail worked its way back to the bluff overlooking the river. I saw two fishermen in a skiff. They were as surprised to see me as I was to see them. They were anchored behind a promising logjam untangling snagged lines. It was the first time that I had seen a boat on Black Creek although it is used for canoe trips from time to time. You can go a very long way down this river with overnights on the sandbars, plenty of firewood, good swimming and complete privacy.

The trail left the bank of the river and it followed an ancient logging road for a while. Then it made an abrupt right-angled turn on a hacked path of its own. It was one of those places that are easy to miss if you don't keep checking the white blazes as you go along.

Just after the turn I had a sixth sense of impending danger and sure enough, not three feet away, a huge moccasin was neatly coiled at the ready right beside the trail. He was big for a moccasin, about three feet, and he was all ready to let go. Beauregard had gone right past him.

As soon as I saw the moccasin I stopped short and backed up taking Duffy and Benjamin with me. Beauregard nonchalantly came back. To my horror he paused to look at the snake and made ready to sniff him. I called quickly and he made it past all right. Probably all the moccasin wanted was to mind his own business, usually the rule with most animals, including snakes, but I have known moccasins to be agressive without provocation.

Duffy was getting ready for action and I quickly picked him up so that there wouldn't be any terriering with snakes. We all made a wide detour through thick brush. This is a great way to get lost but my sense of direction was working all right and we managed to pick up the trail again well beyond the snake.

It was no use trying to dispose of the moccasin, especially with three dogs in the melee, and in years of late my credo has become live and let live in nature, even a snake.

Besides, he deserved a little respect. It must be tough making a living on your belly in that forest. My advice to him would have been to head for the river where the pickings were bound to have been better. Another thing I've learned, though, is that nobody wants advice either, especially when it is unsolicited, least of all a three foot water moccasin whose composure has just been shattered by three dogs and some dude with a walking stick.

The trail then passed alternately through pine forest with a welcome pine needle floor for a path and now and then through the nuisance of some boggy parts. I was grateful for the old Rocky Boots. The dogs didn't mind. They love all the intrigue of mud and puddles and a heaven-sent opportunity to get filthy. They wear the muck like a badge of honor, as if to prove that they've been someplace important in case they should run into one of their buddies.

We stopped by the bank of the river for lunch and I spread the poncho on a sand dune. I had inadvertently forgotten to bring the dog biscuits and no one seemed inclined to share my tuna sandwich or fruit so they went without the customary noontime snack. They didn't seem to care too much, though. They were just glad to take a break after all of the cruising back and forth looking for rabbits or squirrels or whatever the scents had turned up.

Soon after lunch we passed by another couple camped beside the river. They had a tent pitched and a nice campfire going, even a folding chair, and they were about a mile from their shiny new pick-up that we later noticed showed an Iowa license plate.

Shortly afterward we came to the long footbridge that crossed the dismal looking swamp and this time it was above water all right. On the other side I knew then that I had now walked all of the Black Creek Trail. The dogs refused to be impressed, in fact Beauregard had elected to wade across the swamp itself in disdain of the benefit of the footbridge.

The southern portion of the trail, or a large portion of

it, is maintained by a friend of mine who lives in Gulfport. He is one of that select fraternity who have hiked the entire 2,100 miles of the Appalachian Trail. It had been quite a while since he had hiked on the northern/western part of the Black Creek Trail and so I was relieved to find that it, too, is well marked with white blazes that are spotted frequently enough to keep anyone from getting into trouble.

We reached the rendezvous at Hwy 29 near Janice Landing for 1:30 p.m. We were an hour ahead of schedule. It was nice to flop down beneath the trees and think back on the pleasant walk that the Black Creek trail had provided over the three easy sections that we had done from the western start.

The southern section, which I have hiked before many times, starts at that same parking area below Janice Landing on Hwy 29. It heads for Black Creek through pine forest. When it reaches the river it then changes course and heads southwest along the north side of Beaverdam Creek. This is an interesting creek and the trail is well-maintained.

The trail then empties out back onto Hwy 29 and here it is easy to become confused because it utilizes the highway bridge to get across Beaverdam Creek. On the other side it then heads back into the forest and it follows along the south side of Beaverdam Creek until it reaches Black Creek again.

The trail stays with Black Creek for about an hour or so until it takes off in the vicinity of Cypress Creek Landing on the other side. It heads south then through gently sloping pine forest. After a couple of miles it turns east across a gravel road. About four more miles from there it finally arrives at Fairley Bridge Landing, which is where it ends, or begins, if you want to start from there. The trail is very straightforward on this southern end with proper footbridges across the many little streams that flow into Black Creek. It makes for very pleasant walking on mostly a pine needle or leaf covered floor.

The maps to use for Black Creek Trail are from the U.S. Dep't. of the Interior Geological Survey (topographic):

- Brooklyn Quadrangle; Miss. 7.5 minute series
- Janice Quadrangle; Miss., Perry Co., 7.5 minute series
- Bond Pond Quadrangle; Miss., 7.5 minute series

(Order from: U.S. Geological Survey, Reston, VA 22092)

Unfortunately, the trail is not shown on these maps, nor is there any map of the trail itself. By using these topo maps, though, together with the foregoing narrative, it is not difficult to locate the trail at any of the strategic crossings where its blazes can be seen. The National Forest Service has also located signs identifying the Black Creek Trail at major roads as well.

Santiago de Compostela
Santander
FRANCE
Leon
PICOS DE EUROPA
PYRENEES
Barcelona
Madrid
PORTUGAL
Valencia
SPAIN
BALEARIC ISLANDS
Alicante
Granada
Sevilla
Malaga

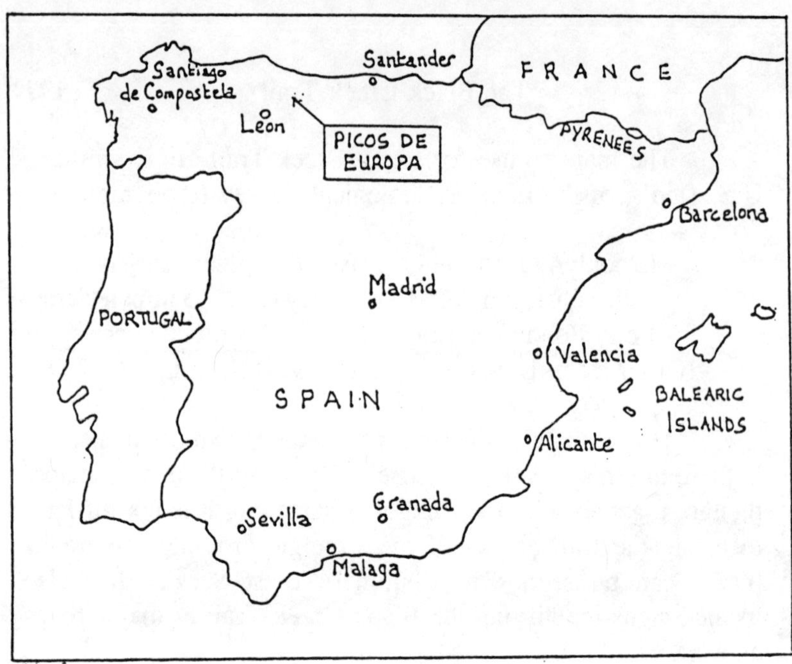

Picos de Europa ~ Northern Spain

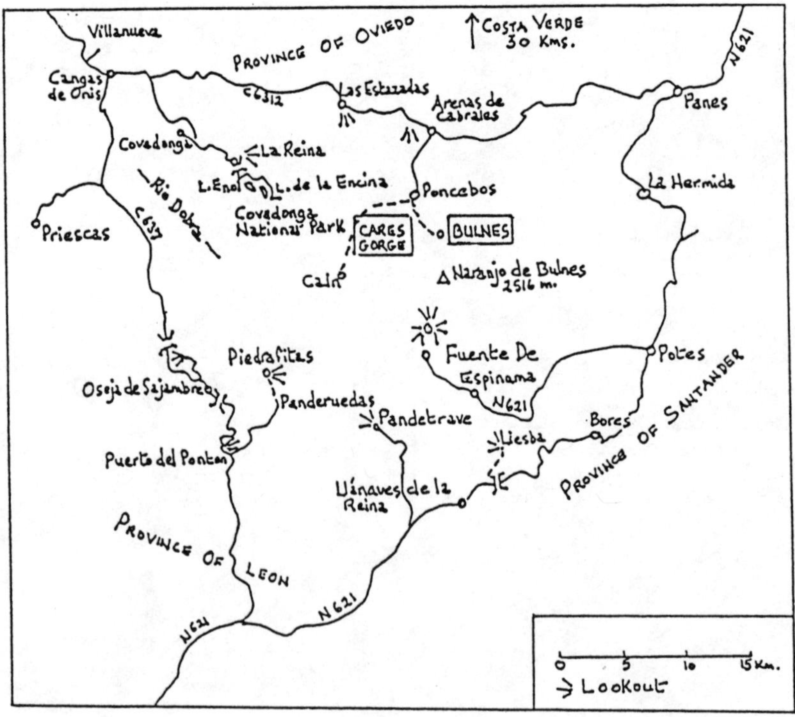

Villanueva
PROVINCE OF OVIEDO
COSTA VERDE 30 Kms.
N621
Cangas de Onis
C6312
Las Estazadas
Arenas de Cabrales
Panes
Covadonga
La Reina
L. Enol
L. de la Encina
Poncebos
La Hermida
Rio Dobra
C637
Covadonga National Park
CARES GORGE
BULNES
Priescas
Cain
Naranjo de Bulnes 2516 m.
Fuente De
Potes
Piedrafitas
Espinama
Oseja de Sajambre
Panderuedas
N621
PROVINCE OF SANTANDER
Pandetrave
Bores
Liesba
Puerto del Ponton
Llánaves de la Reina
PROVINCE OF LEON
N621
N621
0 5 10 15 Km.
Lookout

WALK XI

XI. The Picos de Europa of Northern Spain.

(40 Miles)

The Picos de Europa are located about one hundred kilometers southwest of the airport at Santander on the northern coast of Spain. Iberia flies there and it is also possible to take the car ferry to or from the U. K. out of Santander. The Picos (peaks) are exceptionally rugged and dramatic, like Yosemite, with granite walls, clear streams and ever-green meadows and trees in the spots where vegetation manages to find a foothold. Part of it has been made into a National Park and part a restricted hunting reserve. The area is comparatively undiscovered by the tourist public because of its distant location from major cities or resort centers.

Angie's parents live in southern Spain and we visit them quite regularly. Because of this we keep an old Renault 14 there. We cranked it up in May and we headed north. At the time we knew very little about the area of the Picos, just that we hoped to find some new places to walk in the northern part of Spain. On the way up we visited some towns that were new to us. Those that we liked the best were Chinchon, just south of Madrid, then Avila, Salamanca and Leon, to the north. I think our favorite, though, was Santiago de Compostela with all of its winding streets, ancient buildings and rich history.

In a book about long-distance walking special homage should be paid to Santiago and the pilgrims who flocked there from all parts of Europe in the middle ages. The Apostle St. James preached Christianity in the area for seven years. His remains were buried by his followers and later moved and then rediscovered in the 9th century when James became 'Santiago', the patron Saint of Spain. By the 11th century devotion spread until a pilgrimage to the shrine of St. James became a popular goal for Christians everywhere. Some 500,000 to 2,000,000 pilgrims a year made this excruciating journey on foot. They wore sandals, a wide brimmed hat, and heavy robes. They carried an eight foot stave with a water gourd fastened to it and little else.

In 1589 Drake attacked Coruna and the relics were again lost until 1879 when they were once more discovered and returned to the crypt beneath the altar in the Cathedral at Santiago. They can be viewed there by visitors like ourselves and to this day some two million visitors a year continue to carry on the tradition, albeit not on foot as before.

There were two favored routes for the pilgrimage to take, one across the northern coast of Spain through San Sebastian Donostia and the other, after trekking down through the Pyrenees, to Pamplona and across the inland route. An interesting present day walk can be made out of retracing this path. The distance is some four hundred miles and it crosses some magnificent country.

The northern coast of Spain is largely unspoiled and a contrast to the resort areas of the Mediterranean coast. We visited many of the coastal fishing villages along the back roads and we stayed at the Paradors in Santiago, El Ferrol and Ribadeo. These harbors and coves are a yachtsman's dream for sheltered, picturesque anchorages and rarely did we see boats other than fishing vessels anywhere along the coast. The region seems to be unspoiled by tourism and everywhere we looked we saw sights that we could not believe still existed today. The land is still farmed by hand. The family cow does the plowing with the woman leading the way between the rows while the man guides the plow from behind. Carts are the mode of transportation, sometimes with a donkey, a mule, or a horse for the more affluent, but often as not with the family cow or a pair of cows harnessed together. Nobody is in a hurry.

Many of the people in Galicia wore wooden shoes and

carried an umbrella as a precaution against the prevailing drizzle that occurs from time to time. These wooden shoes are quite comfortable and practical I found. I purchased a pair of them for around ten dollars. Inside the wooden shoes one slides one's slippers so that when you enter the house the mud is left outside with the shoes.

The farms were neat and tidy. The stone buildings and the typical horreo, a corn crib built high off the ground with circular stone rodent protectors, were substantial and ancient. The people of Galicia and Cantabrica, which includes the Picos, seemed to be happy with their way of life in spite of the hard physical work involved. They lived close to the earth where they could provide for most of their needs from the fertile and well-watered soil or from the sea nearby. They must stay in excellent physical condition and good health from all of that manual effort each day and one wonders if perhaps the old ways might not be best after all.

We learned about the Picos de Europa from an English couple seated next to us in the dining room of the unforgettable Parador San Marcos, a 16th century converted monastery in Leon. They had taken the ferry down from the U. K. through Santander and they had stayed at the Parador up in the Picos at Fuente De. It was hard for me to realize that I knew nothing about them until that time. I had carefully researched the book stores in Madrid and also one in Salamanca but nothing could I find about walking in Spain in either language, let alone any mention of the Picos. It was welcome information.

We found that the two best hotels in the Picos area were the Hotel Pelayo at Covadonga in the northwest, three stars, and the parador at Fuente De, reached from the southeast. The phone number for a reservation at the Pelayo is 985-846000, at the Parador, 942-730001. There are a number of little inns in the area, though, and their rates are also quite reasonable, usually with a bath in the room and a good restaurant below. It seems all right to travel without reservations, at least we experienced no difficulty, except for the period of the summer onslaught during mid-June thru August. At that time a reservation would be good for cutting down the time involved in looking for a place to stay. I have found that the best way to make reservations in the paradors is through the concierge (conserje, in Spain), who can pass you along to his mates...for a tip, of course.

Poncebo to Bulnes and return. 8 miles.

We found suitable maps at the tourist office at Covadonga, not far from the Hotel Pelayo where we stayed, and a shop in nearby Cangas. Our first walk started at the end of the road in the deep gorge through which flows the river Cares. It was reached after an hour's drive in interesting country to the town of Arenas de Cabrales. Here we followed a narrow road beside the river in the gorge until we passed a fork off to the left that led to the village of Sotres. Just up the way was a bar and cafe called Garganta del Cares (Gorge of the Cares river). Here we left the car and started walking at 12:15, a late start.

A car with Madrid license plates pulled up nearby and the driver joked to his fun-loving Madrileno friends about a couple of 'peregrinos'. With the bamboo walking stick, the pack, the flea market straw hat, Angie's scarf tied around her head, peasant style, and our boots I had to concede that maybe we could have passed for pilgrims at that. It helped to lend credence to the idea of retracing their footsteps across the north of Spain to Santiago de Compostela.

After about 7/10 of a mile we came to a sign that had been posted with an arrow that pointed across the river to a trail that wound ominously up another steep canyon. The sign read 'Bulnes', nothing more. The bridge we crossed was extremely old. It was held in place through careful placement of the granite stones that wedged its arch into position to support the four foot path above it. The river that flowed below was slate-gray in color and crystal clear.

The trail up to the little valley that held the village of Bulnes was steep and rocky. It had been hacked out of the side of the mountain which soared above. It was four to five feet wide and for much of the way the drop-off to the cascading stream below was five hundred or more feet straight down. It involved numerous switchbacks but the views were breathtaking. It also served as the principal artery to the village and it was used by the residents to pack in their necessities. We found on three separate occasions that it was well to find a wide spot in the trail to let the pack horses squeeze by. The villagers charged on by us like mountain goats headed for the barn.

At the head of the valley a footbridge crossed the stream and up above we could see what appeared to be the village of Bulnes. We took the trail that led that way only to laboriously discover that the little cluster of houses was called Castillo, a sort of suburb to the real Bulnes. A friendly farmer there informed us that the main village was yet another five minutes or so beyond. We also learned that it contained a bar. With this encouraging piece of news we pressed on and suddenly there it was. Set in a sort of a basin, surrounded by imposing peaks, with a waterfall beyond and a clear stream rushing through, it made a post-card-to-send-back-home scene. Green fields swept up either side. The buildings themselves had been put together out of rock and granite blocks centuries ago. They were huddled close enough to spell sanctuary against a climate that was probably harsh, I suspected, for much of the year.

We staggered on down and located the Bar Guillermina. It had taken two and a half hours to make it up there to Bulnes with frequent timeouts for admiring the views and for exchanging greetings with the half dozen or so people that we had met along the way. The proprietress was an affable lady and we enjoyed a beer and a glass of good wine at her bar. She said that there were fourteen families who lived there and that just this year they had acquired electricity. She proudly switched on a naked bulb to demonstrate. I asked her if they had acquired television as yet and she said that they had no interest in it! She said, too, that it was a 'dura vida', a hard life, and that trips down the trail in the winter were dangerous because of the threat of avalanches, a common occurrence. She was proud to point out that she and her husband owned four horses, a white one and three blacks, two of which we had met on the way up, and the other two, on the way down.

On passing through the rest of the village we came to another bar and restaurant which also claimed to be an Albergue, an inn. It looked inviting and a perfect spot for a hideaway with good hiking all around. It would provide a wonderful way to get to know village life and to meet the occasional hikers who might pass the time there.

The village of Bulnes also had a tiny church, a cemetery and a monument beside the trail. In reading the monument inscription we interpreted it to be for someone who had died at one of the shelters up above at the foot of a prominent 2,500 meter peak known as the Naranjo de Bulnes. It stated that he had died in 1928 and that he was the first to have died there from what we assumed was hypothermia. I hesitated to speculate about how many others had since met the same fate or if our translation was inaccurate but it was not difficult to see how it could easily happen with the rapidly changeable weather and the lack of adequate equipment for most hikers in the area.

We found a grassy spot beside the stream farther on down the valley to have lunch. A bottle of Carta de Oro, a favorite red wine from the Rioja area, along with some fresh bread and the local cheese which was usually quite good worked wonders for recharging the batteries for the return trip. The other two of Guillermina's horses paused on their way past us as they went on up the trail. They were unattended and seemed to know exactly where they were going.

It took us only an hour and a half to make our way on down to the car. It was not without a certain amount of trepidation because a stumble in the wrong place could take a long time to be resolved. I wasn't sure about what to mark the mileage exactly. The pedometer wasn't too much help because of the shortened strides in most of the ascent and descent. I would guess it to be about 8 miles up and back.

Refugio de Vega Redonda and beyond. 9 miles.

With Angie interested in exploring the cave and shrine for the Virgin of Cavadonga I took the car on up the narrow but well-paved road that led to the lakes above. The road was a bit hair-raising without guard rails for the blind curves and precipitous drop-offs. It required a certain amount of faith in the oncoming driver's ability to winkle by but it was only 10 kilometers long and the vistas were truly remarkable. It had turned out to be a clear sunny day, the first one we had enjoyed since hitting the Cantibrican coastal area. I had decided to take advantage of it by checking out some of the high country.

Up at the top I reached the first little lake, called Lago Enol, where a rocky dirt road immediately led down and off to the right. After following this for about a kilometer and skipping a road that led up to a cantina and shelter off to the right I came to a fork in the road. It was in a meadow with several stone huts nearby for the herdsmen's use during summer. When I passed by it was full of Brown Swiss cows grazing contentedly on the lush green grass. I took the left fork and parked the car near a sign that warned against traveling any farther by vehicle.

The rough track that continued carried past a flowing spring and a monument. A stone bridge took it across a clear stream and then it wound on up the hill. Up at the top of the hill another dozen of the stone huts stretched out in a row. When I went by the area more of the fat Brown Swiss cows were busy grazing. Some of them wore bells around their necks. All of them seemed docile and sociable. Even the bull was a gentleman.

Then the track petered out altogether but a sign on a

huge rock featured an arrow that pointed in the general direction of where I wanted to go which was up, to the high country. It read, 'A Vega Redonda y Ordiales'. Some upright stones had been placed every ten feet or so and these were helpful. Although the trail turned out to be a bit obscure in spots it really wasn't too difficult to figure out where it was headed.

After about an hour and fifteen minutes I crossed a stream and then I came to two more stone huts. Just beyond I reached a little ridge where the refuge came into view. The old refuge was farther on up in the distance and two new buildings had been located down below it. A number of hikers were airing out their bedding and clothing and generally coming and going. I later learned from the young caretaker that they totaled fourteen in all and that they had been spelunking a large cave nearby. A spunky brown horse with blond mane and tail was moored to the front of the building.

At the refuge itself I ordered a cup of descafeinado and watched the group who were having a 10:30 a.m. breakfast of salami and sausage sandwiches Spanish style. The dining room had a stove in the center with benches around the walls and ten tables and stools. Upstairs was the dormitory with upper and lower bunk beds tightly packed together, sardine style. A separate, smaller room was available, presumably for the opposite sex. The rates were about six dollars for dinner, seventy-five cents for a bunk and a liter of vino for roughly three dollars. Full pension would run about seventeen dollars for everything. At last, a real bargain in the new España.

After leaving the refuge I headed on up toward the peaks towering above. I had noticed the snow on them from down below but I hadn't realized how much of a problem it was going to be. As I worked on up the sometimes indecipherable trail I noticed four chamois up near the peaks. They soon spotted me and took off for even higher territory. The snow was crusty and sometimes icy and deep in spots. I worked around it on the jagged rocks as best I could. I was afraid of a slip and a tumble down onto sharp rocks, or a plunge through a possible snow bridge where it seemed deep in spots. I thought about my broken leg from skiing in college days, bones that had completely fractured in three places and taken nine months in a cast to mend. And I could remember the death of my uncle's brother-in-law when he had fallen into a hidden snow cavity on a cross-country ski trip. And I was solo, too, and I couldn't find any other tracks that had used the path. Even so I worked on up to a basin at 5,500 feet.

The basin was just below the last thousand feet that would have carried me to the top and I still had enough time to make it. I could see some other tracks coming down from up there and a couple of long sitz marks where somebody had slid or fallen. It was disappointing not to continue. I kept thinking that I was supposed to have an ice axe and crampons for this sort of thing or maybe some company in case one of us got into trouble. I asked myself the question that has served me so well over the years, especially whenever it becomes tempting to consider a questionable alternative, namely, 'What is the right thing to do?'

After the obvious answer I sat down on a rock, broke out the bread and cheese, sliced an onion and pulled open a can of tuna. God, it was a lovely day and so quiet up there. I could see all the way to the Bay of Biscay in the distance.

On the way down I again spotted another four of the wild chamois. These were quite close, maybe a couple of hundred yards away. When they saw me they took off like a cannon ball, straight up a sheer precipice that I wouldn't have thought possible to negotiate without climbing gear.

Past the refuge I ran into the young caretaker. He was returning, riding his horse with empty pack baskets. He had helped the group down with some of their gear. He said that his horse's name was Rubio, Blondie, that he was very bad but intelligent, and that the other trail that I had noticed carried over to a lookout spot with a fabulous vista. That was Ordiales, which was also indicated on the map. The refuge was now empty and he had a lot of cleaning up ahead of him. Very polite and agreeable, he was enjoying the sun with only a pair of shorts and jogging shoes.

The car came into sight at three o'clock. I estimated the hike at about 9 miles altogether. Distances didn't seem so long in the Picos because of the steepness of the peaks themselves. I felt that I would like to return sometime when the snow had melted so that I could gain the top and then go on down the other side to the refuge there.

Amieva to Rio Dobra and the Waterfall. 8 miles.

We reached the little village of Amieva perched high on the side of a steep hillside around noonish. The road up was paved and narrow with the usual steep dropoffs but when we tried to negotiate the narrow streets between the buildings of the town the paving turned to straight up dirt and rocks and we finally reached a point where the old Renault just couldn't make it any farther. We had a running try at it three times but we always ended in a sickening wheel spinning impasse. The locals all came out to enjoy the fun and in conversation with the nearest neighbor it turned out that there was another road down below the church that led on up to where we wanted to go. It was worse, she said.

By now the car was overheated and the radiator was boiling away so we went back down to the church and parked in the shade of a tree by the fountain there while it cooled off.

We then tried the other road which was off to the left just as we left the area by the church at the bottom of the village. It was filled with small rocks for traction, but not as steep. We made it on up to the top and followed the road along until we came to a downgrade that looked too steep for the old Renault to make it back up again. We left the car in a borrow pit cut into the side of the bank where it would be out of the way.

Just beyond where we started walking the road came to

a metal plate gate. The gate was ajar and we passed through. Another road led off to the right just before the gate and this we ignored. I was sure that no one would object to passing through this gate in a vehicle if we had one with a little more traction than ours. It should be left closed, though, because it contained horses inside the pasture.

On the other side of the hillside beyond the gate we walked down through alpine-like meadows with fat cattle and a sprinkling of stone barns here and there. Opposite this scene were solid rock mountains that shot straight up from the riverbed to a height of 3,000 feet above.

When we reached the river we passed a small electric generating plant that was fed by a pipe that came straight down the right side of the gorge. Beyond it was another gate which we found open although a sign asked that it be kept closed. The road continued beyond the gate and then it gradually began to climb. Soon we were able to look down on the river Dobra as it wound its way down the canyon.

We came to a bridge over a tributary stream that came in from the left. The clear water flowed through a meadow with free-ranging cows and beyond we noticed a spectacular waterfall that dropped from a canyon between precipitous rock walls. The temptation to hike up to it was too great to resist.

On the map which I had obtained there was supposed to be a trail that led up this canyon and then somehow worked its way on up the precipitous 3,000 foot height to the area where I had been the day before. I had looked for this trail up there at the time but I had been unable to find it. The trail on the map had looked like an interesting hike. I examined the area where it was supposed to lead into the road near us and after a careful search I could not find anything remotely resembling a trail, not even a sheep track.

Angie set out following the stream bed. I followed and we carefully picked our way along from rock to rock until we reached the falls. The falls were about 70 feet in height. They cascaded down into the pool below in a satisfying shower of drops and spray. We spread the poncho nearby and settled into a late lunch.

After lunch and a rest I still felt disturbed about the missing trail. Also on the map was an indication for a large cave. Way up the steep canyon down which the other part of the stream cascaded from rock to rock a deep indent was visible and it seemed as though it might have been the cave. I worked on up there by the hardest. No trail and no cave. There may have been a cave farther on somewhere but I couldn't find any way to reach it without a technical climb. The map's trail became one of life's little unresolved mysteries.

About the missing trail a bit more. On the map there are occasionally red dotted lines with the designation 'Sendas perdidas', meaning lost trails. Why they are shown on the map is another Spanish mystery. And the bartender up at the lake above had looked perplexed when I had asked him about it. "Ni hablar", he had said, ("Don't even mention it"). Trails are seldom marked in the Picos and cows and sheep have a habit of making the issue even more complicated. A trail is nice to have, too, because the weather can change very quickly and up at the higher elevations you can soon become enveloped in cloud. This makes it difficult to check your bearings and the condition may persist for a long time.

We made it back to the car at six o'clock. It was about 8 miles to the falls and return as near as I could guesstimate. It became dark so late, around ten o'clock, that hiking later into the evening was not a problem. Besides, restaurants don't even open before nine o'clock. Spanish hours. When in Rome...

The Rio Cares Gorge. 15 miles.

This was one of the most memorable walks we have ever made. The cover shows a photograph of what it is like for much of the way. We left the car back at Poncebos, just as we had done for the Bulnes hike. To Cain and return is 24 kilometers, 15 miles. Except for the first uphill portion and then descent, maybe a mile, the trail was fairly level or gradually ascending. We hadn't planned on going the whole way to Cain when we set out but the urge to keep going, to see what was around the next bend, was so compelling that we just couldn't stop.

I had to take back whatever I had said about Spanish trails because this footpath was an engineering marvel. No less of an engineering marvel was the accompanying aqueduct that had been drilled through solid rock and made its way above or below the trail and sometimes opened up in close proximity. The canal was some 7 feet deep and about as wide. It moved the body of water that filled it to the brim at around four knots. It did this for around eight miles to gain enough height to drop on down through the huge pipes that send it to the turbines at Poncebos.

What a ride it would be to float down the aqueduct with scuba gear and snorkel! Open headroom is often restricted to just a few inches at times and it would be necessary to stay submerged occasionally. Also it would be necessary to know where to get off, well in advance of the drop to the blades of the huge turbines which would act like a giant food processor on a careless scuba diver.

We set out at Poncebos at noon, another Spanish style start. A vague sign with the lower half broken off read 'Senda a Cain', footpath to Cain, and it was generally pointing to a trail that led steeply up the side of the hill. Another sign, full of bullet holes, pointed on up the gorge, which seemed the logical way to go, but it read 'road out, dangerous'. We later discovered that this was the old trail and something of a nightmare judging from the way it looked when we reached high above it.

After about a half-mile climb we came to a building with the roof missing. In green letters were the remnants of a sign that proclaimed it to have been a Bar. Our hopes were dashed when we discovered that nothing remained save the ruins. Coming up the trail were a young English couple. We stopped to chat for a while. They were taking a six month holiday before settling into the business of becoming caught up in a career, a house, a family, notes to pay each month, the full catastrophe. They had a little caravanette for the campgrounds where they stayed and they made their own meals most of the time. They were enjoying Spain, each other and the people they met along the way. They had been up to the Pyrenees but the snow had kept them from hiking the high country. They were so appreciative and unassuming it was like a breath of fresh air just to hear them talk about themselves.

After working up over the rise we suddenly discovered the immensity of the Rio Cares gorge. We became aware of the precipitous heights of the trail itself as it snaked its way along the side of absolutely perpendicular walls that were several hundred feet above the riverbed. It wasn't until we actually started negotiating these ledges cut out of solid rock that we began to feel like characters from 'Raiders of the Lost Ark'. For someone with a fear of heights like me it was a real problem. We both found ourselves being partial to the inside of the four to five foot wide path with its dizzying drop-off down the outside edge. Every once in a while the trail builders had decided to just burrow through a bend and there they had made a tunnel, a moment of relief.

Everywhere we looked the view was so fascinating that it was impossible not to stop and take pictures. The danger of a stumble over the outside edge somehow added to the excitement of the walk. The only bad incident came when a black snake startled Angie. She has a problem with snakes much the same way that I have with heights. She stepped back instinctively and fortunately there was enough room left to keep her from going over the edge. I don't have a problem with snakes and I doubt that this one was poisonous anyway. He went off into the grass on the inside of the trail and I led her hurriedly by on the perilous outside edge. I am sure that he just wanted to mind his own business the same as we did. The occasions that I have seen snakes in Spain have been very rare, even on the road.

The most difficult part of the hike for me came when we reached two footbridges which spanned the chasm below. For some reason the trailmakers had decided to span the gorge at these two points and the drop was about three hundred feet on the first bridge and around two hundred feet on the second.

My fear of heights stems partially, I think, from Stanford days when I used the three meter platform in the university pool for working off study tensions. Since then I have always had an irresistible urge to dive from great heights. In this situation I was aware that I could have done a triple somersault with a double full twist without any trouble, except at entry into the water below which was about a foot deep on the gravel riverbed. It is difficult for me to reveal that Angie held my hand as we crossed each time. I tried not to look down and she kept up a running conversation, to distract me, about what the probable menu would be for supper that night at a restaurant we planned to try. I managed to resist the temptation with its crazy magnetic attraction to hurtle over the edge, good position, feet together, arms out wide, good arch to the back and ....splat!

One of the diversions along the trail was the occasional appearance of a goat or two. They were friendly and not the least bit intimidated. That baleful expression seemed to want to know what the devil we were doing up there in their territory and hadn't we any better sense than to try to manoeuver like a goat. Their coolness with heights, dangling over a precipice, strolling from rock to rock while looking for that perfect morsel of grass never failed to amaze us. And way up the side of the mountain somewhere would be the lost kid bawling for his mama while she answered back telling him to knock it off the same as every other species does the world over.

The last half a kilometer of the trail was a tunnel. Window-like holes had been carved out of the sides here and there and it was cut a little low so that it became necessary to stoop through parts of it. Water seeped down now and then to form giant puddles but it was fascinating to follow as it wound through solid rock. By then the trail had dropped to the riverbed and the clear, slate-blue water looked inviting as it rushed by. The tunnel opened out onto a dam and a bridge across to the other side. This was where the water was deflected partially into the aqueduct that made its way along the 8 miles to the power plant at Poncebos.

By the time we reached the low bridge that recrossed the river just below Cain it was 4:30 in the afternoon. We stopped for a late lunch and a short rest before heading back.

It was 8:30 in the evening before we made it back to the car and we retired to the bar there for a welcome beer. The whole trip had taken us some three and a half hours but I think it would be safe to figure a little less, depending on how many pictures, goat interviews and pit stops it took. The trail itself was not too demanding once we became adjusted to the terrifying drop-offs. Most of it was fairly steady going after the first mile, so the fifteen miles was not like the usual mountain trek. As I mentioned before, the Rio Cares gorge was one of the most memorable experiences we have ever had on a long walk.

Fuente De

We moved to the Parador at Fuente De with the intention of riding the 'Teleferico' up to the top of the surrounding peaks for a hike into the heart of the highest mountains on the eastern side. This cable car makes a spectacular ride over an abyss of some 4,500 feet and it saves a huge amount of hiking to get up to the high country there. We went up to inspect it and I could see that it was going to be a problem for me, I could just picture myself opening the door about two-thirds of the way up to plan my dive, but that night I had psyched myself up for it. The next morning the weather turned to a hard rain, though, and on conversation with the concierge I learned that the high country was still blocked by snow. We tried to get the Renault up the dirt road that might have carried us on up there or even down to Sotres where I could have approached from another direction but it was too steep. I had very much wanted to hike up to the base of the Naranjo de Bulnes, a famous climbing peak that can be identified from a long way off. It was too early in the year, apparently, so reluctantly we scrapped our plans to do the high country hikes on that side.

May seems to be a bit early for hiking in the upper peaks of the Picos but it is possible to do many other walks in the surrounding area with few, if any, other hikers around. Later in the season there are a number of back-pack opportunities, as well as long day hikes, that are available in the upper areas. A dozen well-built shelters are scattered around between them. The town of Cangas de Onis on the west side and the town of Potes on the east side are good support towns for groceries and supplies and restaurants and both are quite interesting and worth exploring in their own right. The Parador at Fuente De is worth a stay in itself.

Maps are not easy to come by in Spain. Those for the area are:

- Picos de Europa, I, Macizo Occidental O de Cornion
- Picos de Europa, II, Naranjo de Bulnes (Pico Urrielo), Macizos Central Y Oriental.

These are Guias Cartografica, Editorial Alpina, Granollers. We found ours at a local tourist office in Covadonga, near the Hotel Pelayo at Covadonga. They are also readily available at local souvenir or gift shops in the area.

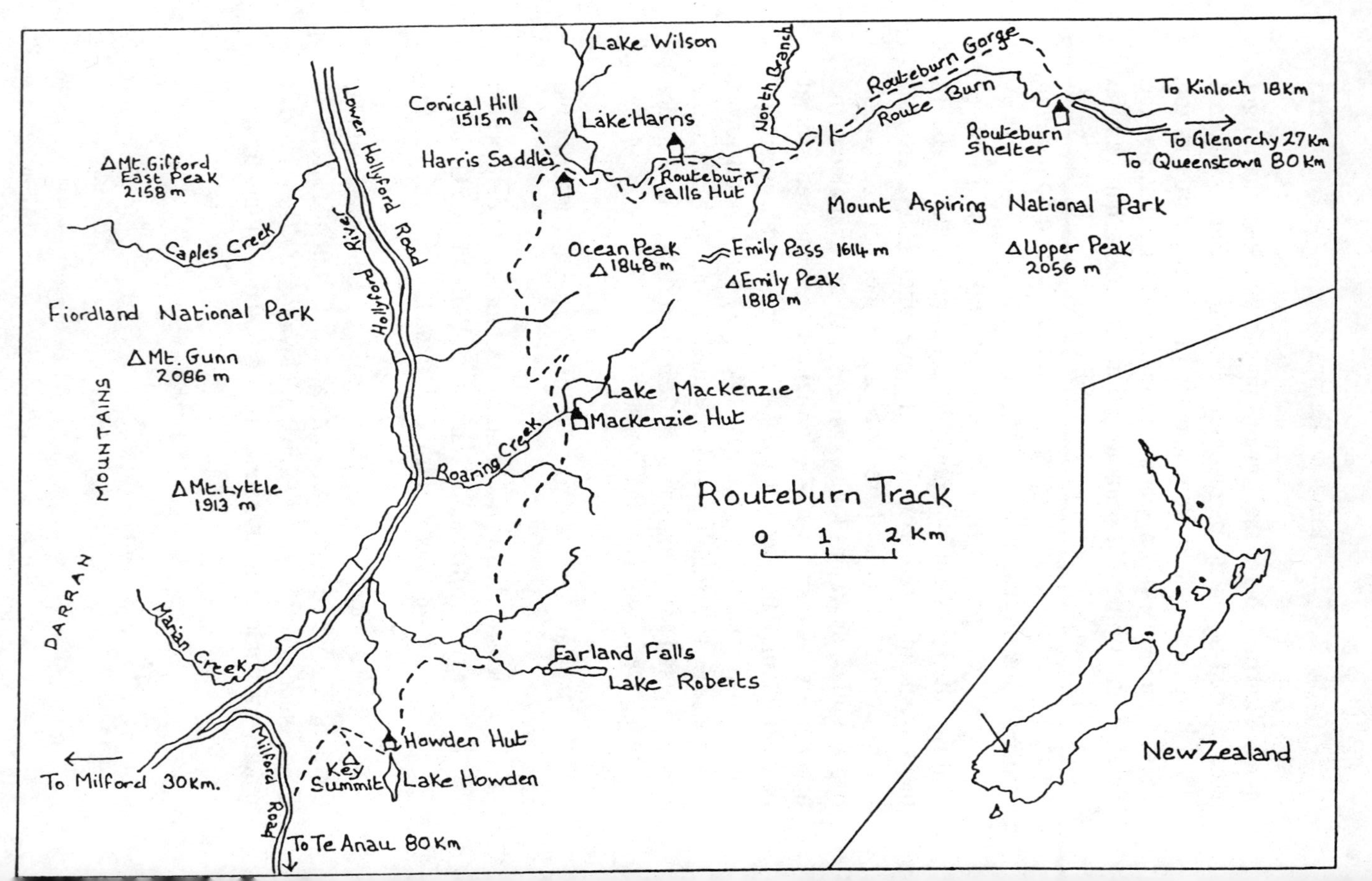

Routeburn Track
0 1 2 Km
Lake Wilson
Conical Hill 1515 m
Lake Harris
North Branch
Routeburn Gorge
Route Burn
To Kinloch 18Km
To Glenorchy 27Km
To Queenstown 80Km
Routeburn Shelter
Harris Saddle
Routeburn Falls Hut
Mt. Gifford East Peak 2158 m
Mount Aspiring National Park
Caples Creek
Ocean Peak 1848 m
Emily Pass 1614 m
Emily Peak 1818 m
Upper Peak 2056 m
Lower Hollyford Road
Hollyford River
Fiordland National Park
Mt. Gunn 2086 m
Lake Mackenzie
Mackenzie Hut
MOUNTAINS
Roaring Creek
Mt. Lyttle 1913 m
DARRAN
Marian Creek
Earland Falls
Lake Roberts
Howden Hut
Key Summit
Lake Howden
Milford Road
To Milford 30Km.
To Te Anau 80Km
New Zealand

WALK XII

XII. The Routeburn Track.

(27 Miles)

The two most popular walks (tramps) in New Zealand are the Milford Track, about 8,000 hikers a year, and the Routeburn Track, with around 9,000 each year. Unlike the Milford track the number of walkers allowed on the Routeburn are unrestricted. This has become a bit of a problem in the peak months of Jan. and Feb. because of the limited amount of hut space available. The huts are quite well built with far more facilities than anything one sees in the States but the Government requires that all walkers sleep inside them at night so it can get a bit crowded at times.

The way around the threat of overcrowding on the Routeburn is to take advantage of the independently owned concession that operates catered huts in the general vicinity of the Government huts. These can be booked through the Tourist Hotel Corp., although they are not owned or run by them. These facilities can accommodate up to 16 trampers in separate rooms with upper and lower bunks. This is better since families or spouses can stay together rather than having to be separated in dormitory type rooms.

In addition to the better sleeping accommodations the package also provides meals with two staff who come along to do the cooking and washing up. Bedding is also provided so that the tramper needs only to backpack his personal goods. Bus service from Queenstown is also included. Queenstown is a good base with plenty of activities for the adventurous and comfortable accommodations for before or after trekking.

Another walk is offered in the area with this same arrangement. This is the Greenstone Track. It actually joins the

Routeburn at one end. It is less strenuous and not quite as long but also three days in duration. It follows a river for much of the way. Fishing along the way is usually quite good.

Briefing for the walks takes place at Millie's Restaurant in Queenstown the night before. One then becomes acquainted with the staff and the other walkers in the group. Backpacks and raingear are provided for those who do not have their own. The next morning the expedition joins other sight-seers on a large bus that eventually deposits them at the trailhead.

At 7:00 a.m. Angie and I assembled with our back packs for the four and a half hour ride to 'The Divide', our destination. Seven other hikers and two staff joined us for the trek.

The ride over in the bus was entertaining. The driver was informative and competent. New Zealand roads were well-maintained, a bit narrow in places but devoid of traffic. Wheeling the big bus around the curves and across the one lane bridges required experience and skill. At the same time he conducted a monologue that was full of Kiwi humor:

"Black sheep eat less than white sheep."

"Oh, why is that?"

"Less of 'em."

Then the farmer who was asked by a tourist:

"Does this road go to Milford Sound?"

"Well, I don't rightly know. If it does it must do it in the night because it's always been here in the morning when I get up."

As we cruised along the shore of Lake Wakatipu we looked across at the huge sheep station on the other side. In the steep surrounding alps the ranch ran 28,000 head of sheep and 2,700 head of cattle on its 100,000 acres! We later visited this ranch on a lake cruise in the coal-burning steamer Earnslaw, launched in 1912 on the same day as the Titanic.

At the ranch we witnessed a sheep shearing demonstration and learned that all of the sheep were Merinos, raised only for their wool. They were sheared once a year and the crop was worth about $35 per sheep, or around a mil from the ranch's wool crop. No supplementary feeding was used in the winter but they did fertilize the mountain sides by spraying with planes, you could see where the grass was greener halfway up the slopes. The ranch ran 40 miles in one direction along its own private mountain range.

At the Te Anau stop we were treated to coffee and a slice of delicious coffee cake in the local cafe. The cake was sprinkled with little chocolate drops and it was served by our two staff, Brenda and Tina. They were both fit, pleasant and easy-going. Normally they would have been in college but this was their summer break.

At The Divide the bus dropped our group of trackers by the side of the road. We shouldered packs and headed into the bush. The trail worked its way up the side of a precipitous mountain. The trees and undergrowth were dense and varied, unlike anything that we were used to walking through in other parts of the world. The track was well-maintained and graded with adequate switchbacks.

The three national parks of the southern alps comprise some three and a quarter million acres. Most of it has never felt the footprint of man. There are no bears or potentially threatening wildlife. New Zealand and Ireland are the only two countries in the world without snakes of any kind, too. The only insect of any concern is a shy spider, much like the black widow, but even this is rarely encountered.

The water of the lakes and streams is 99.4% pure. The off percent is claimed to be the fish, rainbow and brown trout and large salmon trout, too. There is seldom any giardia to worry about and streams are everywhere. The mountains are steep and rocky and the tops were still snow-covered when we were there.

Most trampers seem to go from East to West whereas we went in the opposite direction. Those that we saw were mostly young and fit. They were predominantly New Zealanders, Australians, Canadians and Americans with a sprinkling of Japanese and a few Germans but walkers on the Routeburn come from all over the world. Backpacks were not overloaded since it wasn't necessary to carry sleeping bags, tents or stoves. The trail was not crowded either and most of the time we had that huge expanse of alpine wilderness to ourselves.

Distances were shown in the amount of walking time that it should take to get there, both on maps and trail markers. I guess this was so as not to discourage prospective hikers. 5 hours seems more encouraging apparently than contemplating 10 miles of rocky alpine slogging.

After an hour of climbing a good trail with switchbacks and footbridges across streams we reached a trail junction that headed up to Key Summit. Packs were stashed there and only lunch was carried up to the summit for a view. I was reluctant to leave my pack, though, and become separated from my goods. I just didn't feel good about leaving it unattended so I kept it with me.

The view was magnificent. We looked across the Hollyford Valley far below to the alpine crests on the other side. Beyond the range in front of us, some 10 or 12 miles as the crow flies, would be the Milford Track. Over in that area the rainfall is around 300 inches a year whereas on this side it only amounted to some 30 inches a year. The mountains over there were granite, though, and better for rockclimbing.

The day was glorious sunshine, an event that was not taken for granted even in this area which was also considered a rainforest. It was possible to trace the path of the three glaciers that a million years ago had carved out the valleys in the distance far below.

The next section that led to our first night's lodging was still mostly through forest. All of it would simply be referred to as 'bush' by Kiwis or Aussies. The track just flirted with the tree line, then it worked its way on down a difficult descent to the hut at Lake MacKenzie.

Beyond our own hut was the Government lodge for the

'freedom walkers', those who packed their own food without staff. It had two floors and seemed to have a United Nations crowd in residence. A warden lived there. His principal duty was to collect the nominal $8.00 fee from the occupants. There were 8 tent sites, too, but no random tent pitching was permitted. No dogs allowed either. Dogs might disturb the odd bird or a piece of flora in the 3 million acres of their territory, a concept always difficult for me to grasp.

Crowding in the Government huts was resolved by one innovative warden who was reported to have been seen trimming 1/3rd off the mattresses in an effort to cram more sardines into the pack. It is easy to criticize the system but the truth is that these shelters are far nicer than anything on the Appalachian Trail or elsewhere that we've hiked and there was never any litter. The wilderness itself was always pristine and completely natural because of it.

At the 'private hut' we found comfortable bunks with pillows and duvets in a clean, freshly-painted room with plenty of hooks for hanging wet trail clothes. We had been issued the same clever sheet sack that is used on the Milford Track as well. It doubled as a pillow case and along with it we each received a towel. After a hot shower, no less, in the mixed washroom where separate shower stalls eliminated the prospect of communal bathing I changed to the set of dry clothes that I had brought for after hiking. What luxury!

To my complete amazement the hut furnished a guitar. It was a beat-up Japanese model, resistant to fine tuning with a steel sixth string but it was a treat to play it on the veranda in such a setting. For about an hour Lake MacKenzie and the Kea birds were subjected to what was probably their first strains of flamenco and classical guitar, a sound that interrupted the customary mountain silence.

One by one we came to know our fellow travelers. Katie was a New Yorker, thin, of thirty-something age. She held an executive position with Citibank. She was attractive and independent and travelling by herself. The long legs and slender figure belied an underlying stamina that had taken her up to the 18,600' summit of Kilimanjaro. She had done another walk, too, in the Himalayas, an 8 day trek to Bhuto. She was cheerful and friendly and unmindful of upholding the patent New Yorker image.

The description of Katie's walk up Kilimanjaro sounded arduous enough for the most dedicated masochist. The last push to the top, without benefit of oxygen, started at midnight so that the loose rock scree through which they had to trudge would be in a firmer mode. The top was reached in time for a dramatic sunrise that no Hollywood setting could begin to duplicate.

At the top of Kilimanjaro the survivors opened the tiny foil packet of vodka that had been provided for a celebration. It was similar in size to a fast-food serving of catsup in its little never-enough wrapping. A few sips from the tiny packet at that altitude produced a mind-bending high that could not be equalled in any other way. The trip down to where they had left camp was a loose scree descent of only 45 minutes. Of the seven who had made it up to the top three were in a state of disorientation that later evaporated as oxygen was gained at succeeding lower elevations. It had been an experience of epic proportions.

Another surprise at the hut before dinner was a generous serving of white wine. Dinner was pate stuffed chicken breasts prepared by Tina, with vegies, mashed potatoes and chocolate pudding for dessert, a backpacker's feast.

The next day, after the availability of a huge breakfast if desired, and a do-it-yourself lunch pack, we hit the track that led up from Lake MacKenzie. As the switchbacks worked upward through dense green forest the vista of the small lake became more and more appealing. Finally, up on the rim of the basin we stopped for a breather and waited for Tina and Brenda to catch up with us. They had dealt with clean-up chores at the hut and then hurried to catch up with the group.

Tina had just graduated from college with a degree in Psychology. She was cheerful, tall and strong and knowledgeable about the trees and wildflowers that we saw along the way. She had a contagious sense of humor and a lack of concern about how fast or slow or where the individuals of the group travelled. This non-regimentation made the group travel palatable, besides, New Zealanders figure you can look out for yourself.

On crossing the ridge the track then followed along the sloping face of an escarpment that continued to rise above. It was now above the tree line. Far below could be seen the winding Hollyford valley again and on the other side of the canyon were the snow covered alps of Fiordland. The track here was fairly easy going with an occasional narrow rock ledge scramble to make it a challenge. A misstep then would have been serious because the face was steep enough to insure a non-stop drop of around a thousand feet to the valley floor below. Mostly, though, the trail was well-defined and bench-like enough not to have to worry about the off edge.

We stopped by a stream for lunch and here Brenda made an orange drink. I noticed a stashed butane tank and a cooking ring with a huge 'billy', i.e. cooking pot, for hot water. I guess on cold rainy days there would be the option of hot tea or coffee instead.

Brenda had also just graduated from a small college in South Island. Her major had been Park and Recreation Management. It was easy to see how much she loved the outdoors. She had worked the Routeburn and the Greenstone the season before, too. She reckoned that she had done this same three-day walk about thirty times altogether. Her family owned a sheep station. She, too, was strong and fit with a shy way about her but she was never intimidated by the experiences or life styles of others. I guess rubbing shoulders with so many nationalities from so many parts of the world had kept her from becoming unduly impressed by them. She was worried about finding a job when the season ended in April.

The leaders of the pack usually worked out to be Sandy and Jamie, a local couple from Queenstown. They had been offered the choice of making the walk by friends who had been unable to go but had paid their non-cancelable fee. Sandy's parents had volunteered to look after their two young children and they had pounced upon the opportunity. Jamie was a dentist in Queenstown.

Like the other New Zealanders we had met, Sandy and Jamie were outgoing and friendly. They were firm in their opinions about world affairs and how the country should be run but they were willing to listen to someone else's ideas.

Jamie was tall and he carried a heavy backpack. Sandy was spry and she usually set a blistering pace. They were avid skiers, like almost every Kiwi we met, and they were fond of the mountains. I stayed with them and kept their company on the slog up to Harris Saddle. It was enjoyable but harder going than the usual goat gear I seem to favor on the up sections.

There was a challenge side climb out of Harris Saddle, the pass that was the objective of the long ascent. It was being touted by Brenda and Tina as being worth the difficult ordeal of gaining the top for the 360 degree view that it offered. Conical Hill it was called. I remembered the Conical Hill that I had hiked up on the West Highland Way in Scotland and the soggy sandwich I had eaten huddled in the rain under the poncho there. Today was bright sunshine again, though, with few clouds.

When we reached the pass Sandy and Jamie decided to climb Conical Hill. They went over to the emergency shelter located there to stash their packs inside. I went behind them to do likewise and join them and then I noticed an old Japanese asleep on the hut's emergency cot. I worried about leaving my pack there. Its loss would mean problems on the walks to come and I had grown accustomed to the pack itself, too. It was a familiar companion, like Beauregard. And other hikers would be coming and going as well. I asked Jamie about it and he said, "Well, you just rely on the honesty of the hills."

The climb would be a bit much with the pack and I was reluctant to leave it unattended so I asked Jamie and Sandy to go up without me.

Rowan came up the track next. She was an absolutely stunning sixteen year old. She had a sort of endearing naivete about her that just made you want to protect her from any vicissitudes, real or imagined. Her father had planned to make this walk with her but he had developed trouble with a pulled leg muscle. They were New Zealanders from Rotorua.

Rowan stashed her pack in the shelter, too, and she took up with Sandy and Jamie on their way for the chamois-like ascent of Conical Hill. Then Tina appeared. She simply dropped her pack beside the track and hurried to catch up with the others. By now I was beginning to feel that my fears really were groundless.

As I watched the four of them scrambling up the steep rock scree I focused on Rowan. Underlying her sheltered-like appearance and fresh beauty was a fearless core that had sent her plunging 140' off of a bridge near Queenstown tied to the end of a bungy cord. She proudly wore her bungy-jumping tee shirt that she had been awarded for surviving the jump.

Bungy-jumping has become quite popular in New Zealand. We had talked to one of the two painters at the MacKenzie hut who had jumped 220' off of a bridge that held only a couple feet of water at the bottom. I was curious to know how you become disengaged after the jump. He said that they then lower you down after the bungy cord stops bouncing and your feet are untied by the bottom team. Nude jumpers go free!

A later conversation about bungy-jumping with others we met produced the chilling story of a bungy-jumping effort off of a bridge south of Auckland. The operation was in its infancy when the bridge operator had forgotten to knot the cord around the ankles of his customer. It had been looped but not tied. He had been smoking cannabis. Hopefully the jumper had not had time to register the mistake in the final instant when he was expecting to be jerked back up from oblivion.

When Angie and the others finally made it up to the

saddle the urge to climb the nearby escarpment became too much to resist. I left my pack with Angie and I headed up the nearly perpendicular face of the peak. Katie and Brenda followed.

About two-thirds of the way up I encountered a middle-aged Japanese man working his way back down the rocky cliff face. I was astonished to see an elderly Japanese woman following doggedly behind him. She was thin and wiry and obviously his mother. She looked to be about ninety years old. The old man sleeping in the A-frame down below was probably the father, wisely catching a few winks while his foolish son and energetic old wife sprinted up the peak.

At the 4,900' top there was indeed a magnificent view in every direction. Off in the distance was Lake Wilson and over there could be seen four little white specks of another party that we would join and get to know that night. Up to the right was the formidable Mt. Erebus at over 6,000 ft. The other party's guide, Phillip, who was Brenda and Tina's counterpart, was busy climbing to its top by himself. He would then ski boot down its steep facing snow slope, hopefully stopping before the perpendicular drop-off. Both of the girls gave a triple shout in unison without any response.

At Harris Saddle we shouldered packs again and headed down now, past the welcome tarn that was Harris Lake. Soon after I was astounded to see three fell runners charging up the rocky trail in a sea of perspiration. Tina was with me and one of the trio stopped to talk with us. He was solid muscle beneath the grey hair and he was wearing shorts without even a fanny pack. They had run up the difficult Emily Peak track that morning and now they were headed back over the same difficult trail that had taken us a day and a half to negotiate. One of them was a lean and muscular woman. He figured that it would only take them three hours to make it all the way back to where we had started at the Divide!

Far below I could see Angie moving along at a good clip. She carried a heavy pack. We both tend to carry too much in the way of 'necessities'. Tagging along behind her like a shadow was our Japanese friend Chiyok. She was travelling by herself. She had only a few halting words of English and communication was mostly in sign language with a good deal of head nodding but she was quite determined and a good sport. Several days later we were astonished to meet her in Queenstown with her husband. He spoke English well himself and he was proud of his wife's accomplishment.

The track down to Routeburn Falls hut was less demanding than some of the previous walking. It was a welcome relief to reach the end of the day's hike. The hut was located right next to the falls with a nice overlook on the river.

The other party soon joined us at the hut and bunks began to fill. They had already been in residence there due to a booking mishap whereby they thought they would be spending an extra day at the hut. We had a separate room, though, with six bunks in it and Katie moved in with us to take up the other lower.

Again, the hut held a guitar for visitors to play. This one had a broken string which I managed to repair and after some stubborn resistance I managed to get some sound out of it while sitting on the steps of the hut.

A large Kea came to call. He was a huge bird and completely fearless. He was a handsome parrot green with a layer of orange feathers underneath. He posed on the railing while looking for something to carry away or chew. Boots were removed before entering the hut and to save them from the Keas they were hung just inside the entrance on special pegs.

The Kea is an almost endangered species in New Zealand. There are only 5,000 of them left. They are a tough bird and they live to be quite old but they generally manage to produce only one offspring a year. The infant birds find it difficult making their way in life.

The sheep stockmen accuse the Kea of killing their sheep. Sometimes a sheep will be found with a sharp gash in the back where a renegade Kea, supposedly, has pecked down to get at the animal's fat. Environmentalists say no, these are only sheep that are old or ill or already dead, or maybe attacked by a rare renegade. The argument continues to rage but the Kea is still protected from hunters. KEA is a popular crossword puzzle word. I often wondered what they looked like.

Anyone who had left their socks out on the railing to dry that night had found them missing the next morning. A Kea had carried them off one by one and scattered them around the nearby bush.

A steak dinner, again with wine, was followed by unexpected entertainment. Phillip blithely explained the procedure by which the 'crepes' would be served for dessert. After frying a pancake in a skillet he and Brenda and Tina, in turn, would stand with their back to the table while the recipient, plate in hand, made ready on the other side. On the count of three the pancake was flipped over the head backwards and, hopefully, clean across the table where the dinner guest was supposed to catch it in his plate. Invariably the pancake slipped off the plate onto the floor, if you were agile enough to get your plate under it. Not to worry. Just pick it up off of the floor, brush it off, load it with peaches and whipped cream and pour syrup all over it. Delicious.

The two couples who were already in residence were New Zealanders from Auckland. John was a social worker whose home was right in a section of the area through which we had walked when we had hiked the Coast to Coast Walk of Auckland. His wife Liz was tiny and captivating and a real dynamo. Her legs were strong and muscular. She was a mountain climber. She related a terrifying story about climbing with two friends. They had been roped together and she had been in the middle. The bottom climber had slipped and fallen. When the rope had tightened it had taken her with him. The lead climber had then been unable to hold their combined weight with his own piton and it had broken loose, too. All three of them had then fallen together.

On the way down they had hit a ledge. They had

managed to cling to it while they regrouped and this had saved their lives.

Jeff and Christine were just as friendly. In a discussion about the government and its burdens and the problem of ever-increasing taxes under a semi-socialized system Christine related the story of a part-time maid who was on the dole because of being an unwed mother. When Christine had asked her who the father had been her reply was, "I don't know, missum, In the dark the faces look all the same."

Our two parties walked out together the next morning. The track followed the Routeburn river the whole way. The water of the river was that same crystal-clear slate-blue color that we had seen in the Picos de Europa on the Rio Cares. It was so inviting that a lunch-break swim tempted the girls and Phillip and a couple of the others. The water was cold, though, and their swims were measured more in seconds than minutes.

The forest through which the track passed contained red beech trees and a multitude of ferns. The swinging bridges were good for keeping one's boots dry. They were one-at-a-time affairs. Phillip, the ever-extrovert, made a practice of running across them at full tilt.

Phillip was a fourth year law student with the job of acting as a guide on his summer break. He was considerate and interested in people with a flair for spicing things up, Kiwi-style.

The Routeburn Flats hut was situated in a lush valley with fresh grass and the clear Routeburn stream flowing through it. Sharp escarpments climbed on all sides and a canyon ranged off between higher peaks with deeper snow than what we had seen up on Harris Saddle. A long waterfall cascaded down one side.

In the hut itself, which was for public use, there were 20 bunks, a fireplace, butane-supplied cooking rings, tables and a wood stove. On a table near the door was a log book. In thumbing through the entries over the past several months it was interesting to observe that they had been made by hikers who had come there from all over the world. One entry that somehow touched me had been made by a Japanese on the 5th of December:

"JAPANESE (KAZUKO - FUJIMURA) (this part was in caps with its own parentheses, then:)

I am here.

It is nice weather, and here is nice place. I love here very much. My long holiday (? for a year) nearly finish. It is very sad. But I could get many good experience and many friends. Thank you New Zealand."

The path continued along above the gorge that had been cut by the Routeburn river. It was interesting to note the way it had sliced its way down through solid rock over the centuries and always it had that inviting teal blue color.

Alice and Shirley were the other two members of our party. They confessed to being senior type citizens although age was never mentioned and they both looked much younger. Alice lived in Wellington but she and her husband, Ron, whom I would meet later, had a second home near Shirley in Queenstown. They were both game and full of stamina and glad to be out on the track moving along with a perpetual twinkle in the eye with never a complaint about the steep parts. This was Shirley's sixth tramp along the Routeburn.

When we arrived at the shelter near the car park, the end of the track, it was with reluctance that I jettisoned the pack knowing that the walk was finished. It had been a pleasure to have enjoyed a good long-distance walk without having to deal with the usual logistics and to have met congenial people who led such varied and interesting lives.

On one wall of the shelter there was a pictorial history of the Routeburn Track. It had been an old Maori path in years gone by. It had enabled them to get over into the Greenstone Valley where they would collect the green stones that were prized for jewelry and exchange. In the late 1800's it had been developed by a Richard Bryant. Interestingly enough, he was the grandfather of the current Richard Bryant to whom I had spoken about our own trek. Even more coincidental it had been his wife, Elaine, who had briefed and organized us on the night before setting out. And later it became even more coincidental.

That night we attended a final banquet at Millie's restaurant. I was glad to find myself seated next to Keith, Shirley's husband, who had been unable to get away for the walk. As it turned out he was a part owner of the New Zealand trucking firm that also owned Millie's restaurant and, in fact, the concession itself for the only private huts allowed on the Routeburn and Greenstone tracks. The accommodations and staff had been part of his firm. And never once had Shirley or Alice revealed that they were personally interested beyond the fun of the tramp itself.

Keith had been a director of the Fiordland National Park and he was a member of the New Zealand Alpine Club. When I had asked him about weather conditions in the mountains he had related an experience he had when climbing with three other friends. They had been hit by a blizzard and besides the problem of the adverse weather one of their party had become unable to walk because of swollen feet. They had dug a snowcave into the side of the mountain where they had stayed for eight days until it had cleared enough for them to be rescued. They had stomped a message in the snow so that the search party would wait for favorable conditions. The wind is the enemy, he explained, not the snow.

The banquet was well managed with an excellent meal. Everyone was presented with an enlarged photograph of the group along with an impressive certificate of achievement that was a suitable memento of the walk.

The map of the Routeburn and Greenstone Walks can be obtained at the Dep't. of Conservation on Ballart Street in Queenstown. The best map is: Infomap # 335-02.

Or write to:

Infomap Centre
Private Bag
Upper Hutt. New Zealand

There are a number of other magnificent long walks in the area but these two, and the Milford Track, are the only walks that are catered like the above. They can be booked through Tourist Hotel Corp. as noted in WALK VI, The Milford Track.

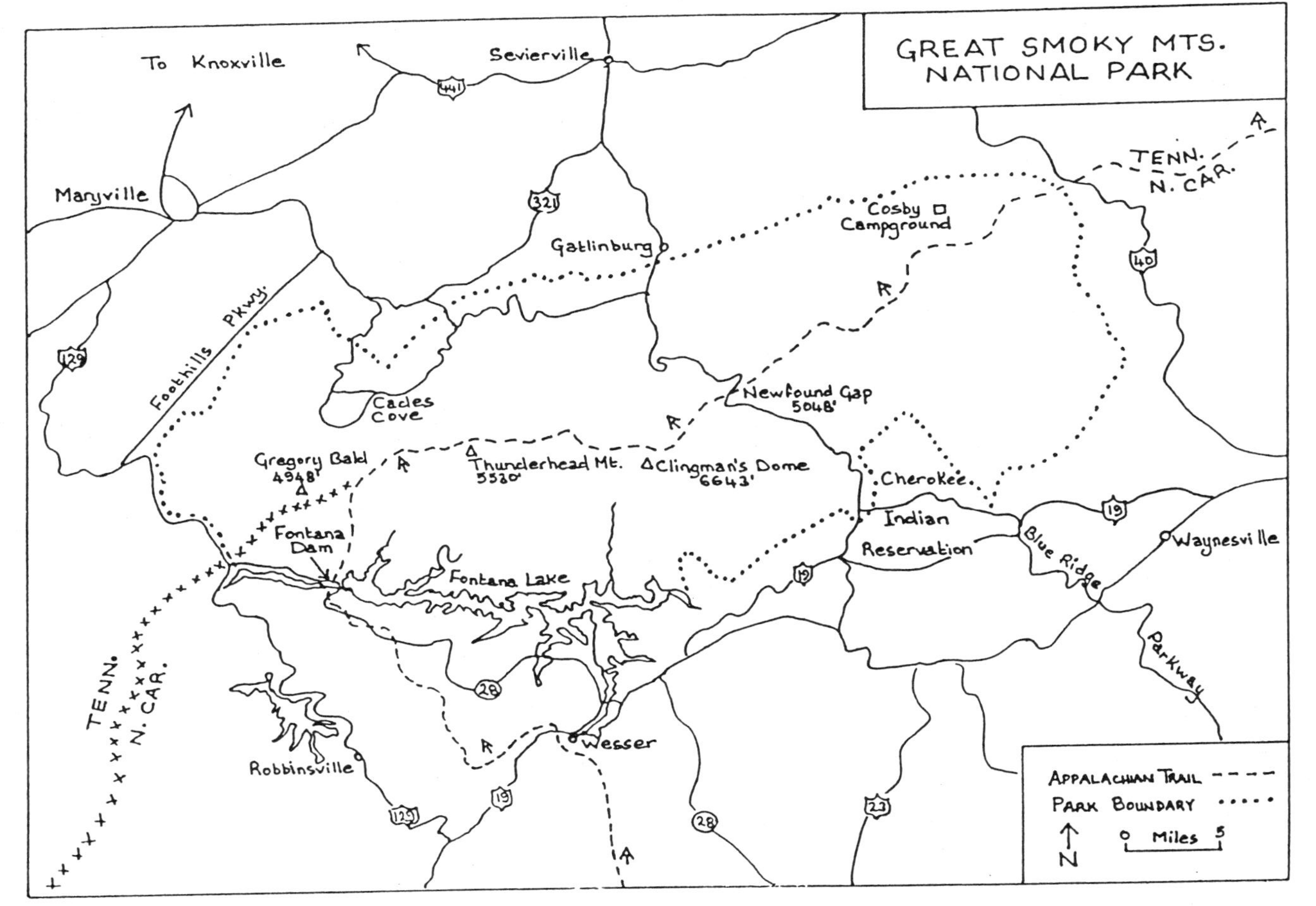
GREAT SMOKY MTS.
NATIONAL PARK
To Knoxville
Sevierville
441
Maryville
321
Gatlinburg
Cosby Campground
TENN.
N. CAR.
40
129
Foothills Pkwy.
Cades Cove
Newfound Gap 5048'
Gregory Bald 4948'
Thunderhead Mt. 5530'
Clingman's Dome 6643'
Cherokee
Indian Reservation
19
Waynesville
Blue Ridge Parkway
Fontana Dam
Fontana Lake
28
Wesser
Robbinsville
23
APPALACHIAN TRAIL
PARK BOUNDARY
N
0 Miles 5

WALK XIII

XIII. The A. T. Across The Smokies.

The First Part

(37.5 Miles)

Most hikers who have walked the whole trail or large parts of it consider the Smokies to be one of the most memorable sections. The trail follows the very crest of the range, as usual, but once up on top the elevations remain more stable so that there is less up and down to do when crossing the Smokies themselves.

My own experiences in the Smokies were divided over two separate trips. In trying to Walk Easy I wound up piecing it together. Because of this it turned out that I was able to enjoy some of the side trails up to the A.T. as well as some of the other amenities of the area.

Fontana Dam to Mollie's Ridge Shelter. 9.7 Miles.

The start for the hike was an 8:15 a.m. departure at Fontana Dam. I had misgivings about the weather, which had been bad and didn't show signs of improvement. The plan was to spend two nights out in the Smokies-type shelters and wind up at Newfound Gap. I was alone. A typical Smokies' mist set the stage. It occurred to me that the Smokies derived their name from this mist so it provided a clue as to what the prevailing climate might be. I walked across the dam and then I turned right up a road. I passed a bear trap where the trail headed off up into the woods. The trap was made out of steel plate. It did little for my peace of mind.

A hard slog uphill in a light drizzle turned into driving

rain. I walked in the cloud mist or rain all morning. Then I stopped at Birch Hill shelter for lunch, my first example of a Smokies shelter. The front side was open with heavy chain-link fencing that stretched across it to keep the bears out. I could see where they had tried to break in around the edges. It had taken awesome strength to have bent the heavy metal supports for that fencing. Rocks and wedges of wood had been chinked into the bent places. The gate had a tricky sliding latch with a chain around it and a hook through the latch. Hopefully, it would be hard for claws to undo.

The shelter was a gloomy place in a little hollow in the woods. It was out of the rain, though. I had lunch there and I rested for half an hour. I tried out the wire-mesh bunk arrangement until I got cold. I was wearing cut-off jeans at the time that did little for warmth when not moving. Then I set out in the rain again wrapped in my poncho.

There wasn't a soul on the trail all day long even though it was mid-July. The trail worked uphill mostly and it made the going fairly slow, maybe 1.5 miles per hour. It took about 7 hours to reach Mollie's Ridge shelter.

The shelter looked out on a grassy clearing and it was a welcome haven from the rain. Someone had left plenty of dry wood for a fire but I had a terrible time finding water. In spite of the rain the spring below was dry. I finally found a little pool of accumulated water down below it and I used the 1st Need filter that Boonie had given me for my birthday.

With the dry wood I made a fire and I put on some dry clothes. The wet clothes and socks and the wet boots I placed near the fire. The bear-proof gate I shut and carefully latched. The bedroll I made up on the wire-mesh bunk. Somebody had left some candles and these I lit. The little fluorescent light and the candles cast a cozy glow around the shelter. They helped to make it the inviting refuge that it was and I looked forward to relaxing and enjoying it.

It was good to stretch out on the mattress and the sleeping bag. I felt secure in the shelter, the door latch seemed bear-proof and cords were hanging from the roof for holding your pack. The cords had tin cans inserted near the end so that the mice couldn't travel down them to get into a pack or food sack.

The clouds kept rolling on by outside but the rain stopped after a while. A patch of sun poked through for a few minutes. I had seen only one squirrel all day long and no other animals. I figured that they had been holed up somewhere out of the rain.

It would have been nice to have had company in the shelter and I had thought that surely there would have been others there, too. It takes a certain amount of effort to backpack the 3 days to Clingman's Dome and then the three or four days to Davenport Gap, though, and the thru-hikers, Ga.to Maine, had already passed by about a month or two before.

Then I can remember thinking, 'Hey, this is great. All the comforts of home'. I started the little gas stove and made a hot toddy. Then I made some soup. I finished the sandwich that was left over from lunch. The six little miniature candy bars I saved for something to look forward to with a John D. McDonald read.

Something happened to disturb my peace of mind over the course of the next two hours. I couldn't quite put my finger on it. I tidied up and climbed into the sleeping bag looking forward to reading about the exploits of old Travis McGee and getting some rest. Darkness set in and the rain commenced again. Something scampered across the tin roof and I heard noises outside the shelter from time to time but I was cozy, warm and comfortable inside the bedroll and I remember thinking how great it was with the fire, the candles and a good book to read and then, gradually, I began to somehow feel uneasy. There I was snug and dry with absolutely no worries that I couldn't contend with and an intellect that knew this beyond the shadow of a doubt. And yet the situation still managed to somehow give me the creeps.

During the rest of that night I alternated between

reading and dozing fitfully. At 6:00 o'clock I got up and crawled into the still damp trail clothes. I stoked the fire and made myself a coffee and cognac, Spanish style. It was raining again. I looked out at it coming down in buckets in the clearing. 'What the hell!' I thought. 'Do I really want to slosh through that for the next couple of days? And I can't stay here because of the schedule.' By the time I'd finished the coffee and cognac I had to laugh at myself. 'Some thru-hiker I would make. And I always thought I loved walking in the rain and being alone in the wilderness. But, you know, a nice hot shower in the camper, a couple of beers and some dry clothes really would go pretty good! And nothing is cast in stone.' The decision to go down the mountain for some creature comforts really took less persuasion than I had thought it would.

Mollie's Ridge to Cades Cove. 8.0 Miles.

After tidying up I had a breakfast of two slices of fried toast, two packages of oatmeal and some more coffee without the cognac. I put the pack together and I headed out to the trail, in the rain, for a 7:45 a.m. departure.

It felt good to be on the trail and moving again. Surprisingly, no one else appeared for the rest of that morning, no tracks even. I had thought that a good many hikers would be up on the A.T. part of the Smokies at that time of year. Maybe nobody else wanted to be out in all of the rain or maybe this section was more remote.

It was good to make Cades Cove campground and the local store for just after noon. It had been an easy hike down through changing types of trees and across clear streams. It had rained the whole way. Then when I had reached the road it had turned into a deluge. It had been hard to even see where I was going and I had become worried about running into the traffic. Finally I had reached the park headquarters where I had gone into the men's room to change into what dry clothes I had left, at least my upper half became dry. I had some ice cream from the store next door and I arranged for a ride to shuttle me back to the camper over on the other side of the park.

The old man who drove me back was an interesting character. His old Datsun pick-up was half full of empty beer cans. I'd always wondered about the economics of the beer can recycling trade. Henry made his rounds for the beer cans early so as to beat the competition. He started out at five a.m. He knew all of the 'hot spots' and they were always best after a big weekend or a holiday. Then he went back home for a nap.

Henry and his brother and sister owned about 50 acres of land. They all lived together on the place. His sister did the cooking. He had tried being married for a few years. Didn't really like it he said. Divorced. Never again. He had Social Security and a small government pension each month. He did the beer cans, shuttled hikers and made crooked canes, engraved, that he sold to gift stores in Gatlinberg. He was a talkative, appreciative man with a thick beard and high blood pressure. His conversation was punctuated with a stream of tobacco juice that was slewed out of the window every so often.

Back at the camper the dogs were glad to see me ahead of schedule. Angie had gone to Asheville on an expedition. It was a real treat to be able to enjoy a hot shower, dry clothes, a cold beer and a respite from the rain.

Clingman's Dome to Newfound Gap. 8.0 Miles.

The sun was shining on my next hike along the A.T. This time I started at Clingman's Dome. Some Boy Scouts from Columbus, Ohio, picked up with me. They were on an outing with their troop. One of them was an eagle scout. His mate, an almost eagle, mentioned how much they would like to do the whole A. T. themselves one day. They didn't know how long it was or even if anyone had ever hiked all of the trail yet. They asked me how many months it would take. We climbed up to the top of the lookout tower to admire the view. Clingman's Dome is the second highest peak in the eastern

U.S., Mt. Mitchell in N.C. being the highest by a few more feet.

After leaving the scouts I set out on the trail. It was grown over in many spots and deeply eroded at times but spruce and fir trees were everywhere and everything was green, like a rain forest. Someone had gone to a lot of trouble to position split logs across the boggy spots. The hike was easy walking in deep forest for most of the way.

Just before Angie arrived to pick me up at Newfound Gap a storm appeared with lots of thunder and lightning and plenty of rain. I huddled in the poncho under a sign with a partial roof for a bit of shelter. After the other experience it seemed perfectly normal. It was good to know that I had a ride coming but in spite of the rain I was reluctant to leave the trail. The A. T. in the Smokies had a magnetic attraction that beckoned as it led off into the woods, especially now that it travelled across the top of them.

Cosby Campground to Low Gap to Davenport Gap to Pigeon River. 11.8 Miles.

It took me an hour and a half to make it up to the A. T. from an early start at Cosby Campground. I had decided to hike down the opposite end of the A.T. across the Smokies in the time I had left.

When I reached the A. T. I saw two of the familiar white blazes on trees beside the trail as it headed north. A sign also read 'Mt. Cammerer 2.5 miles'. I hiked up this trail for 45 minutes and suddenly I realized that I had not seen any white blazes for the A. T. in all of that time. I decided that I could have somehow missed a turn-off or inadvertently taken another trail that actually led to Mt. Cammerer. I went back down again to see if I had missed the A. T. Nope. The same two white blazes at the junction at Low Gap were still there but there had not been any others since then.

The hike back killed an hour and 35 minutes, probably

an extra 2.5 miles. In the distance between the two trail junctions I could find only one white blaze about two miles up the trail. I had learned to become concerned when hiking the A. T. if a blaze didn't appear fairly frequently. The trail was otherwise well-maintained and easy to follow.

At a junction trail just before the long descent to Davenport Gap the thunder began to roll again. I stopped to eat my sandwich before the rain came. Then I worked on down the hill in a light drizzle. I found a welcome spring and I cleaned it up a bit so that the water flowed more freely, my good deed for the day. I used the filter to replenish the canteen.

On the long hike down to Davenport Gap and Hwy. 32 I saw no one else until I reached the junction up from the Ranger Station. Two backpackers had just made it up to the A. T. We had a brief visit. They were enthusiastic about the Shenandoah Valley near their home in Virginia.

When the A. T. crossed the road that was the edge of the park at Davenport Gap it was like driving across the border into Mexico. The A. T. suddenly became a pretty scrawny affair there when compared to the section that was maintained by the National Park service. It had the familiar white blazes in abundance, though, and it was somehow good to be back on the narrow path that I had grown so accustomed to hiking.

On the way to Pigeon River the A. T. wound down through a little glen with a stream that cascaded over rocks. It was hard to resist the urge to dump my clothes and cool off in the clear water.

When Angie showed up in the Blazer Beauregard was sporting a brand new red collar. He was proud of his new outfit and ready to start hiking again, now that we were out of the National Park where dogs are not welcome. I had done both ends and a piece of the middle of the A. T. across the Smokies on this trip and I resolved to do the rest of them when next we could return.

WALK XIV

XIV. The Rest of the A. T. Across The Smokies

(72.5 Miles)

Almost a year went by before I managed to get back to the Smokies. This time it was a more satisfying adventure.

<u>Cosby Cove to Snake Den Mtn. and Return. 12.5 Miles.</u>

At Cosby Campground the trail up to the A. T. started out at campsite number B96, an innocuous beginning to try and locate. A sign nearby read 'Campsites no. 36 & 37 closed due to bear activity. Do not remove this sign. Its removal may cause injury to others.' It looked like the Walnut Bottom bears of the year before were at it again. Walnut Bottom was the location where the campsites were located and the same thing had happened then.

The trail up to Low Gap which joins the A. T. there is heavily wooded and it borders a rushing stream with lots of character. It was the same trail that I had used last year. In a short distance it crossed the stream via a two-log foot bridge. The bridge had a hand rail nailed to it which took some of the sport out of using it. A single-log foot bridge with another welcome handrail recrossed the stream a little farther along.

After about half an hour of enjoying the dense forest and feeling good about being back in the Smokies again I noticed a young couple coming down the trail toward me. The man was using two walking sticks as though his feet were sore. He carried both of their backpacks himself. This included two half-heartedly rolled sleeping bags and a mountain of extras.

His young girlfriend carried nothing but herself. "Few bears up the trail," he volunteered. "Mama bear and two cubs."

"Friendly?" I asked.

"Yeah, but the one last night wasn't friendly at all."

"Where did you stay?"

"Cosby Knob."

They kept on moving. They seemed anxious to get back to their camper after a night out up at Cosby Knob shelter.

'Well, great.' I thought. 'Back in the Smokies for only a half hour and a bear story already.' I had read that there were then 700 to 800 bears living in the park. Apparently this dwindled in the fall when some of them ranged farther afield for a change of menu. I could remember reading that the population was estimated at only around 300 to 400 some two years ago. This seemed to indicate that the bears were thriving well.

At the small stream where I had stopped for water the year before I saw bear tracks but no mama bear with cubs.

At Low Gap I reached the A. T. again. It had started to rain and I had already broken out the faithful poncho. A couple were standing there at the junction putting on ponchos themselves. They, too, had spent the night at Cosby Knob shelter. They said that the bear in question had dropped by in the night. They had thrown rocks at him. They said that he wasn't the least bit intimidated by people. He had finally left. The shelter had been completely full, double six packs, top and bottom.

It continued to rain all that morning as I worked on up the A. T. to the trail that led back down from Snake's Den Mtn. The A. T. was unblazed, as before, except at trail junctions. Now, though, I was better prepared for this departure from the usual A. T. tradition. The rain was more of a light drizzle and not too bad.

The part of the trail along Hell Ridge was fairly level and easy going with occasional vistas on both sides. Then it began a long climb for about an hour which eventually led up to Inadu Knob. This is the Cherokee term for Snake's Den, so named because of the many snake dens supposedly located there. I did not see a single snake, though, and I wondered if maybe Cherokee imagination had had something to do with producing the name.

At noon I reached the trail junction at Inadu, on Snake's Den Mtn. Two white blazes, sure enough, had been located there to celebrate it. I stopped for a sandwich under a pine tree and a welcome drink of water, the first for the day. I kept thinking that the English hiker, John Merrill, may be right. The more water you drink the more you want to drink and the more rest you take the stiffer and more reluctant the joints are when you start moving again.

Even though it was late June it was cold. I put on my faithful Gortex jacket. After about fifteen minutes for lunch I was underway again.

The rain let up temporarily on the way down. I dug out the mittens to help the numbness in my fingers. I crossed two nice streams, one on a single log with a hand rail. This 5.3 miles back down was a very pleasant trail with a gradual descent through spectacular forest with open vistas along the way.

None of the predicted bears showed but I did see more of their tracks and plenty of bear scat, also many deer tracks. I passed only one other couple on the A. T., no one else all day long.

At 3:17 p.m. I made it back to Cosby Campground. It had been an easy hike albeit mostly in the rain. I was beginning to think that it rained almost every day in the Smokies or at least part of each day. Beauregard wouldn't speak to me when he arrived in the Blazer. He was really put out that he hadn't been able to go on this hike. I couldn't convince him that dogs are not allowed in the National Park. $500 fine. Maybe prison. He might disturb the bears.

Our own campground, where we had located the camper, was near Gatlinburg. It was beside a small stream and next to an open field that was handy for walking the dogs. We were there in order to be close to the motel where Boonie was scheduled to stay. She was coming from California to hike in the Smokies with me. Gatlinburg is a well-known tourist center with everything in it that makes for a good vacation visit. This probably helps to contribute to the fact that the Smokies are the most frequently visited National Park in the U. S. My own observation is that this doesn't apply to any trail that is farther away than fifty feet from the family automobile or a fast-food restaurant. The trails themselves are not like Yosemite or the Sierras. They seem to receive little use by comparison and you seldom see others out enjoying them with a private walk in the wilderness.

There are many fine restaurants in Gatlinburg. I can heartily recommend the Open Hearth as being one of the best of them. They serve excellent food at reasonable prices.

Clingman's Dome to Derrick Knob shelter. 10.4 Miles.

My sister Boonie joined me for this hike. We started in the mist and drizzle of the Forney Ridge parking lot, half a mile below the observation tower at 6,643' on the top of Clingman's Dome. I had been up it the year before but there would be nothing to see in the midst of all of the clouds and drizzle this time. We picked up the A.T. just beyond the left of the incline ramp up to the tower. It was hard to locate even though I could remember about where it was supposed to be.

We slogged down through mud and lush vegetation in the wet all morning. We passed three parties and a pair of rangers. Everybody was complaining about the rain. The rangers said that it had been raining every day like this for the past four weeks. They said that it was unusual and that they actually did have sunshine up there for several days at a time. They were carrying out sleeping bags and camp gear for somebody who had abandoned them. They didn't say why.

We reached Siler's Bald shelter. A group of hikers were

huddled around the fire inside. One of them was an older hiker from Arkansas who had been on the A. T. for 17 days. His objective was the observation tower at Clingman's Dome. He said that he was going to wait one more day before hiking in to it in the hope that the rain and cloud would lift so that he could have his view. Each man makes his own objectives. As best I recall there actually was sunshine on the afternoon of the next day so chances are that he did get his wish.

It was crowded in the shelter so we went on down the trail where we found a couple of logs to sit on for lunch. Two younger hikers passed us. They had been in the shelter, too, and as it turned out they would be our roomates for the night later on.

The rain stopped. In climbing up Cold Spring Knob we caught up with a doe and her fawn. They had been grazing on the grass beside the trail. They were not the least bit concerned about us. Since we were slowly trudging uphill they were content to stay about ten yards ahead of us. They let us herd them this way for almost half a mile.

Just as we were about to reach our shelter for the night at Derrick Knob we heard a loud thud. Over to our immediate right, about 50 feet away, a large bear had just pushed over a sealed and padlocked 55 gal. drum. He ignored us. I don't know what was in the drum, probably some kind of emergency provisions for the park service I would guess. He was doing his best to worry his way into it.

Derrick Knob shelter was made of stone with the usual inside fireplace and the two levels of six wire-mesh bunks that are stretched across logs. It looked out over a small grassy clearing where the deer came to feed at dusk. Hanging from the roof logs were the customary cords with inverted cans or lids suspended above the bitter ends. The chainlink fence looked secure on the open side and the shelter was an altogether pleasant place.

The shelter mice, for which the cords are in place, can be very persistent at times. Many is the entry that I have read in the different logs along the way that has complained about them from time to time. Sometimes the more courageous will take a dive out over the can in the hope that he will land on the pack or food sack hanging below. It is best to leave pack pouches unzipped and easily accessible otherwise they may get gnawed through and an expensive pack can soon become ruined. The most outraged entries, though, were for the infrequent occasions when a too enthusiastic mouse scampered across a sleeping face.

The two young hikers who had passed us earlier were named Alec and Matt. They had already settled into the lower bunks that were on the left side by the stone wall. We settled into the lower right bunks ourselves. The bear didn't bother any of us as we went back and forth to the spring, gathered firewood or otherwise went about our business in the forest. Neither did he try to visit the inside of the shelter. Suddenly, seeing the bear nearby, just minding his own business while wc did likewise, what bear apprehension I may have had evaporated completely. It seemed the most natural thing in the world for him to be there hanging out like the rest of us. My observation has been that the same rule almost always applies. Bears, other animals, snakes, big fish and most people won't bother you if you don't bother them.

It had been 4:30 p.m. when we had reached the shelter. About an hour later another young couple joined the group. Ron and Sylvia were from Oklahoma. They were on a short vacation. Their two young girls had backpacked the year before at ages 2 and 4 but this year they had elected a plushier change of scene when they had been given the opportunity to visit their grandparents nearby. It made a nice holiday for Ron and Sylvia and it gave the grandparents a chance to get in a little spoiling themselves, something that grandparents are supposed to do.

Ron was a practicing wildlife botanist for the State of Oklahoma. He was doing a dissertation for his PhD. on fire-generated nutrients in the soil. Apparently it is not necessarily wrong to burn cropland, in fact, it can be beneficial and this was news to me.

With the help of a piece of fire starter, a few dry twigs and a lot of blowing encouragement I managed to get a fire going. I finally had enough coals to burn some of the wood we had scrounged even though it was mostly wet. Alec took a turn at coaxing it into a nice blaze and the shelter developed a certain coziness that it wouldn't otherwise have had.

Camaraderie in a shelter is an original experience, especially where the group is small. The occupants subconsciously realize that they are unlikely to ever see one another again. In fact, first names only are usually customary for an introduction. Little by little each person's life style begins to surface. His aspirations, current problems and plans for the future gradually come forth, sometimes voluntarily, sometimes with a bit of gentle probing from others. There is an innate curiosity involved and there is also a keen desire to know, more or less, who you are bunking down with for the night. And, of course, there are a goodly number of stories that get told, many of them interesting and useful.

Alec was a personable 21 year old just graduated from a junior college in Orlando. He had had a number of colorful part-time and summer jobs for his age. Among them was a summer spent with an eighty year old trapper in the Florida Everglades. He had actually been bitten by water moccasins several times that summer. His mentor had been bitten so many times that his system had built up an immunity to snake venom. Alec played guitar, sax and a 'little keyboard' with a band. He wanted to become a music teacher.

Alec had a bear story of his own to tell:

"When I first tried backpacking in the Smokies last year I stopped in the trail to cook myself some stew for lunch. Pretty soon I saw a little bear cub heading my way with a view toward sharing my stew. I thought, 'Gee, that's a cute little fellow,' and then it dawned on me that where there was a cub around there had to be a big old mama bear somewhere close by. I grabbed the stew and held the cooking tin in my teeth. Then I headed for the nearest tree as fast as I could. I shinied up the tree to a lower branch just in time to see mama bear come lumbering out of the woods.

"I'd spilled a little of the stew on the way up the tree and this encouraged the cub to climb up after me. I threw down branches at him as best I could and I hollered my head off at him. The cub finally demurred. I ate the stew so as to reduce any more temptation. The mama bear shook the tree. She didn't climb up it, though, and finally, after hanging around for a couple of hours, she gave it up. She went off down the trail taking the disappointed cub with her."

Another bear story followed from Ron. He and a large group had been spending the night in a Smokies shelter. He had been sleeping on an upper bunk when he was awakened early in the morning by the sound of a pan being used. He looked down to find a clever sow bear cleaning last night's dishes. She was working on the remnants of somebody's beef stroganoff when Ron shouted for everybody to wake up. The bear must have somehow reached up with her paw and unfastened the chain that held the U bolt in place. Either that or someone had forgotten to refasten it when he had gone out in the middle of the night to answer the call of nature. She had apparently pushed the U bolt up and then opened the door to let herself in.

Amidst the pandemonium the bear took off. She stopped dead in her tracks, though, after going about twenty feet. It was as though a light bulb had suddenly switched on in her brain. She came back, grabbed the tin dish with the remains of the stroganoff in her teeth and trotted off carrying her prize in front of her.

Matt was a likeable young man from a town in Illinois. He was quiet, smoked a pipe and he and Alec had taken up hiking together. Apparently he had just finished a hitch in the Marines and now he was at a crossroads in life trying to decide what sort of a career to follow.

Both Alec and Matt had acquired their gear at an Army surplus store. Everything was olive green. They both looked like combat soldiers but it was a practical and economical way to get outfitted. Alec's boots were jungle combat boots. They had three small holes near the soles on each side. This let the water in when he walked through puddles and streams but it also quickly let it back out again. He seemed to be pleased with the arrangement. They both dried their boots out each night by the side of the fire.

Ron produced another story about a shelter experience he had had with a group of exuberant teenagers who had been celebrating their high school graduation with a walk through the Smokies. There had been much talk about 'Poison Rocks'.

It was not until it became time for everyone to retire that he had discovered the significance of the term 'Poison Rocks'. One of the boys had sprinkled kernels of sugar crisp cereal on the floor of the shelter. They had then stationed themselves on the end of their upper bunks and all lights had been extinguished. After several minutes had passed one of the boys shouted, 'Now!' Flashlights had been quickly switched on and down on the floor below them the shelter's mice population were busy scooping up on a windfall that would prove to be their downfall. Each of the boys had gathered a collection of large rocks that soon rained down on the mice eliminating as many of the little rodents as possible. "Poison Rocks!"

Derrick Knob to Spence Field to Cades Cove. 11.0 Miles.

After a pleasant night with congenial people at Derrick Knob shelter Boonie and I made an 8:00 o'clock start. It was cloudy and eerie with a light drizzle coming down but as the day wore on this changed to welcome sunshine. There were some steep climbs and descents, especially Thunderhead Mtn. on the top of which we had our lunch. Sadly Boonie developed a knee problem which made her progress downhill painful and difficult.

The A. T. blazes here on this section of the trail were more prevalent and the junction trails were well marked. The balds were a nice change, although we worried about being exposed to lightning when we crossed them. The worrisome accompaniment of thunder could be heard nearby.

The trail down to Cades Cove from off of the A. T. was a pleasant five miles, through heavier forest and partly near a rushing stream. Angie was waiting for us along with Duffy and Beauregard. She had a welcome quart of Hagen Daaz ice cream for Boonie and a couple of Dos Equis beers for me.

Newfound Gap to Peck's Corner. 11.2 Miles.

At 7:45 a.m. I left Newfound Gap in the cloud and mist that give the Smokies their name. Boonie wasn't able to make this hike with me as originally planned because of her knee. Beauregard might bother the bears. It looked like it would be another solo campout with a longer than usual second day of hiking over high peaks. To make it more interesting a sporting goods salesman had said that he had been told that Peck's Corner shelter had been closed due to bear activity.

After I hit the trail and after Angie had left with the Blazer so that the dye was cast, any apprehension I had had lifted completely and I immediately began to enjoy the walk.

To make better time I had brought the small pack and lightened up considerably. My cooking utensils were only a spoon and a sierra cup, both carefully bent to fit inside the one small pot that also included the MRG gas stove. I took the small Sigma gas bottle, no water filter and no water carrier other than the small canteen. The ultra-light self-inflatable mattress I replaced with a lighter ridge-foam pad. The rest was just first aid and minimum survival things with a change of dry clothes. Food was 4 sandwiches, some brownies, oat meal and cocoa packets and a freeze dried pack of 'teriyaki chicken and rice'. The piece de resistance was a spinach-mousse stuffed chicken breast left over from dinner the night before.

The other big luxuries that I carried were a couple of

four-hour candles that fit in their wind-proof containers, the small fluorescent light with a change of AA batteries, some crosswords and a Words for the Wild Sierra Club Trailside Reader. All of this was in case I couldn't sleep as in the past with solo campouts. It was a pleasure to swing along with the lighter pack.

Then the sun started to come out. I couldn't believe it. In all of the time that I had spent in the Smokies thus far I had rarely seen it shine through, especially up on the crest where the A.T. runs.

When I approached the Icewater Spring shelter the sound of voices indicated that it was occupied. It was only 9:15 in the morning and I was making good time so I didn't feel like stopping. Just beyond the shelter the trail rounded a bend and as I passed by I noticed a bear only 15 feet away. He was munching on a bush. He looked disgusted somehow. He looked at me and I looked at him and we both went on with our business. This I was to learn was the famous Icewater Spring bear himself.

After another half a mile up the trail I met a young Englishman who had been out on an early morning sortie with his camera. He had spent the night at this shelter. He said that this bear had earlier that morning tried to drop in on them. He had rattled the gate, broke something off it and then he had actually climbed up it like a cat. What he had in mind apparently was to winkle in over the top. I learned later that night that David, another occupant, had hit him on the snout with his walking stick. Discouraged, the bear had left and he began taking out his frustration by savagely attacking a nearby bush for breakfast, "Oh well,...(savage bite)...if that's the way it is...(mighty chewing)...I'll just have to eat this crummy bush...(shake of the head)."

Later I learned from another hiker up the trail that this same bear had performed his routine the morning before. This time a girl hiker inside had snapped his picture as he was standing up against the chain link fence trying to check the contents of the shelter. When he had heard the shutter click he had then spit at her, "Listen...(splat)...no pay,...(splat),...no foto!...(splat, splat)"

It occurred to me that ol' Icewater Spring bear might be in for a relocation jaunt if he doesn't clean up his act before long.

Farther along I met a couple who had spent the night at Tri-Corner shelter and then two others who had been at Peck's Corner shelter. No one else was on the trail.

The sun was warm and the rhododendrons were out in full bloom. Lunch was the piece of Angie's spinach-mousse-stuffed-chicken-breast and a couple of brownies. I felt like I was really roughing it! I reached Peck's Corner for 2:00 o'clock. It was a fine shelter. The gate wasn't too secure but a clean spring was located just below it. I spent an hour gathering wood for a fire but everything that I found was wet. I figured that maybe it would dry out enough for the next occupant if I couldn't get it to burn myself.

By four o'clock it looked like it would be another solo campout. Then three hikers came down the trail. One of them was the young Englishman, Ian, that I had met on the trail up near Icewater Spring. The other man, Art, was a good bit older. He had hiked all over the Smokies for many years. He had first camped out at this same shelter 44 years ago when it had then been made out of logs. He was a Psychology professor from Cincinnati. He had been legally blind since his teens and yet he hiked and camped out without letting his handicap become a problem for him. He was a remarkable man.

The other hiker who was travelling with Art introduced himself as David. He was a younger man, a computer programmer from the same university. He was an experienced backpacker, too, and had been hiking in different parts of the Smokies before as well.

Dinner was not a huge success because I forgot to stir the contents of the foil packet of chicken teriyaki. The rice was bland and then when I got down to the teriyaki part it was soy sauce salty. It was filling, though, and that was the main thing.

I had a peaceful night. I went to bed at 9:30 p.m. and I slept like a baby! I figured that I was at last getting adjusted to life in a Smokies shelter or maybe it was because I had the others for company. Perhaps this is just something that everyone goes through. I remember talking with a friend of mine who had hiked the whole trail, he had put it together in sections, and he told me that it used to take him about three days before he could get to sleeping soundly when he was camping out each night. He had done most of it alone, too.

The National Park reservation system, at 615-436-1231, had said that there would be eleven people for Peck's Corner that night. I don't know what had happened to the others but people's plans change and I guess they had forgotten to call. I had called about my own cancellation for Boonie but the park service didn't seem to really know who was up there anyway at the time. I don't think that the shelters are overcrowded very often. Art had said that they never were.

Peck's Corner to Cosby Campground. 14.5 Miles.

My 5:30 a.m. breakfast was not a success because the stove had become clogged and it refused to pump fuel. I ate my oatmeal and cocoa with cold water. No coffee. Belly full, though. I was off at 6:30 a.m., before the others were up.

A friendly doe was on the trail. She was by herself and she let me get to within ten feet of her before she moved off.

The slog up Mt. Chapman was well graded. It was a beautiful sunny day. What a treat it was to walk the ridge crests and to enjoy vistas on both sides. There were rhododendrons blooming everywhere, even some flame azaleas.

At Tri-Corner Knob shelter I drank the canteen water that I had boiled the night before. It helped to get rid of the taste of cold cocoa that had been hanging in my mouth. I refilled the canteen from the nearby spring but when I reached a nicer spring up on Guyot Mtn. I figured that it had had less chance of contamination from feral animals or shelter occupants. I emptied it and refilled it again.

At noon I reached Snake's Den Mtn. and the trail down to Cosby. I had been startled to see a piece of wreckage from a light plane just off of the trail. I don't know the story but somebody must have perished in it. I met another hiker, Jerry, who had hiked most of the A.T. eleven years ago. We had a long conversation.

Lunch was under a big tree and it was a welcome relief to sit down after five and a half hours of steady going. With only 5.3 more miles to go I polished off the two remaining sandwiches.

At 3:15 p.m. I pulled into Cosby. I was tired but I was two hours ahead of schedule. There was a beartrap on wheels nearby. It was empty and not baited. Then, happily, Angie and Boonie arrived early, along with the Dos Equis. They had brought chairs for a long wait. 'Oh, ye of little faith...'.

By then I was through hiking all of the Smokies except for one little 2.4 mile stretch between Russell Field and Spence Field. It would have been too much to have done it with Boonie's bad knee so we had taken the shorter Bote Mtn. and Anthony Creek trails to Cades Cove. It was the only piece I'd missed from Springer to Roan Mtn. at the time and I was determined to hike it.

Cades Cove to Spence Field to Russell Field & back to Cades Cove. 12.9 Miles.

The final piece of the Smokies A. T. jigsaw puzzle was about to be put into place. I left Cade's Cove at 8:17 a.m. and did the five miles up to the A. T. with its missing 2.4 miles of the puzzle still remaining.

On the way up I saw a little skunk. He was busy about something by the edge of the trail. We didn't see one another until the last moment. He puffed up, raised his tail but didn't cut loose, fortunately. He was a fiesty little devil.

Robin Hood's Bay, Coast to Coast Walk, England.

Roman Bridge Across the Rio Cares, Footpath to Bulnes.

After Eight Days in the Bush, Overland Track, Tasmania.

Feeding The Wallabies, South End of Overland Track.

Kea Looking for Socks to Steal, Routeburn Track, N.Z.

Seagull Riding the Thermals, Way of the Gull, Isle of Man.

Scottish Cattle in Their Fur Coats.

A Gentle Valley Near Rannoch Moor, West Highland Way.

Beginning of the Monteverde Cloud Forest, Costa Rica.

Sierra Bernia Range in the Distance, So. Spain

Bagpipes at an Agricultural Show, Scotland.

The View from Castell de Castells, Sierra Bernia.

Along The Military Road, West Highland Way, Scotland.

Overlook from The Tunnel at Sierra Bernia, Spain.

Ballaglas Glen, Isle of Man

Claude Bushwhacker and Friends, Tchoutacabouffa River.

It started to rain hard shortly after setting out. There was much rumbling with flashes of lightning. I figured that I was too small a target down among the big trees but I hoped it would let up before getting to the top where I knew I would be exposed. One bolt did crash down into the canyon where I was sloshing along. It was a bit unnerving but I was keen to finish the Smokies that day.

Up on top I rejoined the A. T. again and then dropped on down to Spence Field shelter to dry out for a bit. Two teenagers were there. They were just finishing breakfast at 11:30 a.m. They had been told that the shelter would be full but no one else had joined them that night. More no-shows I guess. They were worried about going on to Siler's Bald without rain gear. I suggested that they just hike wet and then change into dry clothes when they got there. If they were still cold they could get into their sleeping bags and warm up. It was a bit late for Siler's Bald, though. I encouraged them to stop at Derrick's Knob, only 6 miles away.

On the way to Russell Field I saw two other parties, one with two men on the other side of middleage, the other with three companions, also about the same vintage. I saw no one else all day.

At Russell Field shelter I stopped for lunch. I took one last look at the Smokies A. T. I had become quite fond of it by then, even proprietary about it. Then I headed down the Cades Cove trail nearby. It was the same trail that I had bailed out on last year. I could remember its idiosyncracies all the way down.

A two foot green snake was crossing the trail and I almost stepped on him. I watched him for a bit. I figured that he must have a hard time making a living at that altitude. Farther on down I had a bad slip on a wet rock just as I came to a pretty stream. My right leg crumpled under me and I couldn't wait to see if everything was working all right. When I launched myself back upright with the help of the walking stick everything was functioning okay, though, much to my relief.

At 3:15 p.m. I pulled into the picnic ground at Cades Cove. It started raining again. I huddled under the Park Info sign beneath my poncho to wait for Angie. I didn't mind. It was a good feeling to know that I had now hiked all of the A. T. across the Smokies. It had taken 110 miles of walking to do the 68.6 miles of the A. T. as it turned out but I had been able to experience all of it and that was what I had hoped to do.

In retrospect I was glad that I did jigsaw piece the Smokies together the way that it worked out. The access trails were very interesting and worthwhile in themselves. I would have missed them if I had just hiked straight across. Once you get up to elevation the A. T. trail is fairly easy walking. To go from Fontana to Davenport Gap without pushing too much is about a matter of six days and five shelter nights, seven days if you take it easier.

Even though you self-register at Fontana Dam or any Park Ranger Station, which you have to do anyway, and even though there are supposed to be three spaces left open for A. T. thru-hikers, and even though the chances are remote that a shelter will be filled up at any given time, it is a good idea to call the 615-436-1231 reservation number for a slot in the shelter. In any event you need to have the self-registry tag with you to be sure to avoid the possibility of a fine. The fine is nominal, though, and I never did see anyone from the Park Service out checking tags anywhere. If a schedule changes for some reason or another and a shelter is actually filled there is always extra room on the floor and rangers and fellow-hikers are all sympathetic and understanding creatures anyway.

Another conclusion I have reached is that the Smokies black bear is really not a threat to hikers. There are some bears that may become interested in your food if given the opportunity and, like any other wild animal or threatened individual, they are capable of responding if they feel provoked or if cubs are involved. Most hikers never even get a chance to see one, though. The bears seem to prefer early morning and evening for their foraging activity. During the day they tend to hole up somewhere which is the period when most people are actually out on the trail. They dislike loud noise. I carry a sharp whistle for peace of mind myself, even though I have never had occasion to use it. A camp pot and a spoon banged together are supposed to be anathema for loitering bears, too, if they become a nuisance.

If you meet a bear on the trail I think that the thing to do is to just keep on walking past if the bear is off of the trail, which is what I have been doing. If he is on the trail using it himself then my plan has always been to just step off of it and get out of his way. When there are cubs around a good sprint down the trail seems to be acceptable. It was in two instances that I know about anyway. There is no way that you can outrun a mama bear but it establishes a proper spirit of territorial respect straightaway.

The big problem with bears seems to be food, including toothpaste or cosmetics, or anything that might be worth investigating in the edible department. Getting fed is the most important part of a bear's day. It seems to be a good idea to keep anything in the pack like that sealed in ziplock bags or a plastic container. And the other old admonition is to prepare your food in the shelter and leave it and your pack on the inside at night or when you need to go outside during your stay. When you camp outside of a Smokies shelter or on the A. T., of course, it is recommended that a pack or foodbag should be strung between two trees so that it is at least eight feet from the ground and eight feet away from both trees. A long overhanging branch will do, though, if you can get the pack far enough away from the tree trunk.

My favorite bear story was a news clipping about a party who had spread their lunch out on a Smokies campground picnic table, complete with plates and utensils and all of the trimmings. An enterprising old bear waited until everything was ready and then he sauntered on over. He climbed up on the bench, sat down and polished off the entire lunch for himself.

I think that the amount of rain that I experienced in the Smokies was unusually excessive. The annual rainfall is often over 90 inches, though, and the higher the elevation and the colder the temperatures the more likely it is for there to be a larger amount of precipitation. The A. T. crosses right across the top, of course, so it is probable that there will always be a certain amount of rainfall and it is best to be prepared for it.

Finally, it would be better to hike the Smokies in company with someone else but in the late spring or summer months chances are good that there will be company in the shelters if you go solo and this, I found, lends a lot to the adventure.

Maps & Guides.

The best maps for the A.T. across the Smokies can be obtained as noted in WALK V. Contact:

The Appalachian Trail Conference
P. O. Box 807
Harper's Ferry, W. VA. 25424

Or by telephone: (304) 535-6331

In addition, an interesting dimensional map that helps to put the trail in overall perspective without as much detail can be purchased in souvenir stores in the area. It is called Tourist Guide to the Heart of the Smokies. It can be ordered from:

Vacationland Maps
P.O. Box 3310
Knoxville, Tenn. 37917

Or by telephone: (615) 687-0933

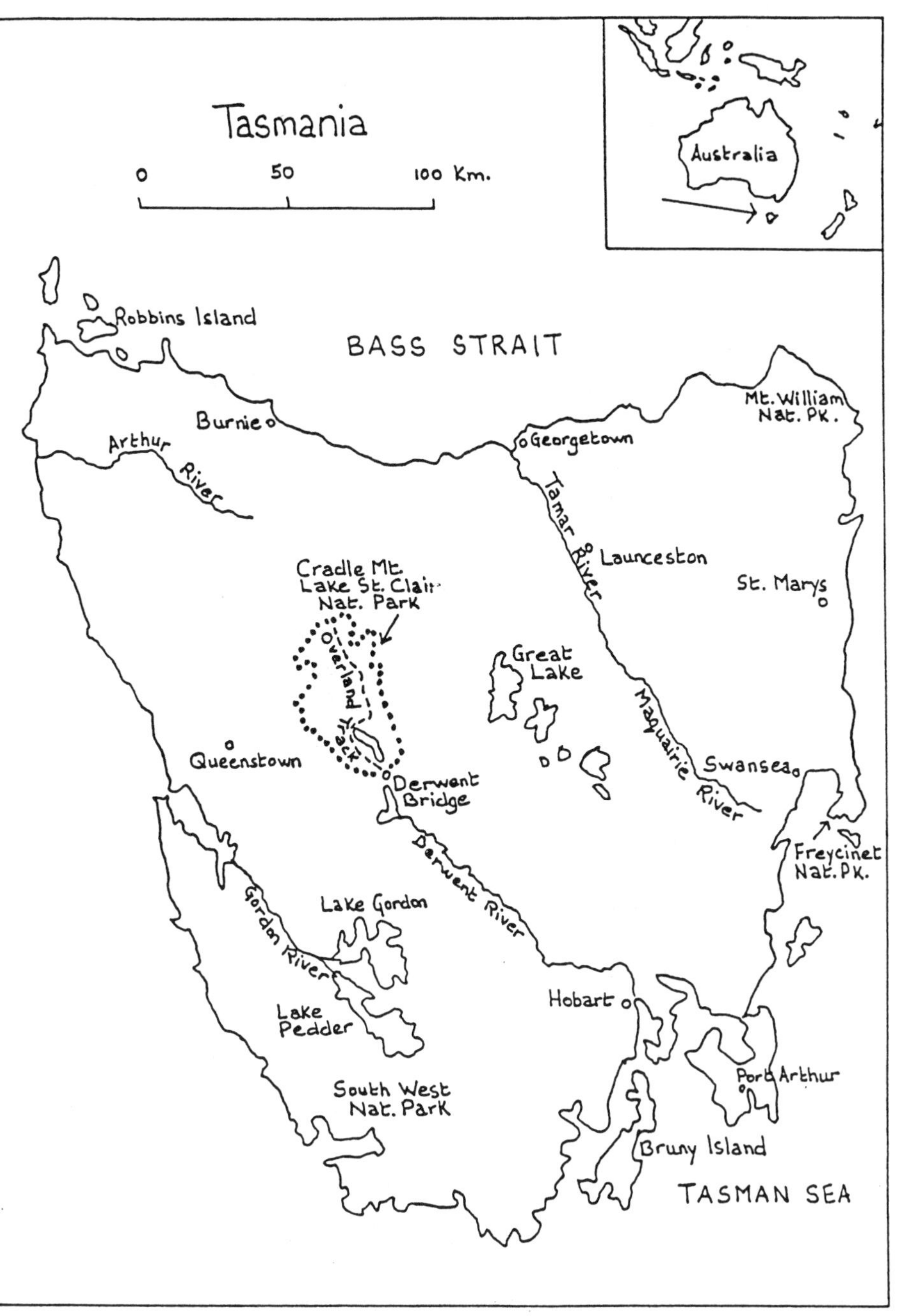
Tasmania
0
50
100 Km.
Australia
Robbins Island
BASS STRAIT
Burnie
Arthur River
Georgetown
Mt. William Nat. Pk.
Tamar River
Launceston
St. Marys
Cradle Mt. Lake St. Clair Nat. Park
Overland Track
Great Lake
Maquairie River
Swansea
Queenstown
Derwent Bridge
Freycinet Nat. Pk.
Derwent River
Gordon River
Lake Gordon
Lake Pedder
Hobart
Port Arthur
South West Nat. Park
Bruny Island
TASMAN SEA

WALK XV

XV. The Overland Track of Tasmania.

Hobart is similar to the San Francisco Bay area as it used to be many years ago when I grew up there. It has rolling hills with nice views of the protected bay, eucalyptus trees, an interesting waterfront with fresh fish for sale and friendly, easy-going people. No one seems to be in a hurry.

Angie and I found a flat to rent in the old Battery Point section where the Victorian style homes are protected by the city. The affable landlord didn't bother to take our name or address, a credit card, or the rent. When we were ready to leave I called his home and his wife said that he had gone to his 'lawn bowls' game so we should just leave the rent under a plate on the kitchen table, which we did.

The city was neat and tidy, the homes were unpretentious but comfortable and well-cared for, it had its share of tall buildings and a long mall stretched down the center of town with lots of shops tucked inside. A grand flea market was held on a Saturday with quality items of interest and the Royal Australian (Tasmanian) Navy Band put on a memorable performance nearby. A large Sheraton Hotel overlooked the waterfront. It was the only one of the customary chains that was represented there. Hobart was delightful.

Overland /Cuvier Valley Track. About 6 Miles.

On the drive out from Hobart to the south end of The Overland Track we noticed a sure enough Tasmanian Devil that had been run over by a car. We stopped to view his remains. He was a cute little fellow in an ugly sort of way. He was about the size of a possum with black fur that had a touch of white running across his chest. He had awesome teeth that were very businesslike for his size. It was easy to see why bones were not a problem. Cars, yes. They are primarily night foragers, carnivorous scavengers, and working the highways can sometimes be a perilous business for them. Tasmanian Devils are really not so fierce. They are actually shy creatures and they can be made into pets.

We found lodging at a bush type lodge at Derwent Bridge, roughly in the center of Tasmania, and then went out to walk some of the south end of the Overland Track. This track is about 50 miles long and it crosses the Cradle Mountain/Lake St. Clair National Park.

In the parking area at Lake St. Clair a group of Wallabies were busy working visitors for handouts. With their soulful eyes and long lashes it was impossible to resist them. We were cautioned not to feed them bread as this led to an unhealthy condition known as 'lumpy jaw'.

At the ranger's office we signed in as required. We were told that if we didn't come out on schedule they would come looking for us. Each evening the license plates in the parking area were checked against the register for the day. Once again I was impressed by an attitude of benevolent concern that was similar to the National Park Service in New Zealand.

The track led out from Cynthia Bay at the ranger station. There was also a speedboat ferry service of sorts that made a run down to the other end of the lake, about 9 miles. Originally we had intended to take advantage of this and to do a hike back. Unfortunately the ferry runs at 9:00 a.m. and 3:00 p.m. and our trip out from Hobart didn't give us enough time to make the early ferry.

The park is a huge wilderness area without roads of any kind. There were two choices of footpaths to take, both of them wound up at the ferry landing at the other end of the lake where the Overland Track then continued on its way. One track bordered the lake for about 9 miles and the other was a diversion called the Cuvier Valley Track. It followed along the

Cuvier river to Lake Petrarch and then up to a gap between Mount Byron at 4100 ft. and Mt. Olympus at 4400 ft. This looked to be a hostile and steep mountain range that would be difficult to cross without a trail.

We walked up the Cuvier Valley track for a while. The chalked-in weather report at the ranger station warned of a possible rapid change to rain and sleet and NW gusty winds. It was cold already and the clouds looked foreboding. Still, though, it was easy walking on a good path and there was no rain.

The first part of the footpath was a nature walk with identification signs along the way. Huge eucalyptus trees predominated in the forest, some of them dead and weathered, killed by a fire ten years previously. They were so large that it was possible to stand upright inside the hollow of the trunk of one beside the track. Angie was intrigued by the range of colors they contained.

The track branched off twice to alternate paths just before it came to a generous stream of clear water. It was a spot where two streams joined and a footbridge crossed just below the junction. A sign aptly labelled it 'Watersmeet'.

The trail forked again for the Overland Track, one route followed along the edge of the lake and the other option continued on up the Cuvier Valley. We chose the latter. The path began to narrow. It was still well-marked, though, with yellow plastic symbols every so often. The bush opened up after a while and the floor became more and more spongy-peatlike with occasional bogs. This alternated between dirt and rocks. The ridgeline of Mt. Olympus could be seen in the distance off to the right.

Birds were everywhere. Some of them were huge black crows and some were dove-like. We saw Wallaby signs frequently. Their mates at the parking area had been rescued by the park staff when they had been found in trouble and become tame. These were shy and they kept out of sight.

Unlike New Zealand snakes are indigenous to Tasmania

and four species are considered poisonous but we didn't see any on our walks in the Cradle Mountain/Lake St. Clair National Park, only later in the sand dunes along the east coast when we were beachcombing.

Down the Track came four weary backpackers. They said that they had been on the Overland Track for nine days, eight of them walking days and the other a weather-bound day. They were up in years a bit and they were looking forward to a touch of civilization.

We went down to the stream that coursed along the valley to find a good lunch spot under a tree. The bush there had a completely different character from any other type of terrain we had seen. After lunch we backtracked to return to the lake fork.

At the fork we followed the Overland Track around the other side of the Mt. Olympus range. The trail there was hard earth in between more of the big eucalyptus trees. It bordered Lake St. Clair. The lake was inviting and it had a number of sandy beaches along the shoreline. We walked the track for a while and then we went back the way we had come.

After returning to the parking area we became acquainted with the young daughter of the lady in the ranger's office. She had been raising a baby Wallaby that had lost its mother. It was a touching sight to see her holding it affectionately because we knew that the family was being transferred the next week and the little fellow was going to be left behind.

That night at dinner in the lodge we were again impressed by how friendly and considerate Tasmanian Aussies were. Somehow one gets a different impression from the outback concept that filters through to America. As much as they seem to deny it their heritage stems from England and Scotland and the place names and surnames are all familiar. Tasmania seems to be an extension of Britain in an early California setting, before my native State became so popular with the rest of the migrating world. Here is the best of both worlds but with its problem of being so distant from anywhere else.

Crater Lake & The Northern End of the Overland Track. 5 Miles.

We arrived at Cradle Mountain Lodge in the early afternoon. We were assigned a Scandinavian-like cabin with a wood-burning stove-type fireplace and facilities that included a kitchen, a generous bathroom, a queen-sized bed and a triple-decker bunk arrangement in a spacious room. Chopped firewood was right outside the door along with an axe for making little ones out of big ones.

We had time to work in a good walk in brilliant sunshine. Cradle Mtn. itself could readily be seen in the distance and hiking up it was entered in the program for future walks to do. At around 4700 feet it would be possible to make it to the top and back in a single day's walk. A number of other interesting walks had been carved out in the area and we chose the northern end of the Overland Track with a detour up through Crater Lake.

The start for the Overland Track was at the car park at Waldheim. The usual contingent of Wallabies were gathered together looking for a handout from a sympathetic visitor. The path led down steps and across a long boardwalk over grassy tundra that probably becomes soggy when wet. It was dry when we crossed it, although a babbling brook wound down the center of the valley itself.

We were startled to see a helicopter come whizzing by overhead with a load of trail building lumber dangling beneath it. This helicopter made repeated sorties during the course of our walk that afternoon. It was obvious that it had replaced the packhorse and that upgrading was being done to a section of the trail up the line somewhere.

We branched off from the Overland Track on the other side of the valley to take the Crater Lake path that would then rejoin the Overland up at Wombat peak. The path up to Crater Lake and along the lake itself was one of the most delightful walks I have ever experienced. It cut into a little glen that was well-forested and climbed beside a clear stream that flowed from the outlet end of the lake. The path had been boarded for much of the way with steps and rails and even a bench had been positioned here and there.

The highlight of the section was Crater Falls, an intimate little cascade with steps that led down to the pool below the falls. After climbing up beyond the falls on some rocky but stepped track in the rough parts we next discovered Crater Lake itself. Here was a jewel of a lake that was completely surrounded by towering rock walls. An old boat shed, weathered and empty, graced the exit shore. It was the only building.

The track then worked its way up and out of the basin on a rocky trail that was in the process of being improved. Up on top of the basin the trail then rejoined the Overland Track. It overlooked Cradle Valley below and off to the east Lake Dove and the distant ranges beyond. The country here is more open and less forested. It seems hospitable but the usual warning sign about taking warm clothing in case of a sudden change in the weather had been posted at the car park.

Behind us we could see a steep scramble on up to a ridge called Marion's Lookout. Several people were up there at the time and I envied them for the fabulous views they must have had. The track beyond followed the ridge in what seemed to be a more gradual ascent as it worked its way along the base of Cradle Mtn. itself. Reluctantly we returned to the car park.

That night we enjoyed a good meal at the lodge in the company of an American couple on a research grant in Melbourne and an Aussie businessman and his wife from Sydney. Aussie's have more vacation time built into their worklife than anyone else in the world. They get 4 weeks and 10 paid holidays a year plus 3 weeks of paid sick leave that accumulates whether you take it or not. Every 10 years you get four months of paid vacation and when you retire all of the unused sick leave that has accumulated is collectible. The original rationale was that Australia is so far away from any place else that the extra time is necessary for a meaningful vacation. John said that he never knew for sure which of his 20 employees would show up for work on a Monday morning.

After dinner we were able to watch the wildlife come out of the bush after sunset to feed on scraps furnished by the lodge. Australian possums were so friendly that they would come right up to be petted and fed on the balcony overlooking the feeding platforms. A Tasmanian devil joined the group, too. He was more shy than the possums and he was only interested in the leg of lamb that was hanging next to the fruit and vegies that were so popular with the others.

Tasmanian Devils are now extinct in the rest of Australia although they seem to be plentiful in Tasmania. They live less than eight years and they are carnivorous enough to clean up the dead remains of other animals. In this way they provide a useful service in spite of their fierce appearance. We noticed a number of them on the highway where they had been hit by cars.

Cradle Mtn. Huts out of Launceston has a guided walk for the Overland Track. They have four huts at different spots along the track. One walk is the six day Overland Track route with the ferry trip down Lake St. Clair at the other end. The other is a three day Cradle Mtn. walk with the option of hiking up Barn Bluff, another peak, on the second day.

The Overland Track this way is about 40 miles all told with 5 days of walks of around 8 to 12 miles and a rest day. Meals, hot showers and beds are provided in separate rooms. You carry your own sleeping bag and personal goods and the group is limited to a party of ten.

The address for these walks is:

Cradle Huts Pty. Ltd.
22 Brisbane St. or P.O. Box 1879
Launceston, Tasmania 7250
Australia
Phone: (003) 31 2006; Int'l. 6103

To obtain maps of Cradle Mtn. day walks or Lake St. Clair or an overall map of the National Park itself write to:

Director of Mapping
G.P.O. Box 44A
Hobart, Tasmania 7001
Australia

The maps are readily available at any bookstore in Hobart, Launceston or elsewhere in Tasmania.

To call Cradle Mtn. Lodge ring: (Int'l code: 6103) (003) 63 5164. (Check with the international operator to get the proper time and day sorted out first).

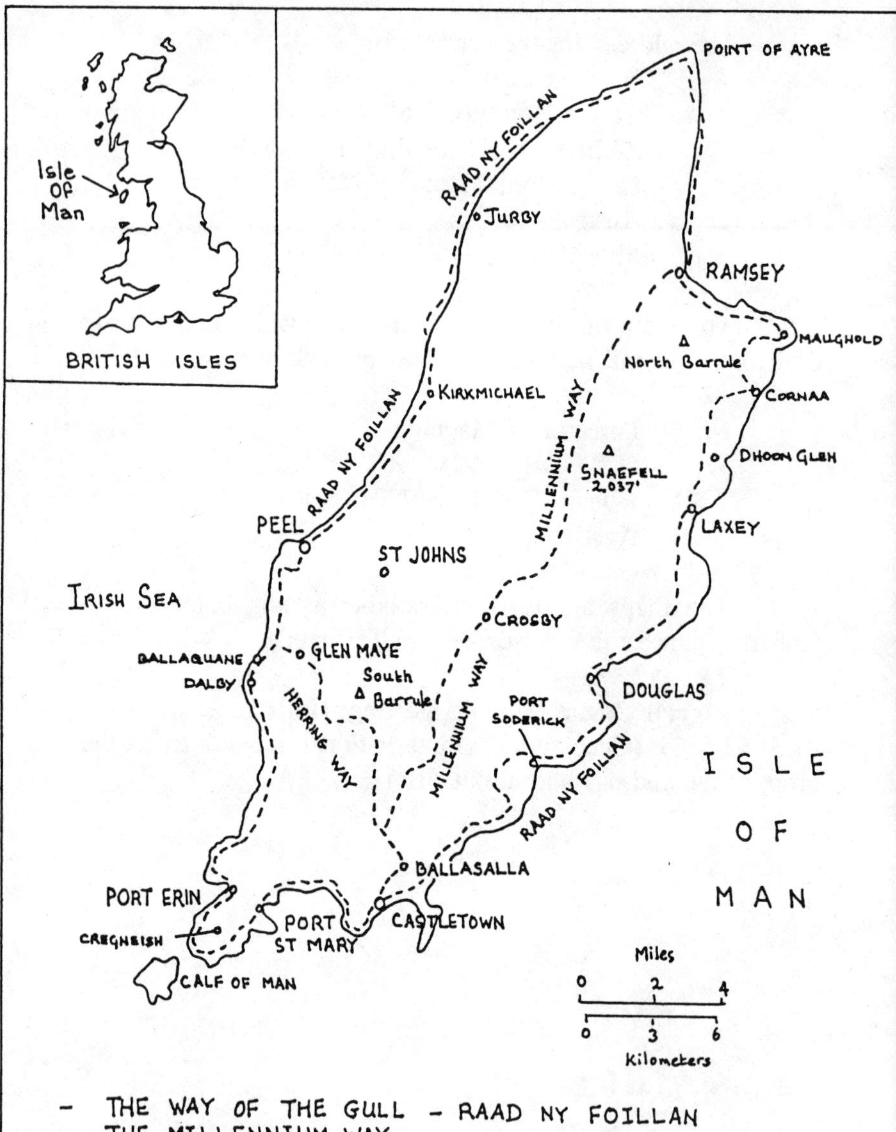

- THE WAY OF THE GULL - RAAD NY FOILLAN
- THE MILLENNIUM WAY
- HERRING WAY

WALK XVI

XVI. The Raad Ny Foillan of The Isle of Man

(96 Miles)

'Raad ny Foillan' is the Manx name for the long-distance footpath around the coastline of the Isle of Man. It means 'The Way of the Gull'. It is appropriately named because part of the pleasure in doing this walk is the accompaniment of seagulls for much of the way. It crosses precipitous cliffs overlooking the sea far below, mountain moors, interesting glens with cascading waterfalls, pleasant little villages with Victorian traditions and long stretches of beaches and dunes in the northern end of the island.

The Isle of Man is located in the Irish Sea between England and Ireland and in good weather it is possible to see either one of them far out on the horizon. Its principal city is Douglas which has a charm all of its own. Here is a tiny slice of an English lifestyle that is reminiscent of a bygone era. The ancient little Edwardian hotels, now Bed & Breakfast inns, stretch for almost two miles along the curving Promenade Street that borders a long beach; horse-drawn trams clip-clop their way along the wide avenue; thousands of decorative light bulbs lend a festive air at night; and the well-behaved holiday-makers on a low-budget vacation rub shoulders with members of the international financial community, the fishermen and farmers and escapees from the mainland who live there.

My daughter found herself living on the Isle of Man for a good while. Our frequent visits to her led to our intimate association with the island. For some ten years the English tourist had been steadily deserting what was once a prosperous resort. The reason for this was the increased popularity of the package tour to the shores of the sunny Mediterranean where wall to wall bodies and topless sunbathers became more appealing. More recently, though, the island is gradually becoming rediscovered, enough to encourage interesting events throughout the summer and better facilities for visitors. It is a picture post card collection of neat farms, tidy lanes, quaint villages and steam train transportation and it offers a variety of things to do without the usual herd of summer vacationers that are so often encountered elsewhere in the U.K.

There are many good walks on the island but the three best known are: the Raad ny Foillan, the Gulls Way, 96 miles around the coast; the Herring Way, 14 miles across the south end of the island; and the Millennium Way, 23 miles down the center and over the highest peak, Snaefell, at 2,037 ft.

The Beginning of The Raad ny Foillan and The Herring Way.

42 Miles.

Dalby. 6 Miles.

My daughter and her husband had painstakingly renovated a Manx cottage over on the southwest side of the island. This charming little house nestled down beside a country lane. It was surrounded by pastures with a magnificent view of the sea from each window. It was only natural that we should start our first walk from there.

Kit and Tim, Angie and I and their two pugs and cocker spaniel set forth from the cottage toward the south. I found the footpath well used for the most part, as it led through grass and gorse along the bluffs high above the sea. The seagulls soared and the dramatic coastline stretched before us. Far below we could see the waves crashing against the rocks.

As we worked our way on up to the slopes above we passed into sheep territory where close-cropped grazing and sheep trails obliterated the regular trail. Located strategically, though, was the beckoning signpost of the walk itself with its distinctive seagull pointing the way and its strange Manx name, Raad Ny Foillan. The route emptied out onto a country lane that wound its way back to the cottage.

Reflecting in front of a cozy fire at Ballaquane Cottage I knew that I would like to do more of The Gull's Way. The next day I discovered a very interesting and helpful guide for the three footpaths at a newsstand in the pedestrian mall in Douglas. I also acquired a detailed map of the Isle of Man at the same time. These make the walks much easier and they are listed at the end of the chapter.

Port St. Mary to Port Erin. 8 Miles.

The best months for planning a trip to the Isle of Man in so far as sunshine and lack of recorded rainfall are concerned are May and June, then July and April and then August. The other months tend to be a bit wet although we have been there twice in September when we experienced a solid week of sunshine both times.

The well-known Tourist Trophy Motorcycle Races occur in late May-early June for about two weeks. Accommodations become fully booked then and crossing the road becomes an adventure not to be taken lightly. The course uses most of the principal roads around the island and bikers come banking around the curves, sometimes practicing, sometimes racing, at speeds rarely less than a hundred miles an hour, even in wet weather. Bikers from all over Europe attend.

In early September car rallies are held but these are less hectic and the old cars from another era are fun to watch as they parade sedately by. In between these two events the island reverts to its customary tranquility but other activities are usually scheduled as well during the summer months. During our most recent visit the International Folk Dancing and Music Festival was in full swing. New plays often try out in Douglas before they get polished for London, too. They are produced in a jewel of an old Victorian theater with superb acoustics and elaborate decor.

For the walk from Port St. Mary we left one car at Port Erin. The other we left at a favorite potter's studio on the seashore at Gansey Bay where we began our walk. We rounded Gansey Point on the paved path and walked along Chapel Bay. It was interesting to note the beach-goers there with their little windbreaks on the sand. The children were as busy as ever with buckets and spades in the universal sand castle construction business. No topless bathers like France, or Crete or the Med, though, Manx folks are pretty straight-laced.

Port St. Mary had a charm of its own as we walked along its streets beside the harbor. The boats were resting on the bottom as we passed. It is an event that never fails to fascinate me. The tide changes as much as 30 ft. every 6 hours and life at the seashore is an uncertain activity when sunbathing. It is even more of a chore for boat owners. Sailboats often have double keels for balancing on the bottom when the tide is out. Other boats have supports fastened to either side like knee stilts. When tied to the quay dock lines become a constant problem. Still though, it isn't necessary to row ashore, you just wait for low tide and walk.

We came to a large shallow pool that had been specially built for sailing model boats. An oldtimer was actually operating his own radio-controlled ketch. This little boat was very realistic. Its tiny inboard engine moved the rudder and it could change the position of the sails as well. Thus it was possible to go downwind, beam reach or close-hauled. With his radio controls he had the fun of sailing his own boat without all of the hard work and exposure of actually going to sea. In our conversation he wryly pointed this out to me and I was impressed with his rationalization. If only I'd known about this the 25,000 miles that I logged with Vagrant Gipsy could have been done right there on that comfortable bench instead.

Next we headed up toward 'The Chasms' as we passed

through our first 'kissing gate'. This is an iron gate that swings in an arc so that two-legged animals with smarts can pass through and four-legged animals with long-type bodies can not.

By way of illustration about Manx notions there is a bridge on the road between Douglas and the airport which is known as Fairy Bridge. According to local folklore, considered gospel, there are a bunch of real fairies who live there and it is well-known by everybody on the island that when you drive by you must wave at the fairies. Otherwise they really get pissed. Bad things can happen. But a friendly wave brings good luck. So... you find yourself waving along with everyone else in the car. You feel a little foolish maybe but better that than having those fairies bad-mouthing you.

We finally worked our way on up between stone fences with stiles and gates until we reached The Chasms. This is a dangerous area and it is important to go there only during good visibility. The path goes very near the precipice edges with a hundred foot drop to the rocks and sea below. When crossing the chasms themselves it is important to stay on the paths or be aware of where you step. Very deep fissures open up all the way to the bottom. Some of them are wide enough to be obvious and you can see down them to the sea and the rocks far below. Others are grown over with vegetation that covers the openings. It would be absolutely fatal to fall down any one of them.

The seabirds that make their nests on the face of these cliffs are varied and abundant. There are seagulls, petrels, kittiwakes, razorbills, shags, etc. It makes for a very secure place to leave one's eggs. I guess when you are a chick you learn to fly in a hurry if you wander outside of the nest. With a hundred feet before graduation it could become a crash course...

A typical old Manx village is located not far from The Chasms. It is called Cregneisch and it is preserved and operated by the Manx National Trust. Here you can see what life was like in the days before modern conveniences. The cottages are snug and cozy with thatched roofs, thick walls and large peat-burning fireplaces. Ladies dressed in traditional folk costume demonstrate spinning, weaving, quilting and life in bygone days. Here, too, are kept some of the rare Manx Loaghtan sheep. These sheep feature four horns growing out of their heads instead of two. They look a little silly but they have been looking like that since Viking days so I guess they know what they are doing.

Beyond The Chasms and Cregneisch we found a sheltered spot in the lee of a hill where we had our picnic lunch. With soft grass and plenty of sun and birds circling overhead it couldn't have been more ideal.

After lunch we worked on downhill to the Sound Cafe for a soft drink. This is an agreeable place with good sandwiches and a cozy atmosphere.

The next two miles to Port Erin were up and down but mostly easy walking with magnificent views along the coast. The path was well-marked and obvious. I suspected that this section sees more use than others. In the large bay of Port Erin a number of pleasure boats were out and about taking advantage of the sunshine. Much to my amazement a number of swimmers were paddling around in the cold water, too. A large breakwater had been built there back in 1864 by a safe maker from Liverpool named William Milner. In gratitude the townspeople erected a huge tower more or less in the shape of one of his keys on a commanding head across the bay. This tower could be seen all the way back near Dalby where we had initially started.

Port Erin held a special interest for Angie because she had vacationed there with her family as a child. She found it remarkably unchanged since then with its wide beach-curving harbor Some of the old hotels have been renovated and put on a brave new air. The same golf course that her father played on was still going strong.

We picked up the car that wc had spotted, our rental car from the island's principal rental agency, Mylchreest, and we headed back to get the other at Gansey Bay. It had been a good introduction into easy walking on the Isle of Man.

The Herring Way. 9 Miles.

The Herring Way is known as Bayr Ny Skeddan in Manx Gaelic. The language is well-preserved around the island. Most of the residences and farms have Manx names. The walk starts at the town of Peel and it follows the coast walk, The Gull's Way, for about 3 miles to the village of Glen Maye. I managed to promote another walk along this footpath with Kit and Tim, Angie and myself and 'the three pigs', Kit's doggies. We spotted a car for the return at the village of Ballasalla and we set out from the cottage which is actually designated on the map as Ballaquane.

The Herring Way is only about a mile from the cottage and when we set out the sky was overcast. We were all wearing our Gortex jackets. We left the little village of Glen Maye behind and we followed the path up a heavily forested ravine next to an inviting stream that cascaded down alongside. The signs of old abandoned mines were noticeable. They had been used to mine lead ore and the shafts had been sunk to a depth of 1,100 ft. That is a very long way down when you stop to think about it. The mines had become uneconomic in 1910.

Off to the north of the footpath is the 1,092 ft. peak called Slieau Whallian, better known as 'Witches Hill'. Those suspected of witchcraft were placed in a barrel laced with iron spikes. If they died from the roll down the hill then the hapless victims had only received what they had had coming to them. If somehow they managed to survive the trip then it proved them to be a witch and they were then burned at the stake.

After working our way on up to the top of the ridgeline we crossed a main road and then headed on down the other side. The next mile was easy to follow until we came to a road where it became necessary to get out the map. From then on the route passed through various farms and down old lanes that needed frequent orienteering. Eventually we reached the main road to Castletown. The route then coincided with the Millennium Way at that point.

Following the main road was a bit of a nightmare. We had to stay aware of traffic driving on the left and there was precious little space on the shoulders. Steep banks or stone fences climbed either side of the road. This lasted for only a short distance fortunately and then the route turned off onto a delightful path beside a stream. The path bordered a number of colorful backyard flower gardens in the traditional English style and finally we came to a stone bridge known as The Monk's Bridge.

Crossing The Monk's Bridge were a pair of sure enough monks in their traditional garb of hoods and sandals, beads and staffs, right out of medieval times. I thought that perhaps we had stumbled onto some sort of Manx monk fairies. I was about to become a believer when I was relieved to notice a movie camera rolling with a sound truck nearby. I don't know what the script was but we kept out of their way.

In Ballasalla we picked up the car near a favorite French restaurant, La Rosette, and headed for home. The walk was really only about 8 miles that were not duplicated by the Gull's Way or the Millinneum Way so I figured that was it for the Herring Way. It made for a good cross section of the island.

Douglas to Port Soderick. 6 Miles.

Incredible as it may seem there are no chain hotels or fast food chain restaurants on the Isle of Man, not even a MacDonalds or a Burger King or a Pizza Hut. No Holiday Inns and no Trust House Forte hotels either. This somehow helps to preserve the old world atmosphere of the place and it keeps the ancient hotels going.

When first we stayed at the Sefton Hotel on the main promenade in Douglas, one of the better of the larger hotels, a 'jumble sale' benefit was being held in the principal barroom. Its purpose was to raise money for the 'Home for Old Horses'. I know of no other place in the world that has a retirement home for aged horses. I bought three large cakes for the good of the cause and then I went out to the farm, which is on the way in from the airport, and my son Bret and I called over some of these old boys and we fed them the cakes. This way they doubly benefitted. One old pinto was very partial to frosting.

Another rarity on the island is its electric and steam railway system. These are vintage locomotives lovingly and pridefully restored and maintained by a dedicated group of railway buff employees. The cars are furnished in old-world upholstery with side-door compartments and up and down picture windows that recess into the doors and which are held in position by leather straps. The system takes pride in operating on schedule right down to the minute. You can set your watch as the steam whistle goes by at your particular crossing.

So I set out on the Gull's Way from Douglas on a partly cloudy afternoon with a view toward a return on the steam train at its scheduled stop at the quaint station of Port Soderick.

The initial walk across the swing bridge of the narrow estuary that serves as an inner harbor for Douglas was interesting because of the vessels that were moored there and the way that they had dealt with the tidal problem in such a confined area. Yachts and fishing vessels and barges and tugs all sat there resting on the bottom. They were ready to float back up near the high walls with their recessed ladders when the tide would once again come in to set them free.

Up above on Marine Drive it was nice to look out over the magnificent panorama of the town of Douglas stretching out along the sweeping curve of beach. A strange castle-like portal was next passed before reaching a section of the road which had partially slid into the sea far below. The route followed this former road for some 3 miles. It was a dramatic coastline of pounding surf and rocks much like the Big Sur of California. Seabirds soared on the updrafts. Out to sea could be seen three fishing boats as they plied their difficult trade and beyond them was the Liverpool Ferry with a fresh batch of customers, hopefully, for the island's partially resurrected tourist industry.

Port Soderick turned out to be only an ambitious name for what was an open roadstead in the sea. An abandoned hotel was located there, its swimming pool long ago drained and its empty windows staring sightlessly out to a cove that no longer brought passengers ashore. I asked directions for the train station from a friendly home owner who was working on his garden. He pointed out the way just as I heard the faithful steam whistle blow as it departed.

At the unmanned station I settled in for a thirty minute wait. The station house had been converted into someone's residence. In peeking in the windows it was possible to glimpse a priceless collection of antiques and train memorabilia. Parked across from the depot was an expensive Rolls Royce, its absent estate owner commuting to town by steam train. A penny saved....

About 3 or 4 minutes before the scheduled arrival of the train, according to the time table I had, a flagman arrived by automobile. He hastily went over to the flagman's shed. I walked over to verify where I was supposed to board and how I should buy my ticket. Friendly but somewhat agitated he explained that right there was where the two trains passed one another on the single track. Whichever train made it to that spot first became the train that had to be switched off onto the siding. His job was to see that this occurred so that they wouldn't plow head on into each other.

Sure enough the whistle from the Castletown bound train sounded first. The flagman hastily threw the switch and then he scurried on down to the second switch so as to keep the other train on the main track.

All went well with the two trains at their rendezvous

except that there were no seats available on the Douglas bound train and I had visions of being left behind. The young conductor ushered me back to his own little compartment at the rear of the train, though, and I had the pleasure of his conversation all the way back to Douglas. The trains are run from spring to fall. Apparently they are just barely self-sustaining although they are well-used by the residents themselves as well as the tourists.

Port Soderick to Castletown. 13 Miles.

The next day I returned to the station at Port Soderick via the faithful steam train. This time I hiked back down the glen below the station rather than continuing on around by the designated Gull's Way path which followed the main Castletown road for about a mile. I assumed that this was because one of the landowners could not be persuaded to allow a right of way across his farm, even if it was along the cliffs. I had noticed a road of sorts that took off from the bottom of the glen in the direction of the cliffs.

With some hesitation I set off up the road that soon turned out to be only a farm road, part of the farm itself in fact. The lane joined up with the familiar sign of the gull again and it pointed down a stone fence toward the seacliffs. I was relieved to have missed the road section and I was glad to be legitimate once more.

Pretty soon I came to a high stile. On the other side of it the footpath led along the cliff at the edge of the fields. It was grown over and little used but it was possible to determine where it went until it came to another field with sheep and cattle trails that had clouded the issue. I headed off in the general direction of the glen that was shown on the map. Eventually I came to a barbed wire fence. This I climbed to get to a path on the other side.

A deep cove called Cass ny Hawin cut into the shore line next. The guidebook suggested wading across it at low tide.

If you didn't mind wet shoes you could avoid the long trudge around. It was high tide at the time and I had no idea how deep it might have been. Besides I didn't relish wet clothes all the way back on the train.

The footpath became an enigma. The little stream that flowed down the cove was too wide to jump across and I began to suspect that it was just a milk cow special. Finally I came to a foot bridge far upstream. Then I was able to work back down again and eventually I came out at a large quarry where a huge tractor-shovel was busy enlarging a mammoth hole in the rocky ground.

Just beyond the quarry the footpath crossed the end of the runway at the island's Ronaldsway Airport. As I was proceeding across the runway in what seemed a safe depression a plane came zooming in at me. Suddenly the pilot aborted his landing. I didn't know why. I worried that it might have been because of me. He circled and then the airport turned on its lights. I guess visibility was poor. I was relieved to think so.

Past the airport I passed along the Bay of Derby Haven It was well protected and many small boats were swinging at their moorings. Then I came to the most immaculate and extensive lawn I think I've ever seen. It went on forever in front of the buildings that were Williams College.

The college had been built in 1830 and it was interesting to note that the request for help from then King William came at a bad time. Short of funds he donated his name instead.

Finally I reached Castletown where I treated myself to a splendid lunch at a favorite cafe called the Chablis Cellar. I returned on the 3:30 p.m. steam train for Douglas. It had been a delightful day with lots of variety in the miles that I had walked and the added treat of a ride on that ancient train that was so much a part of Isle of Man history.

This was all of the Gull's Way that I could fit into our schedule at the time. It was not until much later that I was able to continue.

WALK XVII

XVII. The Rest of the Raad Ny Foillan.

(52 Miles).

In the intervening time before I was able to return to the Isle of Man many changing events had occurred as they often do in the lives of our nearest and dearest. My daughter changed houses, countries, and husbands to find happiness in a new home with 11 acres near an interesting little village on the coast of Oregon, all in about two year's time.

It seemed strange not to have Kit and Tim on the island when we parked ourselves in the old Castle Mona hotel. The hotel is on the promenade in Douglas near the gambling casino and the amusement center. We had a view of the sea from the top floor and wake-up call was provided by the seagulls who came to discuss plans for the day every morning at daybreak...'stingy lot we have here now, no fish or chips bits, just that stale bread they carry off from the breakfast table, etc.'...

<u>Glen Maye to Kirk Michael. 10.5 Miles.</u>

The seagulls got us off to an early start in the rented Ford Vauxhall we had acquired in London. The ferry ride over from Heysham had been fun. The drive over to the west side of the island was through that meticulously cultivated countryside with its green fields, stone barns and colorful hydrangeas that were sprinkled in the gardens along the way. On the bad curves bales of hay and padding were still in place from the motorcycle races, every year someone gets killed in spite of the precautions.

There is a parking area and a pub at the Glen Maye

location where I started. This was where we had branched off before to follow the Herring Way walk across the island. Working down the glen beside its inviting little stream was a perfect way to begin. I could remember visiting it with Kit and the pugs and pausing to enjoy the waterfall about a third of the way down.

The Raad ny Foillan took off across a bridge and it went up a steep bank on the right just past the remains of an ancient watermill. Soon it reached the top overlooking the sea and I was back on the familiar cliff path that is typical of much of the walk. The path followed close to the edge in spots and the 100 foot drop down to the jagged rocks below was a reminder to pay close attention to where I put my boots for each step. It climbed in ups and downs to closer to 300 feet above the sea but this also improved the view. Far in the distance I could see the hills of Ireland. The seagulls soared in abundance in an effort to make the walk live up to its name.

Suddenly far below and about a hundred yards out from shore I saw shark fins cutting back and forth through the water. The fins were quite large and they were numerous. It took a while before I realized that these were big sharks with a high forward fin that was followed by a somewhat lower fin behind. I counted some 9 or 10 altogether. The sharks cruised along in pace with me for quite some time.

Soon I came to a family walking the path toward me. The children passed on by but I stopped to chat with their mother. They had seen the sharks, too. Later that evening we noticed a sign in the window of a marine supply store. It had a drawing of these same sharks with a request to notify a marine naturalist's office should they be sighted. They were basking sharks who fed on plankton, not people, and they were considered harmless.

Eventually the path worked its way on up to a 50 foot tower on the top of Corrin's Hill. The tower had been erected by Corrin as a family memorial. The four corners each pointed to a primary compass direction. He is buried there along with his wife and child.

Behind a marker for a windbreak on Corrin's Hill I stopped for lunch. Below I could see the interesting town of Peel with its river and harbor and in the distance tidy green farms stretched up each side of a valley. Jutting out on the sea side of Peel was its huge castle.

Passing through Peel along the beachfront I caught up with a familiar figure. Angie was there by coincidence. She had been looking for antique shops in the town. I was running behind schedule for the rendezvous so after a quick exchange of notes I pressed on up the road.

The route flanged up with an abandoned railway bed shortly after Peel. The tracks and ties had been removed over twenty years before and it made for easy walking. I followed this old railway bed for several miles until it finally deposited me in a public campground just outside Kirk Michael. The tents that had been pitched there were large and spaced widely apart. I passed three teenage girls lounging with their radio going full blast. Just beyond a young couple were sound asleep on their deck chairs while their radio, too, belched forth hard rock at their feet. Amazing. What a gift to be able to sleep like that.

As I trudged on up the road toward the spot where we had agreed to meet I was glad to find that Angie had second-guessed me. She picked me up and we went looking for a pub at five o'clock opening time.

Kirk Michael to Llhen Trench. 8.5 Miles.

After leaving the campground the route next picked up on the abandoned railway again. Then it turned down a footpath lane toward the beach. A sheepdog saw me up the way and he crouched down trying to decide whether to stay put and guard his territory or to press on with an attack. There was no way to avoid him and I was relieved to see his owner come into view. His owner placed a length of baling twine around his neck and he held him as I came up to them. He apologized for his dog's proprietary inclination toward the footpath. I don't think he would have bothered me, though. I stopped to talk for a bit. He was a Manx farmer with a colorful accent and quite friendly. Soon another dog came trotting toward us. He was an ancient Jack Russell terrier and he had a nasty wound across the top of his head. The farmer explained that the old dog was 13 and that he had been in a fight the night before. He blinked at me a couple of times as he trotted on by but he didn't stop to visit.

The track passed into a field and then evaporated. I followed the edge of the field around and passed into a graveled lane. The lane went through the yards of two houses and then a footpath headed for the beach.

The footpath crossed a small stream on a makeshift bridge and then it worked on up to a grassy knoll with a nice view on a bluff looking out to sea. I could see a long way down the beach, all the way to Corrin's Hill where I'd had lunch the day before. Here I stopped for a lunch break.

The beach was hard sand and pebbles with high bluffs at the shoreline. It reminded me of Southern California around Del Mar and Solana Beach near San Diego. The same problem with high tides was a factor although I would think that it would be difficult to become trapped except in a spring tide with a heavy westerly blowing.

The going was not too bad except that sometimes the pebbles were more prevalent and sometimes the sand was softer. There wasn't much in the way of beachcombing debris. I found a branch, though, that I trimmed into a walking stick. It was far too heavy but it felt good to have something to occupy my hands and arms. The tide was going out so it was possible to walk down close to the edge of the surf and to take advantage of the firmer beach there.

Surprise of surprises, a note in a bottle! The bottle had only recently been washed up since it was not far from the edge of the surf. I picked it up and removed the cork. The note was not a cryptic plea for help from some Robinson Crusoe on a deserted island. It was a request from the Dep't. of

Oceanography at University College in Galway, Ireland. They would like to know where it had been found. They would refund one's postage for a response. I hated to disappoint them. It couldn't have gone far. Ireland was visible off in the distance. I felt like giving it a toss back to sea so it could maybe take up with the Gulf Stream a little better and make it to some exotic place. Science is science, though, and that would have become assisted data. (I responded when I returned home to Biloxi, maybe when they saw the postmark there would have been a brief moment of anticipation anyway).

No one else appeared on the beach during the whole walk. It was a sunny day and it was good to smell the salt air and listen to the surf. At the pick-up rendezvous an attractive blonde lady pulled up and discharged her two well-behaved golden retrievers for a welcome romp on the beach. They were told to sit when the door opened but the excitement was too much for them. They broke ranks about ten seconds later and made a beeline for the beach. It was a familiar exercise. She had been a resident for 14 years and she loved the island.

Llhen Trench to Phert. 8 Miles.

Back on the beach again the next day it was overcast with some suspicious clouds around. A young girl came down a path with her Springer Spaniel. He romped in the surf.

The beach became a bit more pebbly and it made for slower going. Then I made another beachcombing discovery! It was a plastic carrot with a smiling face and a nice squeak to it when squeezed. I emptied out the accumulated sea water and sand and it was as good as new. It would make a welcome addition to Duffy's collection of goods. He is very meticulous about keeping his goods in inventory and he gives each of them an outing on succeeding nights when he brings them up on the bed to share with us.

On the beach walk I had found three successive plastic soccer balls at different spots. I had kicked them along for awhile until a misdirected kick had taken them too far up the beach or out to sea.

The route came to some grass covered sand dunes and behind these was a skeet-shooting range. The firing range was empty and alongside it a path meandered across the dunes. It turned out to be easier going than the beach pebbles and I took advantage of it. Apparently others had done the same thing.

The path emptied out onto a road and then onto a kind of moor with easy walking turf. This seemed to be a National Trust Park called the Ayres. A light squall came up and I broke out the Gortex and poncho. In the distance could be seen the giant candy-striped lighthouse. This is a milestone since it is the northernmost point of the island. Once reached the walk heads on down the east side.

Off in the distance I had seen the Russian cruise ship that had been at anchor in front of our hotel at Douglas. I had seen the huge ferries that connect the island with both mainlands, too, and two brave little sailboats that were making their way to windward in the light squall.

Shortly afterward I came to a visitor's center for the park. It was closed at the time but its overhang made a good shelter from the rain and I took advantage of it for a lunch stop.

After lunch I passed the tall lighthouse. Its fog horns were in business with their three blast drones that loudly sounded a warning to shipping.

In the Isle of Man guide book that is so helpful and informative mention had been made about a water tap in the Gent's room that had been left open because of its handle having gone missing. It was interesting to note that its handle was still missing some three years later and it continued to spout water all over the floor. Change on the Isle of Man does not come easily.

The pick-up spot down the east side was next to an abandoned farm. Not far away were two of the prettiest Manx cottages anywhere on the island. Their stones had been whitewashed, their thatched roofs had been neatly clipped and their hedges were immaculately trimmed. It was easy to see how proud and fond of them their owners must be.

Phert/Dogs Mill to Maughold Head. 6 Miles.

A long rope down a short bluff at Dogs Mill Point made climbing down to the beach a piece of cake. On the beach the tide had dropped enough to produce fine sand for easy walking. I had clipped off a couple of miles of pebble walking that hadn't seemed worthwhile. Dog Mills Point apparently derived its name from the use of a trundle wheel that was powered by a dog in times of drought. The other explanation for the strange name was that an old flour mill there sounded like a whining dog. Manx legends are full of speculations like this.

The promenade at Ramsey put an end to beach walking. Facing the sea were the characteristic old five story Victorian or Edwardian style hotels that give the Isle of Man so much of its charm.

Ramsey is a seaport and two small freighters were unloading their cargoes of cement and building blocks. Although much smaller they reminded me of my own offshore fleet of ocean-going barges before I had sold them all. These were well-painted with a coal tar epoxy coating that I had used successfully over the years myself. They were both resting on the low tide bottom. One of them had the admonition in polite British fashion, 'No Access at this time, please.'

My lunch break I took on the quay near the freighters. It was across from a pub where we had enjoyed a pint of lager the day before. The pub was on the second floor and it had a nice view of the harbor. It had been full of interesting characters including one old fellow with a long walrus type moustache that bushed out on either side of a Sherlock Holmes pipe which he smoked furiously. He read his paper in a determined manner as he put away the traditional pint in between puffs and clouds of burning pipe tobacco. When he rose to leave his table the three piece suit he wore was noticeably greasy and shiny, as though it had not been cleaned in the twenty years or so that he had owned it.

The town of Ramsey is a delightful place and it supports a very good restaurant, The Harbour Bistro, where we had dined some years before. After leaving Ramsey the route followed the main road. Walking on the highway was a bit dicey as usual and I was anxious to get it over with as quickly as possible. The road featured a sidewalk for part of it but that soon petered out. After that it was every man for himself for about half a mile and I've always figured that the pedestrian's cards are stacked against him.

The electric railway between Douglas and Ramsey runs from the end of May until mid-September. It is a pleasant outing with open-sided cars and sedate speeds for taking in the sights as you go along. The little cars run about every hour and they make some seven stops at strategic locations. They also make 'Request Stops'. Because of this it is possible to hike sections between Ramsey and Douglas without separate transport.

On the hike up the Maughold, which is along the cliff edge again with magnificent views to sea and up the coast, including Ramsey, I was elated to come face to face with a pair of the weird Loaghhtan sheep. Instead of the usual four horns, though, this ram had only three. They were both quite tame and they stopped only 40 feet away to scratch their heads on heather bramble.

On the top of the Maughold knoll I paused at a shelter to admire the view and to drink some water. Far in the distance I could see a figure on top of the next hill at Maughold Head. I didn't know it at the time but it was Angie waving at me. She had the binoculars and I was wearing a red shirt that was easy to identify. Besides, there was no one else around.

When I struggled up a lonesome path from the sea side of Maughold Head it turned out to be next to a drop-off beside a precipitous cliff face. Somebody had thoughtfully carved hand and foot holds in the cliff and I was relieved to reach the top.

In fairness to the Raad ny Foillan it was not the scheduled route which followed safely around the lee side of the hill. The climb was worth it, though, because the view was the easternmost point of the Isle of Man. Angie had come up another way and I had wanted to join her.

Maughold Head to Douglas. 19 Miles.

The schedule for the Isle of Man was drawing to a close and it was a sunny day so I elected to finish the rest of the Way of the Gull in one last push. The first part of the walk worked on down a grassy farm lane then across some fields and finally to a delightful little cove with a gravel beach. This was a hidden spot that would only be visited by someone walking the Raad ny Foillan. In the cove were two little stone boathouses. The door to one was held in place with only a stone. I peeked inside. In the shed was a heavy dory with oars. Scattered about were the nets and traps of the coastal fisherman. On the Isle of Man a lock was not considered necessary.

On working around a bluff out of the cove I began to hear some eerie moans as though someone was being slowly tortured to death. It was very disconcerting and I racked my brain to come up with some logical explanation. For a moment I wondered if the fairies were at it again.

When the path rounded the bluff I found the answer to the strange moaning sound. Not far away on the rocks washed by the dropping tide I saw half a dozen seals basking in the sun. A big male was patiently lecturing the group around him. None of his charges seemed to be the least bit interested in the subject matter, though. They looked like they had heard it all before... 'Seals of the world unite! Something must be done about these bloody nets that are screwing up our feeding grounds,' etc...

Then the route made its way up through some attractive houses that were scattered around the little cove called Port Mooar. It reverted to tarmac again on its way up the hill since there was no public right of way along the sea cliffs at that point. This was a little used back country lane between farm fields and quite pleasant for walking.

The lane crossed the double tracks of the electric railway and eventually it reached an intersection where the Way of the Gull turned downhill on an even more remote road. After a short while I came upon some saddled horses. Their riders had all dismounted and they were clustered around one of the horses. A woman leader for the group seemed to be tightening the cinch of one of the young riders. The others were keen on watching. She said hello as I passed.

The western saddle is never seen in England and I'm sure that all of the long hours I'd spent in the saddle as a boy working cattle on my uncle's ranch in the brushy mountains of California would not have counted for much in English eyes. It is a pleasure to see the English ride and horses are popular on the Isle of Man, too. I had often seen riders out on different parts of the island.

Just after the horses and riders episode I came to a narrow turn off into a public right of way called a cart track. I branched off from the Way of the Gull to go on my own for a bit. I had been down to the cove where it then led on the day before when we had driven there in the car.

The cove where the normal route passed was called Port Cornaa. It was part of a huge tract called the Barony Estate. We had enjoyed immensely the spectacle of four little boys around 5 to 7 years old and their sister embarking on their very first boat adventure in an inflatable dinghy. The inlet was completely sheltered from the sea and fed by a clear stream that wound down a grass valley. The two enthusiastic oarsmen had not yet discovered the value of pulling together with the oarblade upright and the wind carried them gradually upstream as the dinghy went in circles. There had been much shouting and discussion and proud waving to mum on the bank. Finally the little girl had jumped ship when they had gone close to a grassy bank. A good time was had by all and little by little they managed to get coordinated enough to head back in the direction from which they had come.

The cart track took me to some interesting houses beside a stream. I headed along the public footpath that passed through gardens and then it followed a wooded glen upstream. It was an enchanting walk that eventually took me to the railway where a station was located for a stop lettered Ballaglass Glen. There was no road there, just the footpath.

Then I dug out the big map and my compass and I headed up a path that soon brought me to an intersection of public right of way paths. I chose an overgrown and little used path that seemed to be headed in the right direction back to the Gull's Way again. I climbed over a gate and picked along a grown-over cart track until I came to a set of abandoned farm buildings on the top of a prominent hill.

The old farm was in bad shape with the roof and second floor of the Manx style cottage completely collapsed. The two small out-buildings were still serviceable, in fact one of them was full of hay. No road led to the farm at all. I walked over to a rusted pump and then I thought better of going any farther as I noticed that the top of the well was partially caved in. A fall down that thing in this remote place, not even where I was supposed to be walking, and chances were that no one would discover me for several centuries to come. The view was magnificent, 360 degrees, with the sea, the coast, the surrounding farm fields and even the peak Snaefell looming behind. The farm had lovely old trees, too, and stone walls. It would make an ideal restoration project and I found the wheels turning compulsively.

Beyond the old farm I dug out the compass and went to orienteering again. Suddenly a shotgun exploded nearby and I wondered if someone was firing at me. Nothing happened, though, and I just kept going. I never did see the hunter.

Soon I noticed some odd stones placed upright in a fenced-in area. I went over and found that it was an ancient burial ground that had been preserved by the National Trust. A path of sorts led down from the ancient graveyard and eventually I picked up an identifiable country lane that brought me back to the Gull's Way.

The next couple of miles were mostly road walking until the route took me down a pleasant path to the charming little beach side part of the village of Laxey. Here I bought an apple to go with my chicken tandoori sandwich for lunch. I sat on a bench by the beach where I enjoyed the sun and the sea air and a fish and chips family down the way.

After Old Laxey the route was forced to follow the most hair-raising part of the whole walk, namely about a mile and a quarter of the narrow two-lane main road again. After surviving this it was a real treat to dip down to the cove of Garwick Bay. A plaque on a white-washed boathouse was located there. It was in memoriam to an 84 year old fisherman who had spent 71 years of his life fishing the coast from out of that same boathouse.

The path then led up the glen to a lane with some lovely homes. It carried on out to Clay Head across pastures until it eventually passed through someone's farmyard to hook up with another country lane.

The Gull's Way then took me down a path that deposited me at a place that was familiar to me. It was Groudle Glen, the scene of our first visit to the island. Here are located some holiday summer cottages where we had all huddled around a coal fire, the only heat during the heart of a gale-blowing winter.

After Groudle Glen the route joined the road again but it featured a sidewalk and less traffic since it was no longer the principal artery between Ramsey and Douglas. A moment of exhilaration occurred when a bend in the road produced the vista of the long-curving bay of Douglas below. I knew I was about to complete the walk around the island. Like all long-distance walks I had mixed emotions about having it come to an end. These were offset by the satisfaction of adding it to the collection.

The route diverged down a steep path on the side of the cliff away from the road. It looked as though it was about to shoot out into space but then at the last minute it veered along a sharp slope toward the edge of the grass lawns of the houses just beyond. Here my walking career almost came to an end again with an inadvertent downhill twist of the ankle that nearly sent me cascading down the 150 ft. drop to the rocks below. Thanks to the strength of my hiking boots the ankle held and I recovered in time.

The route rejoined the road and it took me right down to the long promenade in front of the old-world hotels. About a block away from the Castle Mona I spotted Angie on the balcony of our fourth floor room. She was waving at me. I was about two hours overdue so she was relieved to see me trudging in. I hadn't realized that it was going to be a 19 mile day when I had set out that morning.

That night we dined at our favorite restaurant, Gastone's, over on the quay, and Angie gave me a present of an Isle of Man insignia for my favorite walking stick back in Biloxi. No trophy could have been more appropriate or timely presented.

Guide and Maps for the Raad Ny Foillan:

Isle of Man Coastal Path, Raad Ny Foillan, by Aileen Evans. Cicerone Press, 2 Police Square, Milnthorpe, Cumbria, LA77PY, U.K. (This is also available at newsstands on the Isle of Man. It is full of interesting bits of history along with sketches and diagrams for all three footpaths.)

Isle of Man Public Rights of Way and Outdoor Leisure May. Isle of Man Highway and Transport Board, Douglas, Isle of Man, U.K. (This is available locally, too, with all three long walks marked on this large scale map as well).

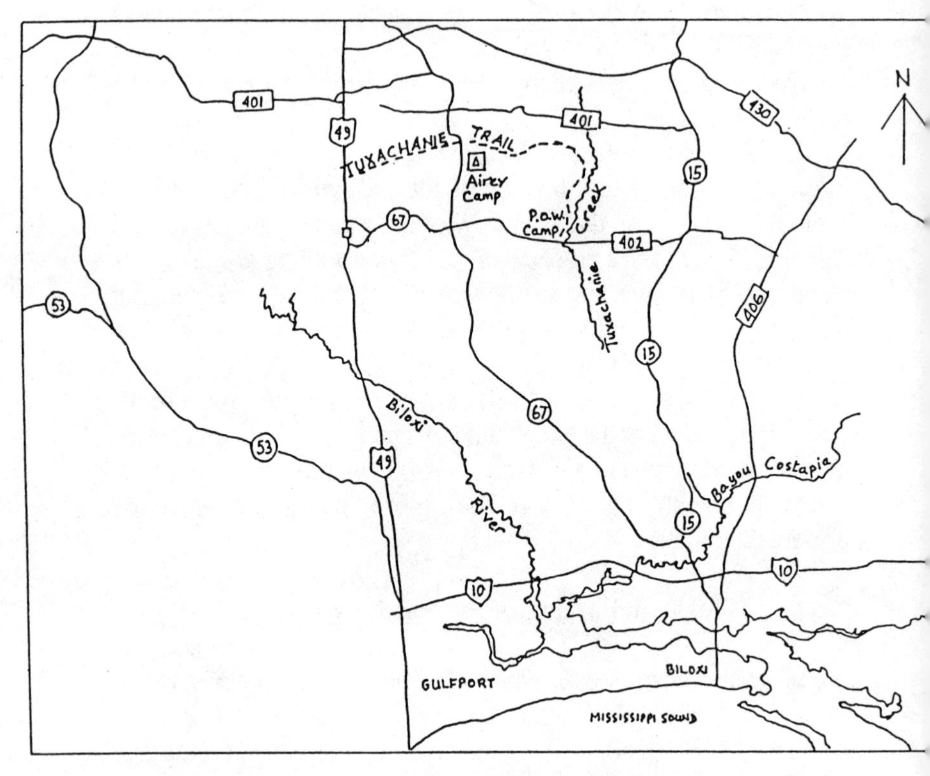

THE TUXACHANIE TRAIL IN SOUTH MISSISSIPPI

WALK XVIII

XVIII. The Tuxachanie Trail of Mississippi

(11.3 Miles)

The Tuxachanie trail is a delightful path through the De Soto National Forest in southern Mississippi. It is well-maintained by the service. Its beginning is just north of Gulfport on Hwy. 49 and it is not far from our home on the Tchoutacabouffa river. Because of its proximity it has long been a favorite for a quiet walk in the woods for whenever we are at home base doing chores.

Over the years we have spent many happy picnics on out-and-return hikes for different sections of the Tuxachanie. A number of offshoot trails and old logging roads branch out from it along the way and these have been fun to explore, too. One day I felt like doing all of it for a change, though. It was a Sunday morning in the first week of April and the scent of spring was overwhelming. The dogs piled into the little Blazer and Angie was kind enough to follow in the big Blazer so that we could spot the small one at the end of the trail which is known as P.O.W. The name comes from the days when it was a camp for German Prisoners during the second World War. She dropped us off for an early start over at the trailhead on Hwy 49.

The dogs shot out of the car and down the trail like someone had just pulled the lanyard on a howitzer. Beauregard first, then Benjamin and then little Duffy taking up the rear. The first five miles of the trail cross over several small streams, savannahs and swamps. These obstacles have been thoughtfully overcome with bridge planks where necessary. In the bottoms I saw pitcher plants and sometimes wild honeysuckle and all along the way the dogwood was in early bloom. This part of the trail runs straight as an arrow as it follows an old abandoned railroad bed.

The former railroad was used to haul logs and personnel from the mill and the 'company store' to the main railway. There it offloaded the logs for shipment elsewhere. The railroad bed itself was built by Irish immigrants using hand tools and mulepowered scoops in the early 1900's. It must have been very narrow-gauge because it is just the right size for a footpath and it makes for easy hiking, the rails and the ties having been removed long ago.

On the ridges and gentle slopes of the trail in between these creek beds the forest is well timbered with longleaf and slash pine. Also prevalent are youpon, galberry, huckleberry and the dogwood, of course, which boasted its welcome display of pristine white blossoms that day. One thing which has always puzzled me is the soft white sand that is found here and there along the way. I can understand its location in the creek bottoms but on the ridges it seems to be an impossibility and yet there it is. Maybe it dates back to a few million years ago when the whole area was probably underwater.

In the countless times that I have walked the Tuxachanie I have rarely seen other hikers using it. Thus it was a great surprise to hear Beauregard's bark up ahead and then to watch the inevitable tail-wag greeting as he attempted to endear himself to company on the trail. A whole string of young girls came slogging down past him. Each had a pack with a tightly rolled sleeping bag tied to it. Also hanging in festoons from the various packs were items of clothing, cups and implements like a collection of country peddlers about to hit town. There must have been over twenty of them altogether. They were accompanied by four grown-ups who were shepherding their flock of Girl Scouts.

It was interesting to note the expressions on each face in the group as they passed on by. I suspect that if that expression could be somehow encapsulated and then tracked to about twenty years in the future there would be a predictable correlation between it and the lifestyle that each girl had then achieved. They had probably camped the night before at Airey Lake, a pleasant campground up ahead. It was probably a weekend that all of them will long remember. My hat goes off to those who organize an outing like that. It is a valuable way to build character and it rubs off on everyone involved.

Farther along the trail I ran into a solo hiker and we stopped to chat. He had lived in Gulfport for over twelve years and this was the first time that he had ever ventured out along the Tuxachanie trail. We discussed the Appalachian Trail and he seemed interested enough to give it a try.

A paved road crosses the end of this first section. A good test of patience has to be trying to cross a highway with two fun-loving labs and an independent West Highland terrier, all on the leash at the same time. On the other side I unhooked the leashes when we hit the campground. Two little girls came over and the dogs became acquainted with them. The little girls' mother was then in the process of nursing their 5 week old baby brother at a picnic table nearby.

Airey Lake is a popular spot that is never crowded. Usually one or two families will be camped there and sometimes you see the odd fisherman trying his luck in the pond. At the time two campers and a solitary fisherman were using the area. A couple of resident ducks waddled along the shore.

The next section of the trail meanders some three miles through gently rolling pine hills with three creek bottoms to cross. Here again the forest service maintains a plank walkway across the soggy areas. About half a mile out from Airey Lake, which is really only a sizeable pond, there is a marked trail to Copeland Springs. The spring is a short distance away and well worth the visit. It is nicely boxed and I have never known it to go dry. The water is crystal clear and full of the many minerals one's body can use. It was named after a gang of outlaws who used to camp there on a regular basis. A plaque commemorates this fact. They would have been amazed had they known that someday it would have been named after them.

Towards the end of this section there is another branch trail that used to lead out around to the P.O.W. by a longer route. This trail is shown as being closed now and it is just as well because it was seldom used and pretty soggy in parts. The bridge for it that crossed the Tuxachanie creek was collapsed, too, I noticed. There is a gravel forestry road just past this turn-off trail and whenever I reach it the dogs reluctantly submit to 'heel' commands. The many enjoyable scents are so distracting, though, that it is always necessary to continue repeating these instructions until the road has been crossed.

Shortly afterward the trail reaches Duck Pond. This is a good stop for a picnic or a turn-around if the car has been left at Airey Lake. On this particular day I found a shady spot on the grassy bank of the dam and settled down to have lunch. It was twelve o'clock on the nose at the time so the eight miles had taken me about three hours to hike.

Lunch was a tin of sardines, some chicken pate from a previous canoe trip and some jalapeno cheese. These went over home-made bread from our new bread-making machine. The dogs had their milkbone biscuits and some of the sardines. The only visitors we had were two blue herons and a scolding crow. After a brief siesta I gathered up any litter I could find and put it in my pack for disposal later. Litter is never an eyesore on the Tuxachanie. It is always a clean footpath. We left Duck Pond and continued on our way.

The last section of the trail works its way on down to the Tuxachanie river itself. It is only a creek at that point and the water is clear with a light tannish cast to it. The stream bed is usually pure white sand. The amount of water varies according to prior rainfall but it is always an intimate little stream and I have never known it to go dry. The stream widens farther on down and we have a couple of favorite canoe stretches along that part of it. Both of them have bridge crossings that make good put-in and take-out spots. What I like about this area is its feeling of remoteness even though it is not far from the coast. There are no houses on the banks and we seldom see anyone else on our way down the river.

The trail follows the bank of the stream most of the time. It joins and leaves a horse trail occasionally and the best way to keep from going astray is to stick next to the bank of the stream wherever possible. It is well-marked with distinctive white blazes in diamond shapes. I didn't see any snakes on the walk but in the past I have come across moccasins on two occasions. Each time the dogs walked right over them. Neither the moccasin or the dogs were very concerned. I don't kill them anymore. They are part of the balance of nature, too.

Just before leaving the creek bed I stopped to pick a sprig of wild honeysuckle to bring back to Angie. It has a fragrant blossom and colorful petals and it will keep for days on end if you get it into water fairly quickly.

There is not much left of the remnants of the P.O.W. camp itself. In the middle of the camp a series of six arched concrete niches are apparent. They look like they may have been large kilns but this is the only structure remaining from those days. I hiked on out to the paved highway that goes on by the entrance to the camp. I had no difficulty with 'heel' commands at this point. My faithful companions were footsore and 'dogtired'.

There is a map of the Tuxachanie Trail. It can be obtained from the National Forest people on Hwy. 49 not far from where the trail takes off at that point. It is marked as a hiking trail with a readily visible sign just before you reach it coming from the south.

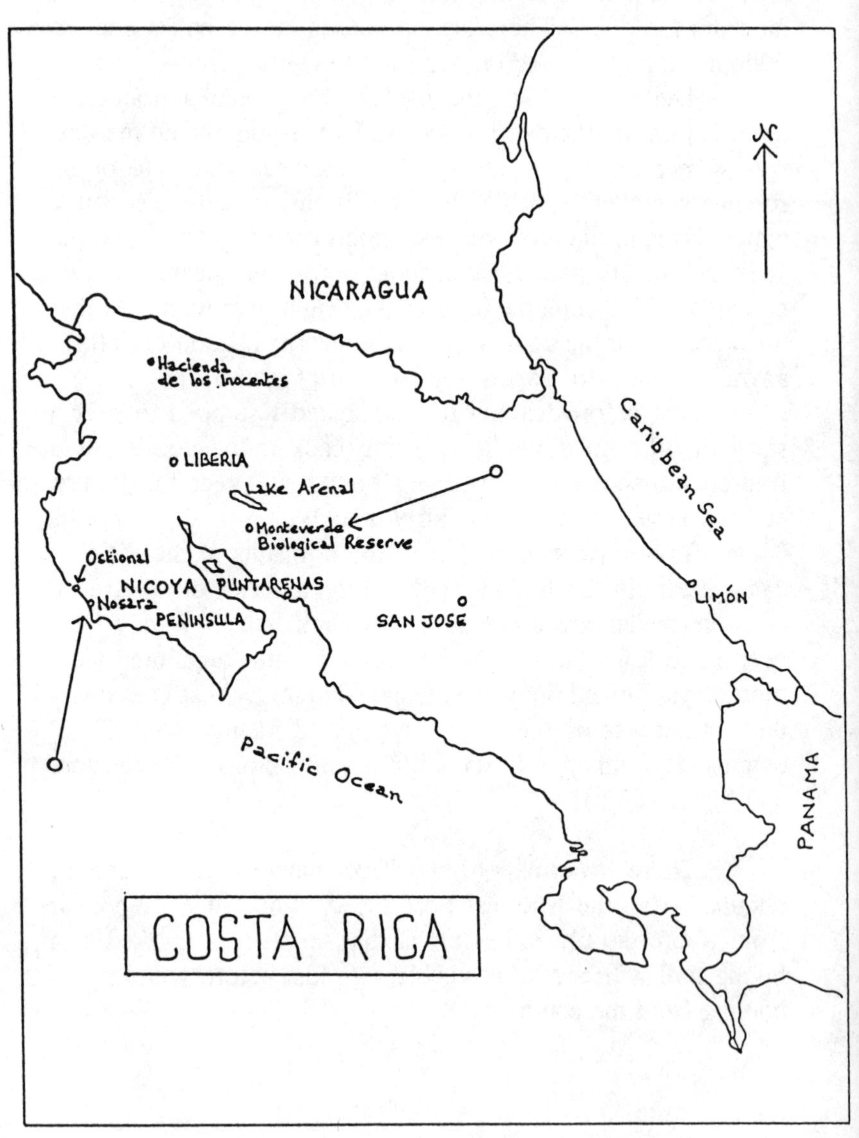
N
NICARAGUA
Hacienda de los Inocentes
LIBERIA
Lake Arenal
Monteverde Biological Reserve
Caribbean Sea
Ostional
NICOYA
PENINSULA
Nosara
PUNTARENAS
SAN JOSE
LIMÓN
Pacific Ocean
PANAMA
COSTA RICA

WALK XIX

XIX. Costa Rica.

Playa Guiones (Nosara)

The dry season for Costa Rica is during the winter months, into April. Hotels, particularly in San José, become booked and it is best to make a reservation. The same for a rental vehicle, 4 wheel drive is a necessity. 'Ticos' are invariably friendly and helpful and crime is usually simple theft or purse-snatching in or around San José.

The drive over to the Pacific Coast is about a five to six hour effort. The last hour and a half or so are over dusty, washboarded and pot-holed dirt roads. These become muddy and more difficult in the rainy season. On occasion there is the odd river to ford, although never a problem, and the trip is a delightful experience.

An example of petty theft would be an incident that occurred on the ferry across the Gulf of Nicoya. Rather than sit in the Nissan Jeep we had hired we had gravitated to a shady spot for pedestrian passengers. It was raised and roofed and a nice spot to enjoy the breeze and the view. I noticed two young Tico's move over to the jeep and squat down beside it. I thought that they were simply taking advantage of the shade that it offered. Later, I discovered that they had removed one lug nut from each wheel. It was really quite considerate, I suppose, because we did just fine with only four lug nuts on each wheel and they could have easily taken an extra set. Three lug nuts would have made it a bit dicey, I kept telling myself.

Another small example of Tico humour was the mileage on the jeep. When I made the reservations on the phone much was made of the fact that this was a 'new' vehicle and they wanted to be sure that it was going to be held especially for me. When later the alternator went out I glanced at the mileage and discovered a total of 175,000 miles there. I mentioned this to the agency when we were making arrangements to get this repaired. I reminded them that they had told me this was a new jeep. Their explanation was that, well, it was new to them.

The Hotel Playa de Nosara sits on a little promontory that juts right out over the ocean. It looks down two magnificent beaches on either side. It is a little slice of paradise, informal, reasonable and completely conducive to relaxation in the tropical isle tradition. Its affable Greek proprietor, John Fraser, does a creditable job of running his 22 rooms, a good bar and an admirable restaurant under difficult conditions. He is fluent in six languages and lives there at the hotel. Somehow he always finds time to visit with his guests, play a game of backgammon, deal with the problems of his help and enjoy the ambience himself.

Guiones Beach. About 6 miles.

This walk south from the hotel is irresistible. We did it several times but perhaps the best way to describe it would be to put down the log for the last time that I hiked it. On this occasion I also went inland a bit to check out some howler monkeys down at the other end of the beach.

First light, around 5:30 a.m., was usually a good time for a walk. With no TV, no newspaper and no anxiety about the world's problems, or your own, the early-to-bed routine helped to generate first light activity. The howler monkeys usually set out around that time and they could often be heard in the distance.

On this particular morning, Angie elected to sleep late and I headed down the long flight of steps to the beach by myself. It was cool, the tide was out and those intoxicating sunrise colors were penetratingly sharp and clear.

Coming out from the little grove of palms and past the

rocky head called Punta Pelada I spotted the usual group of pelicans mustering for breakfast. These pelicans are much larger than those that we are accustomed to seeing along the Gulf of Mexico. They fly with the same effortless grace and flawless timing but those larger beaks are able to hold much bigger fish. I never tire of watching them play chicken with the rolling surf. I've yet to see one trip and get wiped out. It's usually follow the leader across the waves and then a ride up the thermals for a look around. Woe betide any hapless fish that gets too near the surface. Pow! A pelican cruise missile!

In the first part of the walk along this beach the surf is unbroken by any rocks or reef and it is a favorite with surfers. One surfer termed it the third best surfing beach in Costa Rica. I can't remember the other two. We saw only four surfers there at one time, usually one or two, and on this morning the beach was completely deserted.

Four thatched huts had been located about 100 yards apart. Called 'ranchitos' these are available for camping, first come, first served. Only one ardent camper, from California, was taking advantage of the arrangement. With an oversized camper top on his pick-up he and his girl-friend carried a canoe and three surfboards. They were ready for the jungle, the beach or whatever, I guess.

This whole beach area is protected against the encroachment of rampant condo development, something that has ruined so many other prime beachfront areas. It is a protected zone under the farsighted Costa Rican ecological policies.

Next came the challenge of a small stream that drained across the beach like a delta. Only a couple of inches deep it made for the usual set of jumps trying to keep the Nikies dry. Here were rocks and a reef that protected the beach from surf so that snorkeling and fishing were possible. But the Pacific is just not the same as the Caribbean for spearfishing and diving, I'm afraid, at least not along the coast. The water is never quite as clear.

Ahead I saw an oxcart make its way laboriously down to the beach. The two huge Brahmin cows seemed to be enjoying themselves as they plodded along under their yoke. The wheels were solid wood and brightly colored. The driver rode in the cart. I guess he was out to gather beach rocks or sand. Nobody was in a hurry.

Some fairly nice houses had been built along the edge of the beach in the next section, eight of them, their only means of access along the beach at less than high tide.

Shortly afterward I came to a group of thatched buildings scattered along the side of a knoll. Green grass and an abundance of bougainvillea flourished under a sprinkler system. A sign said Guiones Lodge Albergue. I climbed up to the topmost thatch where the owners seemed to still be asleep. What a view! And just below a small swimming pool had been formed out of the rocks. A true Shangrila. Below I discovered the real lodge, a B & B, with the current group just getting into breakfast. The young Tico said she had two thatches for rent, the others were privately owned. What a delightful and remote spot to get away from it all.

Beyond I walked to the end of the beach where another rocky headland jutted out to sea. Here I found a small path that led up a little draw toward a valley beyond. From the direction of the path I heard the unmistakable shriek of howler monkeys. It was too much to resist.

After awhile the shrieks became louder. I had reached some really huge trees. Far above me I could see three of the howlers nonchalantly doing their thing some 70 feet up in the tree tops. One was leisurely sampling some selected leaves, the other two were out in the fork of a large branch. The female was checking out the contents of the hair on the male's back and the male was communicating with one of his cronies off in the distance, either that or he was saying rude things to the gringo down below.

Actually the howler monkey is indigenous to these parts and they seldom come down out of the trees. They travel in tribes of up to a dozen and if a young male gets over the quota he is sent off on his own. All of the howling is often done to announce to a rival tribe that they are about to pass through a certain staked out territory. Property rights are pretty informal but apparently they are religiously observed all the same.

The howler monkey is not overly shy nor is he aggressive. He won't eat a banana if offered and he has a perverse sense of humor, often weeing on the gringo if he gets too close.

On the way back up the beach I travelled along a road inland near the beach. About midway I came to a very old cemetery. Most of the older tombstones were unmarked or too faded to be legible but of the more recent I noticed a couple that belonged to ex-pats from the States. It was a tranquil place, near the sea in a small grove of shade trees, a pleasant place to rest the remains of the owner's life.

Pelada to Nosara Beach and Nosara River. About 6 Miles.

On the north side of the Hotel Playa de Nosara a gentle cove ranged to a high bluff and headland up the way. It was possible to view the long beach beyond from the open dining and bar area of the hotel. This was really Nosara Beach, after which the hotel had been named, in spite of its location, and it stretched all the way to Ostional. Along the famous and isolated beach the Olive Ridley and Leatherback turtles perpetually returned each year to lay their eggs in the dead of night.

The Ostional and Nosara beaches are part of a Costa Rican Refuge where the turtles are protected. During the first part of the season the eggs are allowed to be harvested by the locals, as they have done for generations. Then they are protected by the same locals who act as guardians or guides for those who are curious enough to watch these huge giants of over a hundred pounds as they lumber up on the beach to dig and bury their eggs. This arrangement is a clever compromise.

It assures the survival of these magnificent creatures.

An interesting phenomenon about turtle hatchlings is the discovery that the depth and direction in which the eggs are placed is crucial to their survival, their eventual return and even their sex. An attempt is to be made to transplant some of the eggs to Guiones beach just down the way. The theory is that then these turtles will subsequently return there, since the turtles always return to the same spot where they were born. The deeper eggs become male, the shallower eggs, female. They must all face the same direction, toward the sea. The depth of sand can be measured, of course, but Nosara and Ostional are made up of black sand which generates more warmth. Guiones sand is white. Stay tuned. Maybe one of these days a Nosara turtle will eventually return to Guiones.

At the end of this beach, Olga's bar and Rancho Suizo, there is a jungle trail that takes off from the beach. This is a nice trail that eventually empties out onto a road. When the road is followed north it finally arrives at the mouth of the Rio Nosara. Angie and I did this hike one morning. We also followed along the bank of the river for awhile but we gave it up when the jungle became too dense. We didn't see any crocodiles or snakes of awesome reputation. We did see a strange little fish with bulbous eyes that protruded on antennae-like sticks from the side of its head.

On the way back I fell into conversation with an old woman who was walking her Sheltie on the beach. She had a condo nearby. She was a dry season resident, like so many others of the ex-pat, gringo population. It meant moneyed customers for only a small part of the year and it explained why the infrastructure of the area was still primitive enough to keep the coast from becoming overly-developed and changed.

A walk along the beach in either direction from the hotel provides an interesting two hours at dawn's early light. For companions there are always the big pelicans and the frigate birds. And back at the hotel a good book and a strategic hammock under a palm tree or a thatched hut is always waiting for when the sun gets up too high.

Monteverde Cloud Forest - El Triangulo. About 6 Miles.

We spent a couple of nights at a Stateside-like resort up the coast at Ocotal. Perched high on a bluff overlooking the coast the views were practically limitless. I did a three hour hike along the ridge there and a long swim in the sheltered cove down below but the churned-up sand made snorkeling pretty hopeless. The highlight of our visit was a tame coatimundi who climbed down a tree and made himself at home in the lap of one of the diners. He was a beer drinker. The group he had selected were generous with their beer. Eventually he staggered back to his tree. With some difficulty he made it back up again to what looked like the onset of a monumental hangover.

The trip to Liberia seemed like something out of an old western. The town itself is surrounded by large ranches and the favorite means of transportation in the area seems to be on horseback. We found an accommodating inn just outside of town called Las Espuelas ('The Spurs'). It had an ancient stagecoach parked under its portico.

We went for a long walk down a dry creek bed and along a seldom-used dirt road in the Santa Rosa National Park. It was about an hour north of town. There, too, we visited an historic old house where the infamous gringo adventurer, William Walker was defeated in his attempt to take over the country.

Also north of Liberia we climbed into the saddle for a horseback trip at a ranch at Los Inocentes. This was memorable for several reasons. It showed the ranch operation, 2,500 acres and 500 head of cattle, mostly dairy cows. It was interesting for me to see how the pastures were maintained as they worked their way up the side of a nearby volcano. And at the upper reaches we could see all the way to Lake Nicaragua and Nicaragua itself.

The trail that we followed for much of the ride crossed and recrossed a running stream bed several times. Huge trees bordered the stream on both sides. Every now and then it became possible to observe different tribes of monkeys high overhead. We saw capuchins, congos, large spider monkeys and the howler monkeys that we knew from the coast. I felt that I was definitely making progress in communicating with them. The howlers are misnamed because the male, who does all of the shouting, just emits a deep guttural grunt that is not too difficult to imitate. What it was that he kept trying to tell me, though, wasn't too clear. Probably, "Buzz off, Jack...you're in our territory here!"

From Liberia we went on up to Monteverde over a back road that turned out to be 40 kilometers of very hard going in the high country. It really did require 4 wheel drive for much of the time. The country was full of small dairy farms.

At Monteverde we stayed at The Belmar, recently expanded with a new addition lavishly created out of Pochote wood. It was fascinating to watch the clouds from the rain forest evaporate as soon as they passed our balcony overhead. They had risen up the Continental Divide from the east, hit the warm air from the Pacific and quickly disappeared. An amazing phenomenon.

The next morning we set out on the celebrated hike through the cloud forest of Monteverde. These 26,000 acres are privately owned and preserved for the good of mankind. The pathways laid out near the entrance to the preserve are meticulously maintained. There are three principal trails in the area with another optional trail on a 2 mile returning road. These trails cover only a small portion of the forest and other long trails are shown on the map.

The area was originally settled by Quakers in the 1950's. They wisely set aside some 1,300 acres to preserve for a watershed for their dairies. The area was continually enlarged until it reached its present size.

We quietly walked the opening trail, the Sendero

Bosque Nuboso, constantly looking at the huge trees with all of their companion plants that had taken up residence along the branches and the trunks. All of the moisture from the trade wind clouds as they cross the Continental Divide and then collapse into mist provide the nourishment that supports the lush growth of mosses, ferns, lichens, air plants, vines, orchids and the huge variety of plants that thrive there. These, in turn, support the birds and wildlife who dine on them.

The trail had been carefully preserved with wood stepping stones throughout the walk. Stapled to these crosscut slices were wire-mesh coverings to provide traction. In addition, extensive wooden bridges and walkways had been built, again covered with the wire-mesh. Sometimes concrete blocks and sand and gravel had been used but throughout the three trails the path was always meticulously sculptured. I guess it becomes slippery for much of the time but when we were there, in the dry season, we had no problems.

We crossed over the Continental Divide and worked over to a lookout called La Ventura. There it was possible to see the top of the forest in both directions. I left Angie and followed along another trail marked 'Restricted'. I stayed with it for awhile. It was called Sendero Brillante and it would have been fun to have found where it led.

For a long-distance walking effort or a back-packing expedition there are several trails available. Where we then were I could see what looked like a well-marked trail leading off to the east. Apparently it would be good for some 20 miles until it reached the perimeter of the preserve. You are asked to register and obtain permission for hikes in the preserve. I doubt that there would be many others out there with you. A compass, machete and survival goods would be a must, though, and it would be difficult to find bearings to mark your position if you lost the trail.

We took the Sendero Pantoso fork and passed through a higher section of the forest. We became acquainted with a couple from New Jersey who had already hiked the conventional paths of the immediate section. We passed them again later when they were both sitting back to back on a bench reading away using one another for back rests.

After the end of the Sendero Pantoso we came to another fork option and chose the Sendero Rio. This followed along a small stream and turned out to be the most delightful of the three trails. At one point the stream cascaded down some rocks in a waterfall that was really inviting. Some students had climbed down to stretch out near the pool at the base of the falls.

Finally, we came upon a group of people with a naturalist guide. They were intently staring at something. Eureka! A pair of Quetzal birds! The sighting of this elusive bird is always one of the prime experiences hoped for in a circuit of Monteverde. The female is blue and black and the male is a jungle green with a brilliant red chest. They are huge birds with sweeping tail feathers. The guides are useful in finding them because they can recognize the laurel trees on which they feed.

Even though the actual walk was only six miles we spent some five hours doing it because of the many plants, trees, vistas and neck-craning search for birds and wildlife.

The rain forest is fast disappearing from the world. Already two-thirds of it has disappeared from Southeast Asia. One-half of it is gone from Africa. Latin America now has over half of the remaining rain forest in the world. Some 140 million people live in the tropical third world countries that have rain forest and these people are destroying trees at the rate of about 160,000 square miles a year, about the size of Oregon. And the rate is increasing. The entire Amazon jungle, the world's largest rain forest, will be gone in less than thirty years. ***In less than THIRTY YEARS!***

Bibliography:

The travel section of most book stores have adequate guide books on Costa Rica. Those that we found the most helpful, ranked in the order of their use are:

- Costa Rica by Lonely Planet
  Lonely Planet Publications
  P.O. Box 2001A
  Berkeley, CA 94702, USA

- Costa Rica by Ree Strange Sheck
  W.W.Norton or John Muir Publications
  P.O. Box 613
  Santa Fe, NM 87504

- The Costa Rica Traveler by Ellen Searby
  Windham Bay Press
  Box 1198
  Occidental, CA 95465

- Fodor's Costa Rica, Belize, Guatemala
  Most book stores

- Choose Costa Rica, a guide to wintering or retirement, by John Howells
  Gateway Books, San Rafael, CA
  Have your local book store order through:
  Publishers Group West

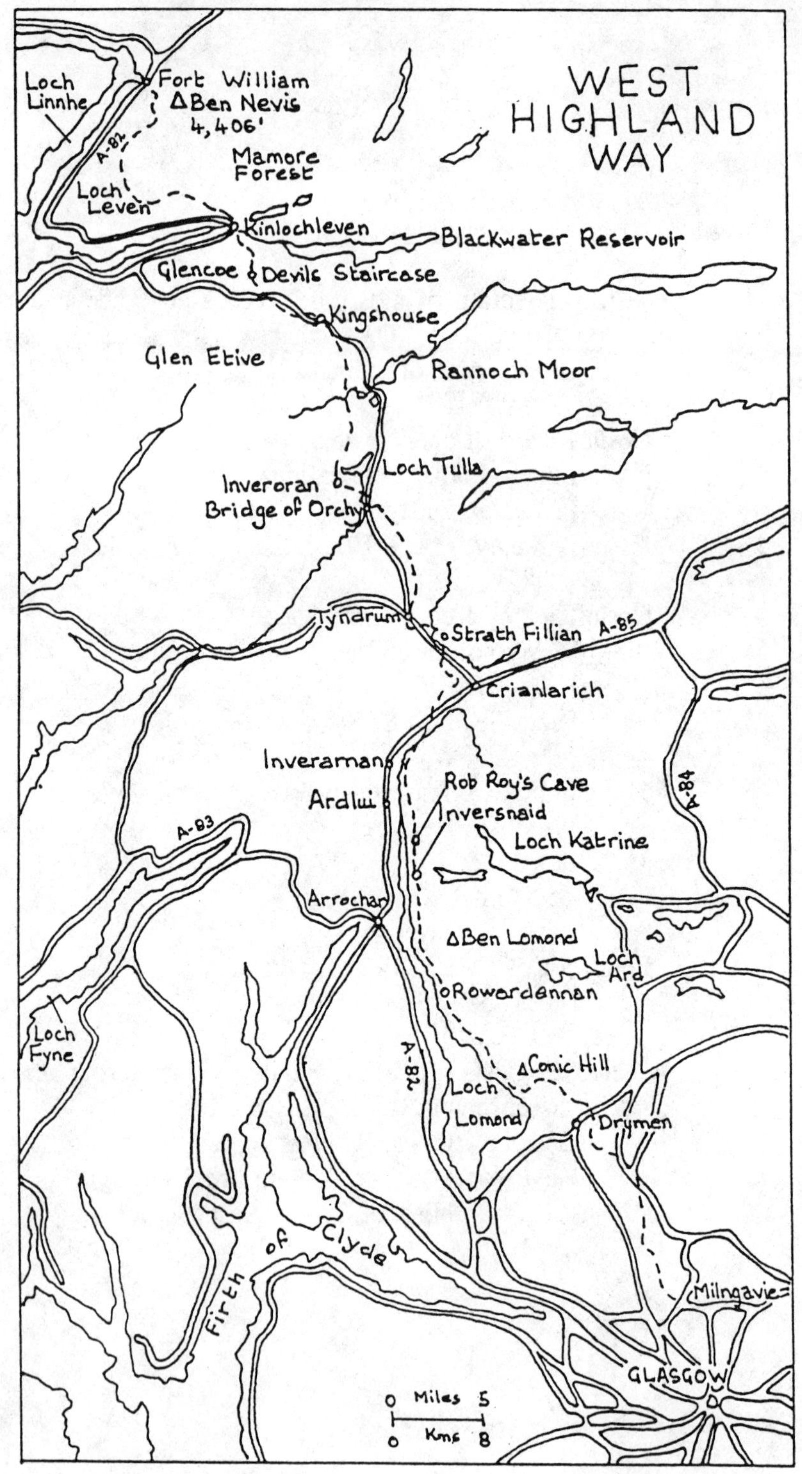
WEST HIGHLAND WAY
Loch Linnhe
Fort William
Ben Nevis 4,406'
A-82
Mamore Forest
Loch Leven
Kinlochleven
Blackwater Reservoir
Glencoe
Devils Staircase
Kingshouse
Glen Etive
Rannoch Moor
Loch Tulla
Inveroran
Bridge of Orchy
Tyndrum
Strath Fillian
A-85
Crianlarich
Inveraman
Rob Roy's Cave
Ardlui
Inversnaid
A-84
A-83
Loch Katrine
Arrochar
Ben Lomond
Loch Ard
Rowardennan
Loch Fyne
A-82
Conic Hill
Loch Lomond
Drymen
Firth of Clyde
Milngavie
GLASGOW
0 Miles 5
0 Kms 8

WALK XX

XX. Scotland's West Highland Way and Ben Nevis.

(94 Miles).

The West Highland Way starts at the railway station in Milngavie (pronounced 'Mil guy') which is a northern suburb of Glasgow. This is handy since it means that a thru-hiker can train up from London, hike to Fort William at the northern end and then train back.

The Way goes from Scotland's largest city to the foot of its highest mountain, Ben Nevis, also Britain's highest peak. It runs along the shores of its largest loch, Loch Lomond. (A loch is never called a lake in Scotland and lakes are never called lochs anyplace else in the world even by a Scotsman). It follows along the edge of its grandest moor, Rannoch Moor, and then it passes through its most dramatic mountain range in the Highlands. It provides an opportunity for intimately experiencing the rolling green hills and precipitous mountains of Scotland. These are interspersed by scattered clusters of stone houses with Bed & Breakfast or hotel accommodations as well as youth hostels and camping sites along the way. It is a wild country at times with many lakes (sorry, lochs) and streams but the track is well marked and obvious for the most part and the majority of the walk is fairly level or gradual in its ascents and descents. Much of it follows an old military road now used only by foot traffic.

The weather of Scotland is rapidly changeable and varied. It can go from bright sunshine to clouds to mist to drizzle to gales and rain and back to sunshine all on the same day. Just because it is overcast in the morning it doesn't necessarily follow that it won't open up to sunshine later on.

And vice versa. This is what keeps the hills so green and the sheep so fat. One soon becomes adjusted to shifting layers of clothing in and out of the pack, though. It can get cold, too, even in summer and it is well to put in the thermal underwear for when it might be needed. The weather is an integral part of what makes Scotland such a friendly place. Being warm and snug inside a remote pub helps to stimulate the hospitality and sociability that is so common among Scotsmen.

Much of our own experience with the West Highland Way was shared with our Scottish friends, Jess and Ian, who live near Edinburgh. They are keen fell walkers who have hiked many of the peaks in Scotland themselves and with whom we have hiked in Spain.

Milngavie to Drymen. 12 Miles.

Jess and Ian and Angie and I managed a late morning start from the railway station, the official beginning of the Way, in nice sunshine. We were accompanied by Holly, Jess and Ian's friendly German Shepherd. She is a sweet dog with good manners and a fondness for meat pies. Each morning Holly accompanies Ian to the bakery in Linlithgow where they live. She has a standing order for a meat pie. This she carefully carries home in her teeth. She eats the pie for breakfast only when given permission to do so by Ian. She eats it slowly with great relish since it is a high point in her day.

The walk out from town passed through a shopping area that was restricted to pedestrian traffic. Then it followed a pleasant stream through a park for a while. It gradually worked up into interesting woods where we stopped to chat with a spry old man who was walking his Springer Spaniel. He was carefully dressed in coat and tie and he revealed that he was in his late eighties. He had made this same walk every day, rain, snow, sleet or shine, without fail for the past twenty years since his retirement. It wasn't apparent quite how far his walk took him but it must have been a key to his longevity and good health.

We passed Craigallian loch, down a back lane and into a long open field with magnificent vistas. We left the track and worked through high grass over to a little knoll with standing stones that dated back to the bronze age over 2,000 years ago.

We rested on the stones for lunch while admiring a handsome estate below us. Two riders were chasing a young horse in a field in the distance and a luncheon party seemed to be in full swing at the turreted Victorian mansion known as Craigallian House. Holly had her meat pie, saved from her morning routine. She carefully lifted off the top crust and after polishing that off she worked her way around the edges saving the meat filling itself for last.

The Way continued along a raised footpath which looked like a dike. We decided that it was really a covered sewage pipe that ran to a treatment plant that we passed later on. Eventually we came to a pub at Dumgoyne called the Beech Tree Inn. Down the way was the Glengoyne Distillery which offered tours and sampling of real Scotch malt whiskey.

Over coffee at the pub I heard about a popular drink called a 'Shandy'. This is half lager and half lemonade. I resolved to try one at the next pub stop.

We came to a stone bridge called Gartness Bridge and paused to admire the river that flowed beneath it. A fisherman had just caught two huge salmon trout and apparently this was the reason for the many cars nearby. The owner of this stretch of the river had just released some of his prize salmon trout for whoever wanted to fish for them, for a fee.

The route followed a back country lane for a while and we passed two backpacking couples from Holland. They both spoke English quite well, an accomplishment that seems to be the norm for the Dutch.

We pulled into Drymen and repaired to a nearby pub to sample my first Shandy. It was delicious! Just the right combination for a real thirst quencher. The pub itself claimed to be the oldest pub in Scotland. The Clachan Inn had been originally licensed in 1734 to the youngest sister of the notorious highwayman, Rob Roy MacGregor. On leaving the old pub the affable proprietor tried out his best southern drawl with, "Y'all come again, ya hear?"

Drymen to Rowardennan. 16 Miles.

Jess and Ian had chores to do at home and Angie had to find and check us into our B & B up the way so it was a solo day. This section is really only 14 miles but I managed to get off to a disoriented start which added another hour and 2 miles at the beginning.

My mistake was in thinking that the route headed back toward Drymen where we had finished with the shandy at the Clachan Inn. When I had passed through town and realized that I had not seen any of the customary markers for a while I asked a gentleman who was pruning his trees nearby to advise me as to the whereabouts of the West Highland Way.

Whether this gentleman had some sort of a bizarre sense of humor or whether he just meant well but was misinformed I shall never know. He directed me across a long field where I climbed a couple of barbed wire fences and a stone wall until I reached a road that had an encouraging walkway with walkers out for a Sunday stroll. All of it was in the opposite direction from where I should have been going to rejoin the Way.

Finally I dug out the compass and then, like a comedy of errors, I didn't discover that the North grid lines failed to run in the customary direction of most charts, toward the top of the page. When I finally made this discovery I was back to my original starting point having made a huge circle and having killed a whole hour.

My stupidity had left me with 14 miles to do in 6 1/2 hours in order to make a 6:00 p.m. passenger ferry ride across Loch Lomond to where Angie would pick me up on the other side. It was the last scheduled crossing for the day. I began to pick them up and put them down with a wee bit more alacrity than usual. If I wasn't on that ferry life would suddenly become very complicated for both of us. Neither of us would have a clue as the where the other would be.

The Way headed on up into the woods of the Forestry Commission. It followed forestry roads for a good while and it was possible to make good time. I passed the two Dutch couples from the day before, one after the other. The road then branched off into a path and finally I came to a huge stile that was some 9 feet high over a deer fence at the edge of the woods. From the top of the stile the route could be identified as it stretched out and up the formidable Conic Hill in the distance. Off to the left was the thrill of seeing Loch Lomond for the first time.

On the slog up Conic Hill a light drizzle materialized out of the morning sunshine. At the top of the hill I stopped for a 10 minute lunch in spite of the pressing ferry departure time. The way down to Balmaha and the edge of the loch was steep but easy with steps in some parts.

The rest of the track along Loch Lomond was interesting because of the shore edge but the 7 1/2 miles were not clearly marked and some of it followed the narrow road with traffic a threat. On the sections that bordered the loch several headlands needed climbing and then descending. Some of it would have been much better appreciated without the ferry departure problem. A light drizzle from time to time wasn't too welcome either but the shoreline area itself was quite scenic with a surprising amount of pleasure boats on moorings.

By pushing hard I was relieved to make the ferry pier at the Rowardennan Hotel for a quarter to six p.m. The ferry turned out to be a little cabin cruiser of only 20 feet in length. I had an interesting conversation with an Englishman, a journalist from Norfolk. He had spent an entire year in Antarctica with a crew of 14 at a weather monitoring station. They had lived on canned goods and dried vegetables. They had been completely iced in so that no one could reach them until the following summer when the ice pack would melt enough for a boat to make it through. He confessed to occasionally cooking penguins and seals for fresh meat and he said that they each took turns with the cooking so that no one would complain about the chef. He had made a short walk and he needed to get back across in order to catch a bus back to his B & B down the way on the other side of the loch.

At twenty after six the ferry operator sauntered on down from the hotel with his dog. There were six of us, a backpacking couple, the Englishman and myself and two girls from West Germany. I fell into conversation with the girls on the ride over and Angie and I bought them a shandy at the local pub on the other side. Then we gave them a ride back to their youth hostel in Crianlarich not far from where we were staying ourselves.

I had been surprised at the water sport activity on Loch Lomond. People had been out sailing and water skiing, even jet boats were in operation. Everyone had been enjoying the water in their wet suits. It was August after all and I guess they were determined to make the most of the summer break. I had been travelling with my Gortex and poncho, myself, and having a difficult time trying to stay dry and warm.

North Loch Lomond to Crianlarich. 9.5 Miles.

The section from Rowardennan to where the little 'ferry' departs at the north of Loch Lomond is strongly recommended not to be attempted when it is raining or soon after a prior rain. I could appreciate the problem. A goodly portion of the 12 miles is up and down scrambling over rocks and through mud to get around the numerous headlands. This side of the loch is precipitous and isolated without a road or track of any kind.

On the day I had scheduled to walk the 12 miles up from Rowardennan it had rained steadily for most of the night. It was raining in the morning as well. Finally, at 10:40 a.m. I reluctantly decided to forego this section as advised but to leave anyway on the 'ferry' at Ardlui to do the part from north Loch Lomond on up to Crianlarich. The 'ferry' was a skiff with a 10 H.P. Yamaha outboard. It is operated 'On Request' by the enterprising Scot and his wife who also offer tent sites on their lawn. The charge was 4 pounds but if I could get another three to go we could split the cost. There was no one else out in the rain so I splurged and we set forth for the other side.

Across the loch a flagpole is situated so that it can be seen by the ferryman. When you run the two big balls up the pole he will come and get you. That is, when he happens to notice them. When we pulled into shore a couple in wet ponchos boarded the skiff after I had climbed out. They had probably spent the night at nearby Doune bothy (a shelter) and they were probably headed for some R & R and grocery replenishment on the road side of Loch Lomond.

Shortly after I had hit the trail from the ferry landing two mountain bikers, a young couple, materialized from out of nowhere. Where they had come from and where they hoped to go in all of the muck was a mystery to me. Perhaps they were headed for the ferry, too.

At first the muddy path was not too bad as it climbed a short hill. Then it gradually became more of a problem as it crossed boggy places where the rain poured down the side of the hill. Numerous creeks had to be waded on the larger stones in the streambed. The trail climbed up and down the wet slopes and good footing was often difficult to find.

Two Scandinavian girls with backpacks and rain gear had paused before a stream that had to be forded. I crossed over to them on some strategically placed stones. They were cheerful and in good spirits and not the least bit concerned about the rain and mud.

Finally I stopped by the Falls of Falloch for a cheese bap and an apple for lunch. The river there was a raging torrent as it pounded down the rocks and through the cut at my feet. The midges came for a visit to help with my lunch but they were not unbearable. Ten minutes was enough. I didn't want to get cold from my soaked clothes. It was no use getting out dry clothes from the pack, what I had would just get wet from perspiration during the rest of the way. They were better saved for an emergency.

The trail finally emptied out onto a dirt road on the pleasant little Derrydaroch Farm and walking became easier. It crossed the river on the farm's bridge and then it cut up under the railroad track through a low sheep run where it was necessary to stoop to get through. Just beyond it passed beneath the highway through a tunnel recently built for walkers on the Way.

After climbing up a short hill the Way picked up on an old abandoned road and walking was again easy once more in spite of the puddles and the mud. It followed along until the old road turned down to the Keilator Farm below. Then it struck off on its own again until it hit a high stile that had to be negotiated to reach a junction trail that led down to Crianlarich. The path finally dropped down a hill through some woods until it emptied out at the railway station where Angie was waiting with the Vauxhall.

This section would have been much nicer on a dry day. It had a good deal of variety to it. It had turned out to be a sample of wet Scottish weather, though. I had asked the ferryman when setting out how much longer he thought the rain would last that day. He considered it for a moment, looked at the sky and then said, "God only knows."

Crianlarich to Bridge of Orchy. 14 Miles.

The B & B where we stayed at Crianlarich was run by an elderly couple who were very thoughtful about our well-being. Even though Frances had had a triple bypass she was up and down the stairs to the upper kitchen and sitting room twenty times a day. She brought my breakfast cereal on a tray and left it outside the door even before we were up. She was an indomitable spirit and full of life. Her husband John had just as much energy, He was a water bailiff and he made frequent checks to see that nobody was fishing illegally in their stream and lake without a permit.

Jess and Ian drove up to hike with Angie and me on the following day. We left one of the cars at our destination and then we were off for a late start at Crianlarich. Holly came along, too, her meat pie ready for lunch in Ian's pack. The first part was an ascent through woods from the railway station. The sun was with us and we could see more and more of the pleasant river and buildings below us as we gained elevation.

After some three miles of enjoyable fell walking through woods and across little streams we dropped down to the main road. Here we had to walk Holly along the shoulder of the road for a mile because dogs are not permitted in that section. Apparently the route passes through an agricultural experimental farm. Why they can't abide a dog on a lead passing by escapes me but ours not to reason why...

We rejoined the Way as it crossed the main road and shortly afterward we stopped for lunch near a stone bridge. It was an enchanting spot with trees and green grass and hills in the background. A fisherman and his dog tried their luck in the stream down the way. Holly had her meat pie and then the little sheep dog came over for a visit. He was a friendly little fellow and he scrambled all around until his owner gruffly called him back.

We walked into the village of Tyndrum and succumbed to a shopping foray at the Green Welly store there. I bought a new Australian leather hat and Ian found some woolen socks that he fancied. We had some tea and tea cakes at the little cafe next door before resuming the trail.

The Way then continued on up a slope where it followed the old military dirt road that is used for much of the West Highland Way. The road paralleled a railway track for the next seven miles. It took us along a pleasant valley. We stopped for the traditional 5:00 o'clock tea from thermos flasks near a herd of shaggy Scottish cattle. They were a handsome group, amber-colored and quite tame. Even the old bull ignored me as I passed right beside him. He was just taking it easy by the edge of the trail. We watched an eagle soar nearby with Ian's single-barreled binocular.

When finally we reached the Bridge of Orchy we ordered a round of shandys at the pub in the hotel. A separate bar was available for walkers who were not permitted in the hotel because of their muddy boots and rucksacks. We had been blessed with sunshine for the whole day and the shandys were the icing on the cake.

Bridge of Orchy to Altnafeadh. 15 Miles.

In the morning we moved our goods to an inn high up on the side of a mountain. It overlooked Loch Leven and the town of Kinlochleven. Mamore Lodge had been built as a hunting lodge around the turn of the century. The interior was finished in tung and groove varnished pine. There were no phones in the rooms and the pay phone in the lobby 'had gone faulty', according to the desk clerk. Large push buttons could be found in the rooms that were marked 'Up' or 'Down'. These had been installed for calling the upstairs or downstairs maids in the good old days when staff was a bargain. A photo in the entrance hall had been prominently displayed showing King Edward VII when he had stayed there in 1909. He had shot the largest stag that year, too, a wise move methinks on the part of the estate's owner.

We met Jess and Ian at the rendezvous spot of Altnafeadh, pronunciation possible only by a Scot. We left their car there and then we returned to the hotel at Bridge of Orchy to continue the Way. A 10:30 a.m. start took us over the stone bridge across the river Orchy and up a steep hill through forest.

The first two miles were pleasant walking up and around a prominent hill with Loch Tulla down below. The earth of the path was punctuated by small streams now and then. We passed some large rock cairns and then dropped on down to the

Inveroran Hotel for tea and tea cakes. Holly ordered a meat pie and was lucky enough to find that the agreeable proprietor happened to have one in stock. The hotel is quite remote but it has been commended for its food for the past three years. It was built in 1780.

The next ten miles were along the old military road again as it bordered Rannoch Moor. The road had actually been built in 1750 but it is now used exclusively by walkers. For a while it was a route for cattle drives, too, before the advent of freestyle trucking. This was a memorable part of the walk. Angie compared it to a Dali landscape because it was so desolate and extensive with its surrealistic light and peaks far in the distance. Here and there a loch or a stream relieved its barren features.

In the beginning we passed Black Mount Lodge the huge estate of the Ian Fleming family. It was easy to picture James Bond at leisure between escapades. On the side of a hill farther along a stone cairn monument had been built that overlooked the moor. It was for Peter Fleming, Ian Fleming's adventurous brother who had died while deer stalking on the estate.

We stopped for lunch at a stone bridge across the River Ba. The day had turned sunny again and it was pleasant to stretch out there on the grass surrounded by steep mountains on one side and the vast moor on the other.

After lunch we followed the old military road on down to Kingshouse Hotel, reputed to be the oldest inn in Scotland. On the way we passed White Corries Ski Tow which offered chair lifts to the top of the nearby mountain all day long. The hotel was an oasis in the otherwise empty moor. We finally reached it after first crossing the busy A82 highway.

We stopped by the edge of the river next to the Kingshouse Hotel and we indulged ourselves in a half-pint of shandy from the walker's pub before doing the final three miles.

The route turned into a muddy footpath which took us

to the car. Our stopping point was just before the notorious 'Devils Staircase' that would be tackled the next day.

Jess and Ian had booked a room at Mamore lodge, too, and that night we dined well in the cozy little bar in the inn with a 'pub meal', orange and carrot soup, battered cod and hot fudge cake and ice cream, all washed down with a couple of bottles of the house wine. The resident inn dogs wandered in to visit, an overweight old lab and a spunky little mongrel. Holly was permitted to spend the night in the room instead of outside in the car in the cold. Scotland is fond of animals and dogs are always welcome.

Devil's Staircase to Blar a Chaorainn (Right!). 13.5 Miles.

The next leg was the Devil's Staircase which Jess and Ian and I tackled while Angie volunteered to gather lunch with a meet on the other side back in Kinlochleven. The climb up was only about a mile. It was steep and rocky with some relief from a few switchbacks but it was really no worse than the average Appalachian trail ascent.

Not far from the start, on up the road, was Glen Coe, the scene of a 1692 massacre of 40 members of the MacDonald clan. The massacre had been carried out by troops under the command of Captain Gordon Campbell on orders from King William III. It was to have been a lesson in discipline for the loose clans of Scotland. What made it so odious was that the troops had been accepting the hospitality of the MacDonalds for the previous fortnight. They had been billeted and fed by them. Then at 5:00 a.m., before first light, the troops had quietly mustered and slayed as many of the MacDonalds as they could find. Most of them were still in their beds. The balance of the 120 members of the clan, including the women and children, had managed to escape by taking to the mountains in the snow. Many of them later perished from starvation and the cold.

The Campbell clan had been enemies of the MacDonald clan for centuries and several members of the troop had actually been Campbells as well as their leader so it has been surmised that this may have contributed to their willingness to execute the orders they had received.

My grandmother had been a MacDonald so it had been a tragedy that could have actually occurred to my own ancestors. With an education in the States it was an event about which I had previously been completely unaware and yet perhaps I could have been descended from one of the survivors. Then the revelation became even more ironic when I suddenly realized that I had actually had a Gordon Campbell who had been working for me for the previous three years.

The way down from the Devil's Staircase was arduous because of the rocky path. Starting sunshine had begun to change to cloud and mist, too. Still, though, it was possible to enjoy the spectacular vistas from up there. Far in the distance could be seen the huge Blackwater reservoir, source of the water for the aluminum smelting plant at Kinlochleven. This plant was the world's original electric turbine generating plant and its pipes still carry water down the steep mountain sides to power its generators. The little village of Kinlochleven was the first town anywhere in the world to have electric street lighting.

Eventually the rocky path emptied out onto a gravel road which took us to the town of Kinlochleven where we met Angie with lunch. We decided to picnic at the lodge itself on a covered porch, sheltered from the mist and drizzle.

The lodge was on a bypass road that crossed the track and after lunch we all hiked on up to rejoin the Way. We were preceded by two sheep who must have thought that they were being shepherded by a German Shepherd and four herdsmen. These sheep have a fondness for hanging out on the shoulders of the roads in the area. It can be nerve-wracking to come whizzing around a curve and suddenly discover several of them contentedly grazing next to the edge of the pavement or wandering across to the other side. Sometimes they are bedded down on either lane itself. They seem to like being near the traffic and they are completely oblivious to the perils of life on the road.

Later I learned that some 60 sheep a year are killed in the Glen Coe area alone. In fact we saw one that had just been hit at the National Trust Visitor Centre nearby.

The Way once again picked up the old military road for the next 7 miles. It was not steep but it was rocky with small stones continually underfoot. This was combined with an off again, on again, drizzle that gave us another taste of what Scottish weather can be like at times. It was eerie, too, with parts of clouds ominously floating right down the loch between steep mountains.

Somewhere along the way the midges came to call. These tiny little black insects usually travel in swarms. They seem to prefer late afternoon and misty conditions but it was the only other time that I experienced them on the whole walk. Descriptions of the West Highland Way had frequently warned about them but I did not find them too annoying. We broke out the Avon 'Skin So Soft' lotion which works well back in the States and Jess and Ian sprayed with a special insect repellant designed for mosquitoes and midges. We seemed to walk away from them quickly enough so I was unable to understand why they were considered to be a problem. Maybe we were just lucky.

We made the area with the impossible name and gratefully took off our boots for the ride back to the lodge. We had a farewell drink with Jess and Ian since they were headed south to get ready for a visit to their other home in Spain. We had enjoyed their company immensely. It is sometimes hard to find two couples where each member relates well to the others.

On television the next day we chanced to tune in on some Scottish Highland games that were being held at the picturesque town of Oban over on the coast. We had visited there on a rainy non-walking day three days previously. Some burly contestants, all dressed in kilts, were competing in the caber toss. (I had made the gaff sometime previously of calling it the "caper toss" which is a bit deflating since capers can be tossed with the flick of a finger of course). The huge pole weighs some 125 lbs. It is lifted from a vertical start and then run to a launch mark where it is then chucked upward so that hopefully it will come down end over end to fall forward after achieving some worthwhile distance.

All went well for a while with a bagpipe band parading by in their kilts and with succeeding contestants having a go until one competitor ran into trouble. Like a character from a John Cleese comedy he hoisted the heavy pole at the appropriate time only to have it fall over backwards behind him with an embarrassing thud. It was a caber tosser's worst nightmare come true.

The Final 6.5 Miles of the West Highland Way.

This little stretch of the Way was really one of the most memorable of the whole walk. It left the rocky military road which turned into a newly paved access route between Fort William and a loch campground nearby. The clue for reaching it by road is a sign pointing to Achintore at the roundabout just before getting to Fort William on the A82.

The path went up an easy hill between Scotch pines, the Christmas tree variety, with their wonderful piney fragrance. The trail was well-maintained and it made for easy walking. After about two and a half miles it crested and the bulk of Ben Nevis towered beyond. It was even possible to note some of the switchbacks that worked their way up the lower side of it.

The day was radiant with sunshine again. This section again reminded me of the Sierras or the Rockies. Then the track dropped down through older, taller trees until it hit a non-vehicular forestry road. Until then I had not seen any other hikers.

As I walked on down the dirt and grassy road at a good pace I saw other walkers out for a stroll. The Way left the dirt road and cut down across a field next to a very old graveyard. It emptied out onto the sidewalk of a main thoroughfare. I walked along this for about a mile until I reached the official end of the West Highland Way at Nevis Bridge. I sat by a fence post to wait for Angie and I reflected on the walk and the parts of it that came to mind. It had been a different type of countryside, more rugged and desolate without as much forest, but the old military road and the well-travelled footpaths had made it easy walking. Best of all it had been a way to get to know Scotland that couldn't have been duplicated from the seat of a car or a tour bus. I felt lucky to have had the experience.

Ben Nevis, Britain's Highest Mountain. 9 Miles.

At 4,406' Ben Nevis is located right next to the finish of the West Highland Way. The temptation to climb it was too much to resist.

The mountain rises abruptly from Loch Linnhe at Fort William. In the valley at its foot is a large Hostel with nearby caravans and a pasture that was filled with tents pitched by backpackers. The backpackers were everywhere in and around Fort William. It seems to have become a very popular way to travel in Scotland. The many that I became acquainted with were from all over the globe. All of them spoke English with varying degrees of fluency but well enough to carry on a good conversation and everyone was friendly, helpful and well-behaved. It was the same observation I had made so many times before. The bad element always seem to hang out in the densely populated urban areas of a country where the action is and where it is easier to blend into their own kind. Backpackers, walkers, cyclists and rural residents are generally a healthy and honest lot that can be trusted as a rule.

The day before we had attended a country agricultural show. It was fascinating. Here the local high school band performed with drums and bagpipes. They looked very smart with their kilts and tartans. The livestock was judged, the ponies sailed over the jumps with their intent young riders, the dogs were judged and the best egg, the best decorated cake, the biggest vegies and the most interesting paper plate drawing for youngsters were all selected and a coveted ribbon awarded for each. There was the sheaf toss, a 16 lb. bag over a 16 foot bar with a pitchfork, a tug of war with six burly Scots on either end of a huge rope, and a knobbly knees contest for the best male knees. It was all good fun and it was a way to appreciate the Scottish life style which is now so much more gentle than the past thousand years of its bloody history.

The start up Ben Nevis was at Achintree Farm parking area for a 9:30 a.m. departure. There is another start which is steeper but a bit closer to the main trail at the Youth Hostel area. I fell in with a young New Zealander. He was backpacking with his attractive younger sister. They were camped in the field below.

The New Zealander's sister fell back to her own pace and another English backpacker joined us. I walked with them for quite a while. The trail was steep and rocky. Finally I stopped to take pictures and they went on ahead. The vista was worth the struggle. I could see across the valley to the trail that I had so enjoyed on the last lap of the Way. Far beyond I could also see the long loch and part of the town of Ft. William off to the right. It looked like a three-dimensional map of the peaks in the area.

Around 3,000 ft. the views were annihilated by a thick cloud that habitually hangs over the top of Ben Nevis. Then it became a grind up the rocky switchbacks which gave little relief to the climb because of their own steepness. It became necessary to pay close attention to the trail, too, so as not to go astray in the cloud or to twist an ankle on the sharp rocks.

The ascent is 4,300 ft. in 4.5 miles. I was pleased to have reached the top in 2 hrs. and 40 minutes. At the summit a gale was blowing and it was bitter cold. It was for me anyway, some Scandinavian types hiked in shorts and tee shirts, although most of them brought out their sweaters and rain jackets when they reached the top.

At the highest point of the mountain a huge cairn had

been erected. Several engraved memorial plaques had been imbedded into its side. One had a stone from Everest and another had one from Kilimanjaro. Both had had bits chipped out of them by souvenir hunters. A patch of snow was still in evidence even though it was late August. The shelter had no roof, just rock walls. I found a spot in a lee from the wind and I changed into the luxury of a dry tee shirt, a thermal underwear top and a sweatshirt. Then I ate my tunafish bap and savored the oatmeal chocolate-covered Hob-Nobs cookies that had become a weakness recently discovered. I replaced some of the perspiration lost with several good swigs from the canteen and I thought about the experience.

The climb up Ben Nevis is an arduous affair. And yet countless others were out making the climb on that same day. It was a Monday but all kinds of people were trudging up that steep rocky path. There were fathers with babies on their backs, fat ladies red in the face, youngsters with their Dad and Mum, oldtimers; some carried briefcases or handbags for packs; there were Nordic types who went zipping by like chamois, a team of mountain climbers with climbing gear, a Leicester Square type girl with blazing violet hair, purple nails and flashy hot pants, and lots of couples where the man pulled ahead macho-like with his mate dutifully following, panting and sweating and trying to be a good sport.

A couple back at the lodge had said that it had taken them over nine hours to get up and back. They were both a little heavyset but like so many of the others they had made it up and back and they were proud of their achievement.

On the other side of the coin were the fell runners. A Fell Run had been scheduled for the following Saturday. It would go from Fort William to the top of Ben Nevis and back. Some of them were in training for the race that day. As my New Zealand friend commented, they were 'disgustingly fit'. They were actually running up that steep path. Coming down had to be another nightmare for them. Ten thousand lightning quick decisions had to be computed by the brain in order to determine where best to put each foot so as to avoid a stumble and a twisted ankle or a tumble over the side into oblivion.

The trip down took almost the same amount of time, some 2 hrs. and 45 minutes. It was a relief to drop out of the cloud around the 3,000 ft. level. There had been a light drizzle up on top, not enough for the poncho but enough to be glad for the Gortex jacket. It was reassuring to warm up again and to gain a respite from the wind. Then the moment of exhilaration finally came when the parking lot was reached and Angie and the car were there waiting. It was a good feeling to realize that I, too, along with all of the others that day, had climbed Ben Nevis because it was there.

Maps & Info for The West Highland Way.

1. The pocket map of the West Highland Way that is the most convenient is put out by: Footprint, Stirling Enterprise Park, Stirling FK7 7RP, Scotland, U.K.; telephone: (0786) 79866.

2. Also useful and more detailed is: The West Highland Way, by Robert Aitken. This includes the Official Route Map and the Official Guide which contains much interesting history and general information as well. The address to contact is: HMSO Publications Centre, PO Box 276, London SW8 5DT, England, U.K.; telephone (71) 622 3316.

3. The large Ordnance Survey Maps have the West Highland Way actually marked on them and these also show the surrounding area. Those applicable from south to north are: Ordnance Survey Landranger maps: #64 Glasgow; #57 Stirling; #50 Glen Orchy; #56 Loch Lomond; #41 Ben Nevis.

These can be obtained from: The International Map Centre, 22-24 Caxton St., London SW1; tel. (71) 222-2466.

WALK XXI

XXI. The Oregon Coast.

Drift Creek. About 6 Miles.

Drift Creek runs through a jewel of a wilderness area that is located about 9 miles north of the Alsea River in the central part of the Oregon coast. It is close to the town of Waldport.

To reach the trailhead, start at Waldport and head east on Hwy. 34. Look for a bridge a few miles up the way that crosses the Alsea River. Across the bridge a State Forest Road, No. 3446, heads on up the hill in front of you. Continue on this partially paved road for about 4 miles until you find a sign that says: 'Harris Creek Trailhead 1 Mile.' Here you have an option. The trail down to Driftwood Creek at this point is a bit steeper than the other trail farther east. The creek itself is only about two miles down either trail.

The other trail is reached by continuing on Forest Road 3446 for three more miles until a sign indicates a turnoff to the left: 'S. Horse Cr. Trailhead, 2 Miles.'

A description of what to expect for this hike can best be illustrated by a hike that a group of us made not long ago. We went down the steep trail and came back up the easier trail. This made a pleasant circuit with a hike along the creek itself as well. Kit now lives out there in Oregon. She and Fred have a hydrangea farm near Waldport. Brian and Kim came up from San Diego and Bret came out from New Orleans. We spotted one car at the South Horse Creek trailhead and then came back to set out at the Harris Creek trailhead.

It was a halcyon day with bright sunshine. The steep trail down took us through magnificent old-growth forest. Some of the trees were five to six feet in diameter, huge firs that shot so far into the sky that it was impossible to see their tops. Stately hemlock, spruce and cedar joined them in Jack-in-the Beanstalk heights. The steep path was springy and soft from years of accumulated needles that had dropped from the giant trees.

Down at the bottom a narrow valley contained Drift Creek. It was an ideal place for hanging out, not too wide so that it was easy to cross on stones, or to wade across, but wide enough with a pool here and there for a refreshing dunk. The creek was full of crawfish. Unlike Louisiana crawfish these were bright orange, as though they had already been boiled.

At the junction with the stream someone had pitched his tent. It was a perfect campsite. We worked on up a little meadow with lots of blackberries that were begging to be picked. The trail then crossed the stream. We met a couple with their two small children and they warned us that a hive of bees were waiting in ambush just up the trail. We recrossed the stream to avoid the bees and after awhile we found a super spot for our picnic. We had four dogs with us, Kit's two Pugs and Husky and Kim's German Shepherd. They had a grand time splashing in the creek.

About midway through lunch we did our best to adjust to the view of a couple upstream who nonchalantly removed all of their clothes to enjoy the water and a sunbath.

In the space of about two hours after lunch we managed to catch a small ice chest full of crawfish. We used bacon on a weighted line with no hook. The crawfish, like crabs, were determined enough to hang on until reaching the surface. We could then grab them with tongs or fingers cautiously placed behind the claws. We gathered enough for a nice étouffee. They were so plentiful that we didn't even make a dent in the crawdad population.

In a bit of exploration I found the other trail that comes in from the north, another way to reach the area. I also found several good campsites, all meticulously clean and unspoiled.

On the way out we stayed with the creek for awhile

until we picked up the trail that led on up to the car that we had spotted at the Horse Creek trailhead. It was an easy climb up the 1.100 feet through magnificent trees that wwere similar to those that we had enjoyed on the way down.

Newport to Yachats on the Oregon Coast beach. About 34 Miles.

The Oregon coast is 350 miles long and it is possible to walk the entire length of it. There is, in fact, an effort underway to establish a bonafide trail all the way from the Columbia River to California. So far only a portion of 'The Oregon Coast Trail' has been marked up at the northern end.

A good sample of the Oregon coast can be enjoyed by walking in the center section from Newport to Yachats. My own walk here was all in sunshine, not always the case in Oregon.

Newport has a world-class aquarium that is worth a visit. Not far from this aquarium the road under the bridge extends out to the South Jetty for the entrance channel to the Port of Newport. I left there on a well-marked trail that wound through the sand dunes and then emptied out on the beach.

The beach was firmly packed sand, good for easy walking, and it stretched without a headland break for some 8 miles to the south. Like the Thames River the beach seemed to attract people only near the town of Newport and other urban areas, otherwise it was shared only with the seagulls, molted crab shells, driftwood and an occasional otter swimming along in the surf.

In setting out I noticed a man who reached down and picked up a small rock. He examined it carefully and then he put it in his pocket. I asked him about the rock and why he had saved it. He explained that he would put it into a continually operating tumbler with others and after a month or two it would have become smooth and shiny and desirable. In this way nature's work would have been shortened by a couple of million years or so.

The Oregon coast is generously laced with sections of State Parks. Because of this a pristine wilderness feeling is experienced for much of the time. In between the park sections attractive homes perch on the bluffs overlooking the beach and the sea. Years ago a clever Oregon Governor had the beach itself declared a state highway so that no land owner would be able to claim any portion of it for himself. Similar to the British philosophy, the beach now is public domain along the whole of the Pacific coast shoreline of Oregon.

After about an hour of beach walking I crossed a little stream emptying across the sand. Soon afterward I passed a trio of sunbathers, the first I had seen that morning. They were partially buried in sand.

After another hour I came to Beaver Creek which is a more serious flow of water. I waded across on some lightly submerged rocks. Then I reached Seal Rock for a rendezvous with Angie and a vegie-burger at the Whale's Tale in Newport.

At high tide for Seal Rock I had some interesting dashes between waves in clearing the headland there. Soon, though, I gained the next unbroken stretch of beach that went for some seven miles. After a couple of hours I came to a beach development on the north side of Waldport. Here it became necessary to work on up to the graceful bridge which spans the Alsea River as it flows out to sea.

In the middle of the bridge I stopped to watch a seal far below me. The water was so clear that I could follow his efforts with no trouble at all. He never did locate a fish for lunch, though, in spite of all of that good visibility. Maybe a crab would have to do.

The walk down to Yachats, (forget the 'c)', is equally enjoyable with two more little streams to cross and lots of weathered driftwood to admire. From time to time an otter will sometimes swim along in the surf and on this occasion I had the pleasure of one little fellow's company for almost half a mile before he grew tired of the game or went after a fish.

There are a number of accommodations in the area, most of them fairly nice and not expensive. In the summer they become pretty well filled, though, as people come for the beach life and to get away from the heat of the interior. Oregon is still unspoiled. It seems to be filling up gradually with refugees from California but there is plenty of room for everyone. And hiking in Oregon is superb.

Bibliography.

The best place for acquiring hiking books in the area is at the Aquarium in Newport. Their gift shop has a book section with an excellent collection of walking books, especially for the Pacific Northwest.

The best book for the coast is:

Oregon Coast Hikes, by Paul M. Williams

Other good books:

Hiking the Great Northwest, Ira Spring
The Mountaineers
1011 SW Klickitat Way
Seattle, WA 98134

Walks of the Pacific Northwest, Gary Ferguson
Prentice Hall Press

These books are usually available at the aquarium or they can be ordered through your local bookstore.

WALK XXII

XXII. The Coast to Coast Walk of Auckland, New Zealand

(13 km.)

The flight from L.A. to Auckland on Quantas is a twelve-hour, non-stop jump that leaves at 10:40 p.m. Somewhere along the way the International Dateline gets crossed and a full day evaporates, making wristwatch readings a struggle until they get reset.

The Park Royal Hotel in Auckland turned out to be a comfortable place with an accommodating staff who are used to letting guests sleep away their jet lag.

After a nice lunch at a charming little quayside restaurant, 'Chin Chin's', Angie and I went for a walk around the downtown area, before going back to deal with sleep needs. The restaurant itself was located in the old Ferry Building, not far from our hotel and close to Queen Street, the principal avenue in the downtown area.

Walking up Queen Street we found The Visitor's Information Center and it was here we discovered that the city had a well-marked walk called The Coast to Coast Walk. A map of the walk was readily available, too, and it seemed just the thing to work off any remnants of jet lag. We resolved to get a fresh start in the morning and to begin from the other coast which would enable us to wind up back at the old Ferry Building where we knew we would be able to find suitable refreshment at the end of the trail.

The next morning we set out for The Coast to Coast Walk by catching a bus on the corner of Victoria Street and Queen Street. The walk was especially appealing to me for two reasons. First, the Coast to Coast Walk across Northern England was one of my favorite walks and I liked the idea of walking from one coast to the other, even on such a reduced scale, the other being 192 miles. And secondly, it had to be the perfect way to become acquainted with New Zealand and Kiwi's themselves.

The bus followed Manukau Road for the most part until it reached the suburb of Onehunga. Many of the passengers that boarded were descendants of the original Maoris or Polynesian emigrants who came in search of a better life only to find that the better life was what they had left behind.

We left the bus on Quadrant Road and we walked on down to the start on Norman's Hill Road. The walkway travels through a series of five parks and along suburban streets in between the parks until it reaches the main part of the city. It travels through the grounds of a Teacher's College and later, the University of Auckland. It ends back at the quay of the old Ferry Building, a walk of about 13 kilometers, or about 8 miles.

In the early stages of the walk we became intrigued with the huge variety of plants, flowers and magnificent trees that we saw. Each home had its own share of color in carefully tended gardens, English heritage showing through. Cornwall Park held some impressive trees, including varieties that were unfamiliar to us. The eucalyptus, monkey pods and magnolias that we knew were exceptionally large.

The walkway took us past a cricket match in full swing. Seated sedately with his owner was a Westie taking it all in. He gave us his independent gaze in typical Westie fashion and I was certain that he knew the fine points of the game far better than I did.

A little farther along we passed the extensive trotting horse trails off to one side of the park. Nearby a pair of blond labs were being taken for a walk. They reminded us of Beauregard and Benjamin, except that they were more English, lower to the ground, stocky and not as large. Just as endearing, though. One of them headed our way, with his stick, of course, until his owner corrected him. He knew a soft touch when he saw one.

After crossing the busy Manakau Road, we stopped in a small café for a carton of juice. The young attendant was surprised to learn of the walk we were following. He was friendly and interested and like many locals in their home territory unaware of the things that visitors find to do.

When we passed through a suburban stretch that surrounded the Auckland Teacher's College we again became even more enthralled with the wide variety of plants, trees and flowers in profusion everywhere, even fruit trees.

A slog up Eden Hill produced the highlight of the walk. The summit provided a 360 degree view of all of Auckland and its surrounding area. We could see the ocean in the distance and the high rise buildings of the city. We could view the many suburbs that stretched neatly in all directions and the parks that were generously scattered in between. Auckland is a city of over a million people. It comprises one-third of New Zealand's entire population.

Eden Hill is also the site of an ancient Maori temple and in a carefully preserved circle the remnants of whatever rites were performed bring to mind the fact that the original civilization and culture of New Zealand existed long before the Englishman arrived.

The homes that we saw in the suburban part of the walk were mostly traditional in style and not overly pretentious. They seemed comfortable and often the front door was wide open. The yards were usually well tended and pride and contentment seemed the dominant traits.

The walkway wound through another huge park and down a little glen with ferns and a babbling brook that reminded us of those in the Isle of Man, a completely unexpected and welcome treat.

The walk took us through the grounds of the University of Auckland. The grounds and the buildings were extensive and well-maintained and the students were out enjoying the sun and conversation in between classes.

Finally, we passed through downtown itself and we ended up on the balcony of the Harborside Bar and Grill which overlooked the docks and the water. A couple of New Zealand Stein Lagers went down with ease. We watched the big cruise ship of the Royal Viking Line leave its mooring. A couple nearby had just left it and they waved enthusiastically as it moved out of the harbor.

The beer seemed only appropriate in deference to the tradition of the finish of the Coast to Coast Walk across England. I thought of Robin Hood's Bay and the pub at The Bay Hotel with nostalgia.

Map:

The walk is marked by yellow signs from time to time and it would be possible to make one's way from Norman's Hill to the Old Ferry Building without a map but The Visitor's Information Center on Queen Street does have them readily available and they are quite useful.

WALK XXIII

XXIII. The Alabama Beach.

(27 Miles).

The beach across the southernmost part of Alabama makes a sea air walk worthwhile. It provides the gentle surf of the Gulf for a companion and the now and then reward of a beachcombing find for a dividend. It is good for a walk any time of the year but my preference is during winter.

For an example of what to expect, my own walk started at Fort Morgan on a sunny day in February. Beauregard and Duffy helped us to explore the interesting old fort with its cannons and thick walls. The sense of history it produces is a welcome recognition of how far mankind has come since the days of muskets and bayonets. Its occupants could never have dreamed that in a little over a hundred years their sanctuary could be blown apart by a ship out on the horizon, a warship that wasn't even visible from the ramparts of the fort, or a silent plane high overhead, like a huge pterodactyl, something else completely incomprehensible. And what do we have to look forward to ourselves, another hundred years from now? A computer button that can just erase the offending structure off of the face of the map?

Angie turned us loose at the edge of the fort. We were camped at the well-maintained Gulf State Park campground, just east of Gulf Shores. This RV park is full of choice hook-ups with views over water, or beneath large pines. It has ample recreation facilities, including scenic hiking trails along the extensive marsh and through the woods. It has been discovered by the northern crop of snow bunnies, though, and during the prime winter months a reservation or an early arrival can sometimes be advisable.

Walking along the beach at an early morning hour the dogs became instantly busy checking out the scents that only dogs can translate and enjoy. All sorts of messages have undoubtedly been left behind by former four-footed visitors. Every now and then a long scent letter seems to take more time to examine than others. Often Duffy will then come over to read it, too, or vice versa. I often speculate about it. Maybe it is a favorite bulletin board, like the side of a 55 gallon drum trash barrel, obviously a popular place for communication, with multiple postings. Or, a driftwood log that has been situated on the beach for a long period of time. Perhaps a gorgeous female, in need of attention, has indicated that she was there and where were you when I needed you? Whatever the message I notice that usually a leg is raised in response and a reply is posted or an announcement made for subsequent four-footed travelers.

Soon we rounded the point and set out down the long beach that stretched to the horizon in front of us. Tragically we came to a scene that really shook me up. Two dead pelicans lay side by side. They were somehow tucked up against a grassy dirt shore far enough away from the high tide level so that it was apparent that they had both died there. It was not a matter of having been washed up on the beach. I speculated that one had died and the other had grieved itself to death nearby.

We continued walking for the rest of that morning. We came to the beginning of the section where beach homes have been constructed. Many of them were tastefully done, not palatial or pretentious, with comfortable verandas and picture windows built for views of the sea and an informal beach life. Most of them were empty. The more important season seems to be during the summer months. Strangely enough we had the beach to ourselves for the entire morning.

A little after noon we came to a comfortable gazebo at the edge of the beach. No one seemed to be in residence in the houses nearby and I couldn't ask permission to use it but it was too inviting to resist. We settled down to share my lunch in the usual routine. Duffy is always more persistent and he requires the first offering. Beauregard is more discrete and polite but what are you going to do? I have learned that two pairs of longing brown eyes are impossible to ignore and it is best to bring along some dog biscuits, or extra sardines, something, to take care of the guilt basket when you bite into your sandwich.

Another hour of additional walking after lunch brought us to our designated rendezvous. Angie soon appeared with the welcome Blazer. About ten miles, an easy beachcombing walk.

The next day was much the same, another ten miles, but here we reached the amenities of Gulf Shores. This is a pleasant little beach town with several restaurants and stores for necessities and mementos. The sand of the dunes is quite white and clean and fine. The water of the Gulf in Alabama is generally much clearer than it is next door in Mississippi.

On the third day we rounded out the walk by doing the remaining seven miles to Perdido Pass. On the other side of the pass, spanned by a fixed bridge, another 13 miles of beach walking is also possible on Perdido Key, all the way to the Pensacola ship channel. This becomes Florida territory, though, and dogs are not permitted on beaches in Florida. Duffy and Beauregard try to be law-abiding citizens so we elected to forego the pleasures of Perdido Key which looked to be a very inviting section as well.

Summer beach walking along the Alabama coast would be pleasant because a welcome plop in the ocean every so often would help with the heat.

A number of good motels and other campgrounds abound in the area around Gulf Shores. Just take State Hwy. 59 down from I-10 and look for vacancy signs, preferably on the beach itself. In the spring people come from all over the country to attend the Arts & Crafts Festival in the nearby town of Foley, Alabama.

A standard Alabama Highway map is the only thing necessary for locating the walk.

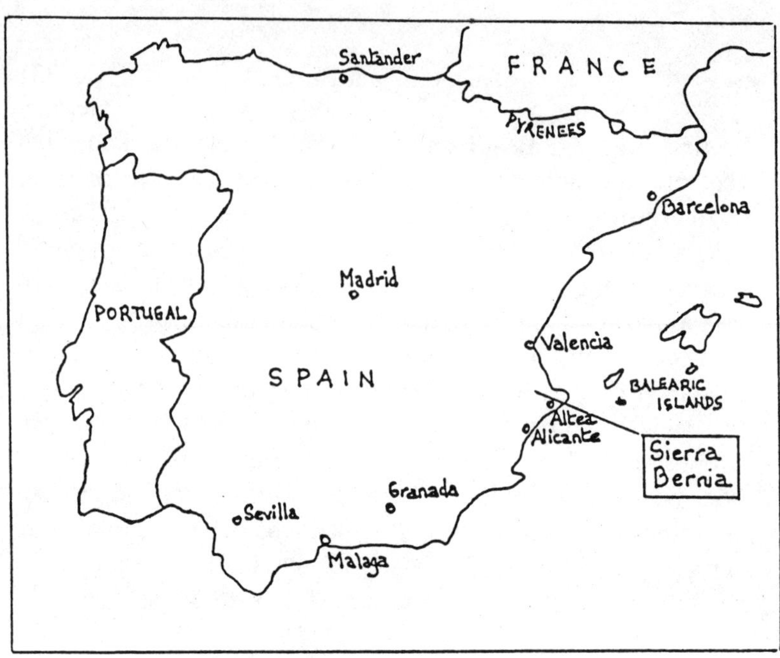

Sierra Bernia in Spain

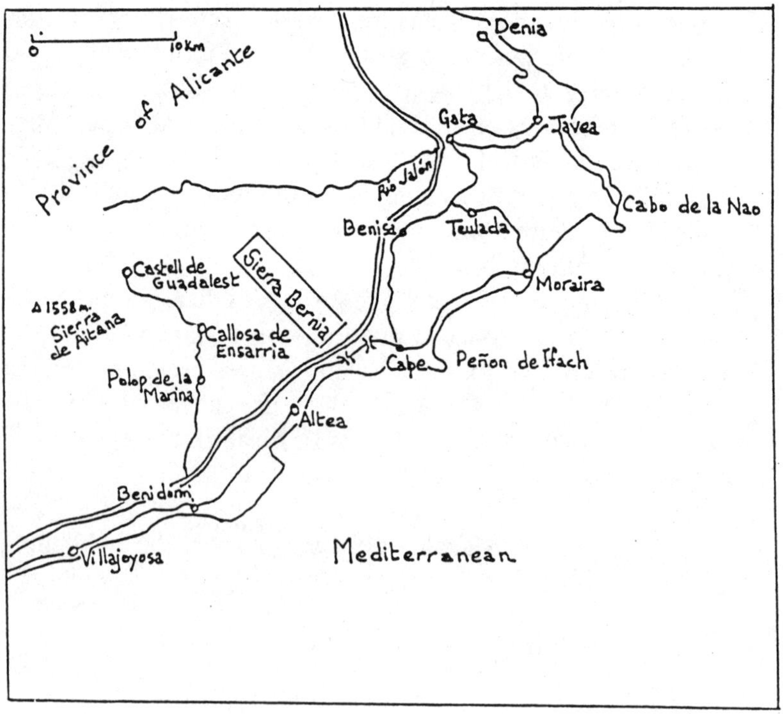

WALK XXIV

XXIV. The Sierra Bernia of Southern Spain.

Bernia to Sella. 30 Miles.

Of the walks that I seem to do on a repeat sort of basis I think that the walking in the Sierra Bernia area is the most dramatic of the lot. Angie's folks have lived on the Costa Blanca, the southeastern coast of Spain, for over twenty years. They have a lovely house in the Spanish tradition near the ancient and picturesque village of Altea. We go to visit them each year and we have come to love the surrounding area itself. Altea is ringed by mountains with the south side facing the Mediterranean. The Sierra Bernia range rises majestically along the eastern side.

When I first came to Altea I had heard about a tunnel that burrows its way through one of the Sierra Bernia mountains but nobody could tell me quite where it was. I looked for this tunnel for four years, that is to say on four different trips. Duffy usually accompanied me on these walks but we could never find it. The mountains themselves are very precipitous and impossible to cross without it.

One day Duffy and I were exploring on the back side of the Sierra Bernia. We were following a faint trail that worked its way on up to the base of the formidable cliffs towering above us. We finally came to a deep cave that seemed about right and I was sure we had found it at last. The cave narrowed and died after a bit, though, and I was beginning to wonder if the tunnel really did exist or if maybe it was just somebody's bid for attention during cocktail conversation.

Without much hope we climbed the rocks on up past the left of the cave and then we continued along the base of the towering cliffs above. Suddenly, Eureka! There it was!

The tunnel itself is a natural cave that extends on through the mountain to the other side. It narrows to about thirty inches in height but it is not too difficult to slide along on your rear end while you pull your pack behind you. It is about a hundred feet in length and the other end opens up into a very large chamber that then looks out over one of the most dramatic and moving vistas to be seen anywhere in the world.

From the vantage point of the other side of the cave the whole of the basin stretches out before you. Off to the left is the Mediterranean that goes on forever and far in the distance is the package-tour mecca of Benidorm with its never-ending cluster of high-rise hotels and apartments and its choice of amusements in the sun for any budget no matter how large or small. In the floor of the valley are the fruit orchards, just like Southern California used to have. They are interspersed with the houses of the Spaniards some of whom have given up their land, albeit profitably, to the foreigners who have come to retire and live the good life in their own pseudo-Spanish style houses side by side with their gracious Spanish neighbors. Here and there, too, can be seen the villages, typically Spanish, that serve as the hubs for service to all of this prosperity. The river Algar flows down the center of the valley and the picture postcard town of Altea with its distinctive and famous church perched on the top of its hill is visible like the jewel that it is far in the distance. All of it is a breathtaking sight.

On the day of the present hike we left my faithful 'moto' chained to a tree and hidden in a grove of young pines about halfway up the ambitious little road that climbs to the terrace at the base of the Sierra Bernia on the Altea side. The 'moto' is a small Spanish motorcycle favored by most of the peasants and the younger set, most of whom are too poor to afford a car. It sports a set of pedals which is the way to get it started, if it is feeling in the mood, and it is very practical and fun to ride. When I take it to town there is never a problem with finding a parking place, another of its fringe benefits. It lives in Sydney's garage until we come to visit and it always starts right up whenever it is needed.

Without a moto, or a long-suffering spouse, or a friend to pick you up, an Altea taxi would be more than happy to meet you at this spot or any other that is roughly in the vicinity. The distance through the Sierra Bernia from the start to this point is some 10.3 miles.

The way to find the beginning of this original and unusual walk is to first go to almost any service station in southern Spain and purchase a copy of Firestone Map No. 28 which shows the Costa Blanca area. Look on the map and note highway N-332. Follow this north from Altea along the coast route. When you come to a little road that branches off to the left just before you reach the town of Benisa cross over and go down it until you soon come to a fork that says 'Los Pinos'. This is a good road, a little winding but well paved and scenic. On the map you have obtained it probably will not show that the road extends beyond Los Pinos and connects with 'Bernia' as yet but it actually does and this is where you want to go.

At its highest point the road deadends into another road that indicates 'Jalón' to the right. Take this road to the right and just after you have made the turn notice a sign in crude letters that says 'Refugio Vista Bernia, M. Magdalena.' Turn in here and park your car near the restaurant. It will be quite safe there and this is the starting point for this spectacular hike.

As you go through life, every once in awhile you are privileged to experience a cherished moment that you will always remember. One such moment occurred for Angie and me on a winter day some years back when we stopped at the bar and cafe there which is, in fact, the whole of the would-be town of 'Bernia'. The place is an example of the term 'tipico', rustic, friendly and inland country Spanish, unlike its more tourist-oriented cousins on the edge of the Med far below. In addition it has a magnificent view of the surrounding mountains with the distant sea far off in the background.

It was cold outside at the time that we stopped for a coffee and cognac by the fire. A group of Spaniards were seated at a long table. It was midmorning and they were likewise fortifying themselves against the elements. Suddenly the whole group burst into song. They shared the song together and then they left. The old couple who owned the place came over and visited with us. Dolores and Francisco.

Francisco went into the bedroom which was just off of the main room of the bar. He returned with his most prized possession, an ancient guitar. He played for us. I was unable to recognize the songs that he sang but they were moving and appropriate. When he stopped to acknowledge the appreciation that we showed I told him that I, too, played the guitar. He passed it to me and he seemed appreciative as I played some of the traditional flamenco that I knew. I sang the Mexican song El Jinete as well, one of the few songs that I manage to sing in Spanish.

When we told Dolores and Francisco that we had come from Los Estados Unidos it was apparent that they must have thought of it as being somewhere just on the other side of Benidorm, about an hour away. Francisco proudly remarked that he had travelled, too, all the way across the Sierra Bernia once to the river Algar, a distance of under fifteen miles which I was now getting ready to hike.

After we finished our coffee and cognac we waited while Dolores went to pick some of her giant string beans for us. By the time we had settled up for the beans and our drinks it was twelve o'clock, noon, a bit late to be starting out on the hike. It was a lovely day, though, as it is most of the time in this corner of Spain, and Angie left me in our old Renault 14.

To duplicate the walk that follows just bring the book along, or rip out the chapter itself. It can serve as a guide.

After leaving the cafe I walked back to the road where we had turned right and this time I took the road which would have carried on to the left. This is paved for a short stretch and then it continues straight ahead along a dirt track that carries past an old finca on the right. About a hundred yards farther along a fork presents a choice. On this occasion I headed off to the left. The other direction actually carries on up to a trail that skirts around the crest of the Sierra Bernia at the northern end. It continues on to a well-known 'ruina', an old fortress that has a commanding view of the basin stretching out far below it. This vista is just as rewarding as that found on the other side of the tunnel.

It is possible to make a circular walk out of this section which would start and end at the fork, or the cafe. It will become more apparent a little farther along from the description that continues. The circular walk would be around eight and a half miles with a dramatic picnic stop at the other side of the tunnel or up at the ruins of the old fortress.

After about a mile and a half along this dirt road I next came to a large spring with clean and drinkable water. It is readily identifiable because of the built-in laundry tubs for scrubbing clothes as they used to do in the old days. When I reached the spring I went up the steps there. These brought me to a trail off to the left. The trail was by then well-used. Others had discovered the route to the tunnel since I had found it originally. It must have been written up in the local Costa Blanca news, the area's English-speaking paper, or become popular with some of the walking clubs.

When I started out along the trail I noticed that some kind soul had taken the trouble to mark it with red spray-paint markers every now and then. Usually the marks were in the form of a two-inch dot but occasionally a red arrow had been drawn where it had seemed appropriate. These little red markers become more and more important as the trail leads on up the side of the Sierra Bernia where the rock scree makes the path less obvious.

About two-thirds of the way on up to the tunnel I reached the large overhang that I remembered as being the site for one of the world's most perfect campsites. The ledge beneath it is reached by climbing about eight feet up from the trail. A natural hollow is located there. It is completely sheltered from the prevailing wind and the top of the overhang extends far enough out to take care of any rain. There is a spot for a fire at one end and a bedroll will fit far enough back to keep from rolling over the edge. The coastline ranges into the distance and beyond is the deep blue of the Mediterranean. Innumerable little fincas are scattered in between.

The false cave came next. Then a steep scramble up the rocks beyond it brought me to the tunnel itself. On this particular day it took an hour and twenty minutes to climb up to the elusive tunnel. My pedometer showed a reading of 3.1 miles.

The tunnel is not dark, like some caves, but the wind tends to whistle through it and it can become a chilly trip in the winter months as you slide along on your posterior. The reward is worth it, though, when the cavernous chamber on the other side is reached. From there it is possible to look out over the entire panorama of the whole basin. The Mediterranean is on one side, the mountain ranges are to the west and north and down below is the countryside that I know so intimately. For years I have jogged or ridden the faithful moto down all of its back roads.

There are a couple of lonesome pines down below the entrance. This has usually been the site of the many picnics we have had with the friends and family that we have introduced to this experience in times gone by. It makes a perfect spot to indulge in the paté, cheese or sardines, the bottle of vino tinto and the ritual siesta. On this particular day, though, I was by myself, without even Duffy to share my lunch. I skipped the vino and the siesta and I soon headed off down the other side.

Off to the right of the tunnel as you leave the entrance red markers offer a bit of encouragement as the trail heads off to the right. More red paint indicates 'ruinas' and just below it a welcome arrow points in the appropriate direction. What it doesn't explain is that it is well-advised to be wearing hiking boots with good soles. The rocks and shale that need to be crossed are unforgiving. It is best to slow down for the sections that require scrambling from rock to rock and sometimes climbing as well. Still, though, it is not impossibly difficult and all the while there is the drama of the sheer cliffs of the Sierra Bernia that rise up beside the trail.

There is another, easier, option at this spot. A scramble down open shale and the mountainside, albeit a bit steep, leads to a dirt road that travels along a long terrace that heads out to where it runs into the road that comes up the mountain. It is about 200 yards worth of effort but the two miles of rocky trail that are avoided make it a good trade-off.

After working along the two miles of rocky trail I came to a small wooden ramp that must have served as a ski jump at one time. At this point it became necessary to decide whether I wanted to continue on with the trail itself as it worked its way on up to the remains of the old fortress, or whether I was ready to head down to where I had left the trusty moto.

If the choice is made to do the circular walk back to the cafe it is only about a half mile on up to the old fortress ruins. From there an easy trail carries back around the far end of the Sierra Bernia as previously mentioned. It joins the same dirt road after about a mile of pleasant walking. Another mile along the road will then carry back to the fork down from the Bar Bernia. The 8.5 miles are a bit slow going in parts and the views are so impressive that it would be well to allow some 5 hours to do it. This would include a leisurely lunch and the traditional siesta.

After the old wooden ski ramp a well-travelled path ran toward a road that leads to the two houses on the mesa just below. On the way I came to an ancient iron door that had been installed in a carved rock niche in the side of the mountain. It had a worn latch and a handle on it. On the door was the reminder: 'Por favor cierren la puerta - Gracias'. I opened this door and inside I treated myself to a welcome drink from the crystal clear water that flowed from the enclosed spring inside. This water is pure and safe to drink. The spring has been there since time immemorial. I remembered to close the door as instructed and I headed on down the well-worn trail leading up to it.

Shortly after the spring I passed through a small orchard of almond trees between the two houses and an enclosed shed. The shed was for the sheep that still winter up there. The road down then became obvious and all the while I could admire the orchards and houses that stretched out far below. Off to the northwest and rising up from the basin I could see the mountains that this walk would cross as it progressed on its distant way to Sella. To the north was Mt. Aitana, the highest peak in the region. It was readily identifiable because of its radar and television parabolas and its tall radio towers. Its height is registered at 4,700 ft. The Sierra Bernia themselves only achieve an altitude of 3,400 ft. They do so more abruptly, though, and this is what gives them such a dramatic appearance.

After plodding along the road that wound its way on down the side of the mountain I finally reached the spot where I had left the moto. It was well-hidden in a grove of pine trees right where the opulent houses of the 'extranjeros' begin, the ex-patriates from northern Europe who are slowly filling up this little slice of paradise. I arrived there at 4:30 in the p.m. The distance was 10.3 miles and it had taken about four hours of walking with a half hour break for lunch up at the tunnel.

To locate this spot proceed 2 km. to the north from the town of Altea La Vieja on the Firestone map. Look for a lone pine tree on the left, just before a sharp curve to the right. You will see an unmarked but paved road that takes off up an incline to the right. Wire fences border each side. Follow this road up the mountain for some 1.4 kilometers. This is where I ended my walk that day but any place in the vicinity will do.

The next day I promoted a ride back to the spot where I had stopped and I continued walking down that same paved road until I reached the highway that goes on to Callosa. I crossed the highway and followed a dirt road for about a hundred feet until it came to a fork. I turned down to the right and after about a half mile I came to a red and white bar that was used to close the road. It said ‘privado’ on it but it was open and I knew from past experience that this bar is seldom down across the road. Just to the right another little-used road was closed with a chain that had been stretched across it. I walked around the chain and followed this path down through the orchard to the Rio Algar. Spaniards are used to people crossing their land and I have never had anything but a friendly greeting from anyone but it is polite to respect the privacy of the casa de campo itself and there is usually a territorial dog of sorts wanting to do his job. The family dog is almost always on a chain so he won’t wander off, in fact many of them spend their entire lives on that chain. You never know for sure, though, and they can set up an awful racket.

At the time I found that a little dogleg to the left turned out to be the best way to avoid disturbing the privacy of the two little houses off to the right. I went on down to the river Algar. Usually it is just a gentle stream. In Spain every drop of water is carefully preserved and monitored for use in the fields and the towns nearby. Very little is left to fill a streambed, especially at the point where I was. It was not far from finally emptying into the Mediterranean. Each farm and house is deeded its hour to open and close its sluice gate, around the clock and on its proper day of the week. Water rights go with a property and they are jealously coveted because they make the difference between fruit trees, flowers and vegies or just barren ground.

The Algar can become a torrent at times, in spite of the diversions, but this time it was gentle enough to make use of exposed stones. I managed to cross without getting my boots wet. On the other side of the Algar I turned right on the gravel road that borders the river. I followed it around until I came to a junction of three roads that branch off in a triple Y. I took the rightmost branch of the roads and I followed it across another stream which is the Rio Guadalest which flows into the Algar at that point.

Just after crossing the Guadalest I came to another three branch fork of roads. I choose the leftmost road and I followed it on around past a gravel plant. Soon I found yet another three road choice as I followed along the stream. This time I continued straight ahead along the graveled streambed.

For the next three miles I just followed the streambed. There was a road of sorts that wound its way along this streambed. This I used. The hike up this canyon was refreshing because of the many groves of bamboo and fruit trees on either side. The stream had decided to use the roadbed for much of its meandering course on that day but it was shallow enough so that my boots managed to keep the water out. The bullfrogs were out in full voice. I saw no one else on the whole passage.

Eventually I came to an overhead highway bridge that carries traffic across the Guadalest. This is the road from Callosa to the town of Polop which was the day's destination. I climbed up the road that ran off to the right. At the top I reached the main road and the east end of the bridge.

The bridge was a bit narrow. I confess that I ran across it so as to present a moving target to traffic for a minimum amount of time (so many pedestrians and so little time). On the other side I had the same competing traffic problem along this narrow highway for about a mile. I found myself stepping off of the pavement whenever an approaching car headed my way. Soon I reached an overhead viaduct and just on the other side I came to a narrow concreted road that dropped abruptly down to the left. This took me off of the highway and in the distance I could see the quaint little village of Polop. I followed this road right on up to the village itself, about half a mile. After I climbed up the last steep slope, which was concreted for traction there, I reached the first street of the town. I took a right there. The name of the street was Calle Teniente Teuller.

In walking down this street I passed the door of a charming little village house that belongs to a friend of ours.

Here we have been privileged to dine on occasion in years gone by. The interiors of these little town houses can often be richly attractive, warm and cozy, with several different levels. This place was like that. I have often felt tempted to hole up in one of these village houses and just let the rest of the world go by.

The street emptied out onto the village plaza with its interesting fountain in the center. Here I sat down on a park bench to eat my sandwiches while I watched village life come and go. The walk had taken only three hours and I made use of the nearby phone booth to call for an early ride back. It is also worth noting that a walk on up the narrow streets of Polop is rewarding,too. At the top of the village hill a very old cemetery is located. It has a magnificent view of the surrounding area. Altea can be seen far in the distance and even farther the Sierra Bernia themselves from where I had just walked.

On down the road that leads off to the right I came into the square that is known as the Fuentes de Polop. It was only a couple of blocks away. The fountains of Polop are the most elaborate in the whole area. A multitude of pipes spout water from beneath a panorama of tiled insignias for the many towns of the region. At one end of the plaza a bust of the Spanish poet Gabriel Miro rises above a tiled quotation of his which praises the water of this fountain which he had been drinking for over twenty years at the time of his poem. The date was 1924.

This seemed a reasonable spot to end the second leg of the walk. It had been 8.3 miles. Some local bars and 'cafeterias' are available for drawing sustenance but the water of the fountain itself is always cool and delicious. In fact, the residents for miles around come regularly to tote it back for their own drinking water at home.

The next leg on the following day was even shorter but it climbed on up to the pass that led over onto the other side of the mountain range ahead. It followed roads for most of the way and it was not too steep at any one time. It was well to have been wearing jeans, though, because of the thorns on the heather and gorse which grow beside the trail up near the pass across the mountains.

After leaving the fountains at Polop I continued on ahead up to the road that leads into the village. After a couple of blocks I reached the main highway. I went on across at the intersection there and I headed on up the road to Benimantell. This is a fairly well-travelled road on Saturday and Sunday afternoons. The restaurants up in the mountains are popular on the weekends. Fortunately it is only necessary to do about a mile and a half along this highway. When I reached some bamboo windbreak fences that stick high in the air I took off on a concrete road that departed just where the asphalt road made a sharp curve to the right. This way I continued straight ahead instead of following the curve along the highway.

I stayed with this road through the orchards with their bamboo windbreaks and past a large reservoir. I ignored a fork to the left just after the reservoir and I headed on up the road where it had become demoted to dirt. The road climbed on up the canyon through the mountains on either side for about 2.5 miles.

When the road brought me to a house in a small valley with another reservoir off to the left I continued on past the house on its right-hand side. I ignored the rough road that took off to the right uphill. I stayed with this road for the next mile as it wound on up through olive and almond trees.

At the very top of the road another country house overlooked the reservoir. The name of the house was 'Casa de Dios' (Heaven?). Just beyond was a road that took off to the left. The road usually has a chain stretched across it to prevent its use by vehicles but it is okay to walk on it.

A ride could drop you off or pick you up here at the chain, or you could leave a vehicle there. The route for an automobile is either the same as just described or it could take the road that leads off to the right. Access to this road is 5.7 km on the highway from the Polop intersection where you started. The clue as to where to exit is a sharp S curve which is where this dirt road takes off to the left just before you are about to go into the second curve. If either of these roads are wet and muddy, though, it is probably better to just walk. They can be very frustrating to negotiate without four-wheel drive and the ruts you make don't help the road any when it drys. It is also a long way down if wheels get caked and the car decides to slide on over the edge.

After stepping across the chain, I followed the road until I passed a small reservoir. Just beyond was a small 'casa de campo' shed. A trail took off up to the right there. I followed this trail. It was somewhat grown over but well-worn and fairly obvious. I have used it before and it is preferable to finding your own way up to the pass above. When the trail soon came to a newly made orchard road I took a right and I followed the road until it petered out. The trail took off to the right there and while it was not marked it was fairly easy to follow. After awhile I could see the pass itself. The objective was to go by the large knoll in the middle of the pass on its righthand side. I discovered this the hard way some years before by climbing up the rocky draw nearby before I found the trail described.

Just before I reached the pass I came to another of the world's most perfect campsites in a shallow cave just up and off to the left of the trail. Some shepherd had built a small windbreak wall at one end. The ledge was protected from the weather and it boasted a mighty view of the surrounding mountains. This could be a good candidate for a lunch spot.

When I reached the pass I had a choice of how to go down the other side. A trail off to the right led to the scenic route. It was not very well-defined but I had learned to just keep going until it became more distinct. When I reached a 'Coto Privado de Caza' sign for the no hunters advice I knew then that it was the footpath that makes negotiating the high route much easier. I followed the trail along for about a mile until I reached a spot where it petered out altogether on the rocky mountainside. I could see the farmhouse that is usually unoccupied just to the right down below. The vistas up on top there are truly spectacular. On a clear day it is possible to see all the way to Alicante, almost an hour's drive away.

This was a good stopping point. It had started out to be a rainy day and then it had changed to sunshine. I had my sandwich and then I walked on back to Polop to the fuente for a total of 14.3 miles. It had been possible to see Sella itself, my next day destination, by letting my eye sort of follow the dirt road as it wound on down in front of me.

While waiting for Angie to pick me up I again sat at the fountains at Polop. It was interesting to observe the activity. Having gone all day in the mountains without having seen anyone, with the exception of a friendly Dutchman who was hiking with a coat and a tie on and wearing the customary driving cap, it was good to see people for a change. I sat on the sidewalk and enjoyed the sun. My back leaned against a building on the corner there and I could watch the nearby bar across the street. It was full of Spaniards, all men, gathered together on a Sunday afternoon. They were busy discussing the events of the week. This is typical of all Spanish villages on all Sunday afternoons. The local bar is their club and it is part of the ritual. Here they get away from the women and the children. They enjoy some just-men talk, maybe some dominoes or cards, a little vino or a cerveza, maybe a cognac if things are going well, and all of the tables are full and reserved for village members.

Also at the fuente people would come and go. Some would just sightsee or stop for a drink from one of the multitude of spigots. Most of them came to fill their containers with drinking water, though, and they were usually ex-pat couples. Unlike the Spaniards in the bar they spent Sunday afternoons together doing chores or nattering away at one another. I wondered who had the better system.

On the next day of the hike it was rainy and overcast. The dirt road up on the steeper grade past the reservoir was a bit sloshy so I had Angie leave me there. From a quarter to nine to a quarter to twelve I climbed back up to that same ridge where I had so enjoyed the view with my sandwich on the day before.

From the lunch spot the trail just evaporated but I made my way on down over sharp rocks to the dead end road below. Water flowed from a spring on the lower side of the house nearby. I followed the road on downhill for some two and a half miles. It passed through the usual olive and almond trees and pine forest. When I reached the road that it ran into I turned right. This road, hopefully, would take me to Sella itself.

After about four miles on the road to Sella I stopped for a sandwich in a little clump of pine trees. I could catch a glimpse of the cemetery and church of Sella that were perched high above the town. The road had passed between precipitous cliffs and everywhere I looked I was surrounded by mountains. It was quiet and the birds were singing. Again, no one else was around. Perhaps it was the rain, which had been only a now and then drizzle, or the problem of dealing with a slippery mud road, but mostly I think that the area is remote enough so that it seldom sees anyone around anyway.

After lunch I reached a dirt road that came down from a canyon that led on up to the right. I could remember the road from once before when we had used it to cross this range of mountains. The road had been very difficult up near the top. It had been so steep on the other side that I had had to turn around and go up it backwards. It had been the only way that the old Renault could gain sufficient traction to carry it on up to the pass over the top.

For the next two miles down this road to Sella it was good to see the casa de campos here and there. Most of these little houses had been built in the days before better transportation made it more convenient and more pleasant for the women and children to live in the village. They still house the farm implements and supplies of the orchard owners but for the most part the houses themselves are vacant. Occasionally one of them has been purchased and restored by a non-local. I have often thought that it would be satisfying to do likewise.

After another two miles I came to a well-travelled road that forked off to the left. I took the right fork that carried uphill. In another half mile I passed by a modern castle with a high wall and an iron gate. I was told that this ambitious project belongs to a Belgian who has become a sort of benefactor to the town. The building of this edifice has generated a good deal of work for many of the people who live there. It would be nice to meet him and to see inside. A peek through the mammoth gate revealed statues in niches in the walls and lovely gardens in an inner courtyard. The castle itself commands an impressive view that overlooks the town like the fortress of some feudal baron.

Just beyond was a short piece of tarmac to the left that led down to the main highway. On the main highway I took a right. There are two fine restaurants there. The one that we know the best is the first one, called Bar Fonda. If it is a sunny day the restaurant serves out in the patio with a fine view of the valley below. It is famous for its homemade sausages and it is quite reasonable. The town itself is quaint and picturesque and well worth a stroll up and down its narrow streets.

This section, from the chain at the 'Casa de Dios', on down to Sella, is about 12.1 miles. Except for the initial two miles it is all downhill and fairly easy walking. My own hike was 14.5 miles with a good bit of it under the faithful poncho and under the old Gortex jacket. The boots stayed dry, though, and apart from the added weight of the mud on the soles now and then, it was an easy five plus hours. Angie met me on schedule and we retired to the Fonda for a couple of coffee and cognacs to ward off the chill. This corner of España is renowned for its surplus of bright sunshine, ordinarily, and normally the indulgence would have been more in the nature of a couple of cold *cervezas*.

The Costa Blanca area of southeastern Spain has other

interesting mountains in the area beside the Sierra Bernia and a very informal group has been loosely formed to take advantage of them. The group does regular hikes in the mountains of the area once or twice each week. The group is called 'The Costa Blanca Mountain Walkers'. Anyone can come to join a guided hike and it is free. The date and meeting place for each hike is listed in the area's two local weekly papers for the English speaking ex-patriate. The Costa Blanca News is sold at any newsstand in the area.

As you can imagine we have done a number of interesting hikes in the area. A few of my favorites can be identified with the Firestone map and appropriate enquiries or, if your Spanish is a bit rusty, by obtaining maps from The Costa Blanca Mountain Walkers. Worth considering:

Peñón de Ifach. 5 Miles

This is a huge Gibraltar-like rock located at the edge of the town of Calpe. It is a landmark and readily visible along that section of the coast. An obvious path leads through a tunnel and out to the precipices that overhang the Med. For the more ambitious a steep climb with some rock scrambling will carry all the way to the 1,000 foot top. The magnificent view is well worth it.

Fuentes del Algar to Tárbena. 11 Miles.

The Fuentes del Algar can be found on the Firestone map by noticing a short road that takes off to the right just beyond Callosa. At this spot a swimming pool with several restaurants in the vicinity receive a lot of activity during the summer months. You can leave your ride here or park your car and continue just beyond this area across a bridge over the stream. Going up the hill is a narrow paved road. This road eventually leads all the way up to the picturesque village of Tárbena, also on the map. Small orchards and farms and good views of the surrounding mountains provide a worthwhile backdrop along the way. With not too late a start the prospect of a good lunch at one of Tárbena's restaurantes is incentive enough for a good pace.

Confrides Castle. 4 miles

This is one of our favorites for another incredible view. The Moors built their castles on the top of isolated peaks that were easily defended from the Christians for so many centuries. The remnants of this structure lie below the Aitana on its southeastern flank. It is an ideal spot for a picnic after the climb up to it. The trail is not difficult. The ruins are readily visible in the area of the village of Confrides, again on the Firestone map. Directions are available from the local restaurante there, El Pirineo, or the locals. We have visited the castle several times and we have yet to see anyone else in the vicinity.

This area and the walks described are the last of the walks covered. I think I put it last because it is probably my favorite area for walking.

Summary:

Of the walks themselves I would rank The Appalachian Trail, The Coast to Coast Walk in England, and the Thames as the most memorable, probably because they are longer than the others and consequently, I guess, I became more attached to them. I'm still hiking the A. T. as time permits.

The most dramatic and spectacular would be the Rio Cares Gorge in the Picos de Europa, the whole of the Milford Track, the Overland Track of Tasmania and the tunnel walk in the Sierra Bernia.

The walk at Ordesa in the Spanish Pyrenees, where we almost lost our lives, and the walk around Grand Cayman, where my sons came within a few feet of being taken by sharks, were sobering experiences. They provided a good reminder about being properly prepared.

The walk around the Isle of Man and the West Highland Way in Scotland were both impressive because of the sense of old-world history that is so prevalent there.

The cloud forest at Monteverde in Costa Rica is unique because of the abundance of tropical plant life. The monkeys made interesting companions along the beach at Nosara. The huge trees and plentiful crayfish of Drift Creek in Oregon are worth a visit, too.

Each walk has its individual character, though, and they are all a pleasure to experience. I can wholeheartedly recommend any one of them as a worthwhile milestone along the winding path of life itself.

About the Author:

JAY B. TEASDEL has a home base on the Tchoutacabouffa River near Biloxi, Mississippi. He has owned and operated a number of businesses over the years. His avocation long centered around a 53' ketch he designed and built in Belize and sailed to different parts of the world. More recently he developed an interest in long-distance walking. The narrative chronicles some of the walks that he and his wife Angie have done. They are partial to their dogs who accompany them whenever possible.